"FROM PARIS TO NICE"
FIFTY YEARS OF LEGAL INTEGRATION IN EUROPE

"From Paris to Nice"
Fifty Years of Legal Integration in Europe

International Pallas Conference, Nijmegen, May 24, 2002

Edited by

MARTIJN VAN EMPEL

Pallas Consortium

consisting of the universities of
Barcelona (Spain), Bologna (Italy), Essex (Great Britain), LUISS Guido Carli (Italy),
Jean Moulin Lyon 3 (France), Konstanz (Germany), Münster (Germany)
and Nijmegen (the Netherlands)

KLUWER LAW INTERNATIONAL
THE HAGUE / LONDON / NEW YORK

A C.I.P Catalogue record for this book is available from the Library of Congress.

ISBN 90-411-2058-0

Published by
Kluwer Law International,
P.O. Box 85889, 2508 CN The Hague, The Netherlands
sales@kluwerlaw.com
http://www.kluwerlaw.com

Sold and distributed in North, Central and South America by
Aspen Publishers, Inc.
7201 McKinney Circle, Frederick, MD 21704, USA

Sold and distributed in all other countries by
Turpin Distribution Services Limited
Blackhorse Road, Letchworth, Herts.,
SG6 1HN, United Kingdom

Printed on acid-free paper

Printed and bound in Great Britain by MPG Books Ltd., Bodmin, Cornwall.

Table of Contents

Foreword

The Pallas Consortium is proud to have provided the forum for these contributions. Participants in this volume, and to the conference which preceded it, have been asked to reflect on the basic lines along which their field has been evolving. The objective has been to provide a framework that would enable readers to see for themselves how the European project of market integration has developed alongside the evolving policies of Member States, some of which complement the Community's priorities, and others which cut across them. As the Community works with the task of harmonizing laws while giving its due place to Member State autonomy, it has to balance disparate concerns across a variety of fields. Some of these concerns can be brought into a constructive balance, and others risk provoking the despairing thought that apples are being compared with oranges with little by way of principle to guide the choice.

This disparate and shifting set of considerations that make up Community law reflect the emphasis that Pallas has sought to give to its teaching and to some of the research that such collaboration has spawned.

The Consortium draws teachers – both academics and practitioners – from most of the Member States of the Union. Its basic strategy has been built around the idea that European law is not only made vertically, via the initiatives taken by institutions of the Union, but also horizontally, via practice that has grown up between Member States, and has produced norms across Europe in matters covering the environment, financial services, and corporate law and many others. To capture this second, horizontal feature experts from each country have been brought into contact with one another, so that they can build a common series of courses among themselves and then teach to the materials thus produced.

The Europe that emerges in this teaching is more mixed and multi-layered than we are used to seeing. Its law is not simply fixed between the extremes of nation state and central bureaucracies: but comes from the practices of multi-national law firms, trade associations, corporations and trade unions. It encourages a form of functional representation that widens the participatory democracy that Prof. Van Gerven points to, arguing that it has become an important part of the project of harmonization in the Community.[1]

We hope that the readers can draw on this collection for reflection on their own fields, and that they enjoy reading it as much as we have in organizing it.

Sheldon Leader
Professor of Law, University of Essex
Chairman, the Pallas Consortium

[1] See Walter van Gerven, Harmonization Within and Beyond, this volume, p. 1

Introductory Remarks

*Martijn van Empel**

I feel very privileged to be allowed to chair this conference. I readily admit that I have been involved in the choice of the theme for today's discussions: the European experience with practice-driven legal harmonisation over a period of 50 years. I wish to stress that I felt gratified, indeed, when having the opportunity to read the written notes of today's speakers. These confirmed my firm belief that discussion of legal harmonisation allows us to go to the essence of the role which the law has to play in our society.

This immediately brings me to the point which I feel we should always keep in mind when discussing legal harmonisation. The process of harmonisation is of course frequently a fascinating exercise in academic terms and we should be thankful for all the time which is spent by so many eminent academics in charting the similarities and differences which appear in this process. However, we should never lose sight of the fact that this process is never a neutral one. It is a political process, where certain groups and interests aim at changing the regulatory environment. This, to my mind is true to the point where a harmonization project which is not actively supported by economic interests is condemned to remain a dead letter, whatever its academic merits. Sadly enough, we don't have to look far afield for examples.

Let me try to illustrate this point by a few references, borrowed from today's contributions, which relate to the subsequent aspects of the process of harmonisation.

First, there is the object of harmonisation, the choice of focus. In the field of patent law, there is the stark difference between the success of the European Patent, created by the Munich Convention, and the dismal story of the Community Patent. The former was broadly supported by the future users of the system, who took an active part in drafting the texts. As for the latter, the European Commission may be forgiven for perhaps feeling that many of the legal criticisms which bedevilled its gestation for so long were in fact largely inspired by economic motives, such as the wish to avoid automatic extension of the exclusive right as granted by "Munich" to all EC Member States, rather than confining it to the obvious few major economies. Or, in simple terms: industry was by no means sure that it wanted a Community Patent in the first place.

---

* Professor, University LUISS Guido Carli, Rome.

Another example: Somewhere in the near future we will be able to assess to what extent the amount of time taken to achieve a "Societas Europea" was really due to a lack of interest on the ground.

Turning to the issue of the procedure and the participants in the harmonisation process, EC lawyers tend to think almost automatically in terms of the well-known procedures of working parties within the Council Framework, staffed by national experts from the capitals of all the Member States.

Here again, however, we are bound to find a large variety, which is, I would suggest, largely conditioned by economics and political considerations.

For academics it is a gratifying thought that sometimes one single name will be linked to a particular project: Sanders for the Societas Europea, Beier for the European trade mark are just two examples. But then, we should also be prepared to recognise the merits of certain cases of downright lobbying: Would we ever have had the 1992-Programme for the Internal Market without the Industrial Round Table?

A relatively recent phenomenon is the reliance on what can be referred to as a specific form of subsidiarity, but also as neo-corporatism. The Social Protocol introduced the concept of Community legislation basically agreed upon between the "social partners", i.e. the trade unions and the employers' federations. A somewhat similar concept based on expert bodies has been recently proposed by the Lamfalussy Report on Capital Market regulation and has duly met with much criticism, because of its "undemocratic" purport. The answer to this is that the markets cannot spare the time claimed by the politicians.

I also wish to mention here the specialised agencies, set up, organisationally and physically, at some distance from the standard Community pattern. Some take mainly executive decisions, such as the registration of trademarks, others are clearly meant to prepare the ground for, and hence to influence, future harmonisation measures.

Then, of course, there is the variable scope, in time and geographically, illustrated by the Schengen experience.

The third aspect of harmonisation in this regard is that of the legal form. I shall only mention in passing the phenomenon of Conventions between the Member States being "internalised" in the form of EC Regulations (e.g. the rightly famous Brussels Convention of 1968). Perhaps more interesting is the role played by soft law. Here I would turn to Competition law. Is it not a fascinating experience to see all Member States, one after another, falling in line and sometimes virtually copying, or simply referring en bloc to, the EC legislation? There is no legal obligation to do so, only the obvious finding that with EC Competition law now so important to trade and industry, it simply does not make sense not to follow the pattern, at the strictly national level also.

Finally, there is the content of the harmonisation-texts. Here of course, the lawyers have a prime responsibility. But even here, the outcome is largely conditioned by economic considerations, as well as – I should add – concern with sheer practicality. I would refer here to the case of the harmonisation of prudential supervision in the insurance field. As of old, there was a clear and principled opposition between the German system relying on administrative checks *ex ante*, on the one hand, and the British system which in essence confined itself to imposing certain rules of substance on the industry. I would dare to suggest that the outcome of this confrontation was, to the neutral observer, a forgone conclusion: it simply is so much easier to level down to liberalisation than to agree on the details of a common denominator at the higher level. Or, from a different angle: administrative control requires much more in depth harmonisation than agreement on objective normative texts.

As we shall see, Professor Van Gerven, very rightly emphasises the need for a comprehensive approach to harmonisation, rather than confining oneself to what is directly and immediately required by the needs of transborder trade. This is a message which is indeed crucial to any lawyer: no individual law can ever hope to be just and secure when isolated from the body of law generally. Beware of the specialists!

As I see it, this point is well illustrated by the developments in the various Member States regarding privatisation, notably the telecommunications sector. As we shall hear this afternoon, this has been a saga of the public authorities being drawn into a quagmire of ever more detailed regulation on a case by case basis. Legal security has suffered accordingly.

Let me conclude. In its CILFIT judgment the ECJ whilst allowing in principle for the notion of "acte clair" offered a revealing catalogue of all those factors which might lead to different interpretations of one and the same text. This then is a warning note with regard to harmonisation of laws. Uniformity of texts indeed is but the beginning; any serious effort to go further requires first of all a consciousness of the variety of backgrounds from whence we come and then a willingness to internalise those differences and look for a common denominator which we can all look at and call "law".

It is for this reason that I feel that it is particularly apt that specific attention is paid in today's programme to "Legal Education and International Exchange" and that I invite you to congratulate ourselves with the presence here of a substantial number of students who have taken advantage of various international exchange programmes to acquire the sort of instinctive openness without which legal harmonisation can never hope to be complete.

Chapter 1

Harmonisation Within and Beyond

*Walter van Gerven**

I have been asked to speak on the subject of objectives and realisations of legal harmonisation in Europe. To explain what I intend to do, I can do no better than refer to two recent books: the first deals with *The Many Faces of Differentiation in EU Law* and has been edited by B. De Witte, D. Hanf and E. Vos;[1] the second discusses *The Harmonisation of European Private Law* and was edited by M. Van Hoecke and F. Ost.[2] In line with these two topics, I will first deal with harmonisation as a component of Community law and then with harmonisation in a broader context as a component of a larger convergence of national and supranational legal systems. Having compared these two variants of harmonisation in general, I will then in the following sections bring these two approaches together by referring to the ongoing harmonisation efforts with areas of consumer and contract law, and with regard to private and public enforcement which those efforts should entail.

Harmonisation within the EU

In the initial version of the (then) EEC Treaty the word harmonisation was hardly used (only in Article 99, now 93, relating to taxation). The (then) Articles 100–102 constituted a separate chapter on "rapprochement des legislations", in German "Angleichung der Rechtsvorschriften", later translated into English as "approximation of laws", a heading which is still used. Harmonisation as a term was introduced by the Single Act in Article 100a, paras 4 and 5, EEC (now Article 95 EC). In my understanding harmonisation refers to approximation of laws by way of directives as opposed to approximation by way of regulations which leads to uniformity.

In a Europe of six Member States uniformity was the prevailing paradigm, so much so that there was no serious opposition against the practice of the Community institutions to (mis-)use directives by making them as precise and detailed as regulations were intended to be, a practice which allowed the ECJ later on to attach direct effect to such precise directives at least as against Member States. With the gradual enlargement,

---

* Professor of Law and former Advocate General at the European Court of Justice.

[1] Intersentia, 2001, 390 pp.

[2] Hart Publishing, 2000, 255 pp.

M. van Empel (ed.), "From Paris to Nice": Fifty Years of Legal Integration in Europe, 1–14.

geographically, and broadening, subjectwise, of the Community, uniformity of laws became less evident. As a result, and to cut a long story short, the ruling paradigm became rather one of differentiation (and flexibility) than of uniformity.[3]

An important factor in this shift of paradigms has been the acknowledgment in the eighties, as announced in the Commission's White Paper of 1985 on the completion of the internal market, that harmonisation through directives needed a new approach, away from detail and over-regulation and towards mutual recognition. The new approach was triggered by the ECJ's ruling in *Cassis de Dijon*.[4] In that judgment the Court prohibited Member States, in the absence of harmonisation, from imposing restrictions on the marketing of products which are lawfully produced and marketed in another Member State unless such restrictions are necessary in order to protect mandatory requirements. In the Commission's understanding, from then on, legislative harmonisation was to be limited to laying down health and safety standards, in view of which European standardisation committees were established.[5] Also, as a consequence of this new approach, the relationship between, on the one hand, the general prohibitions in the EC Treaty to effect freedom of goods, persons, services and capital and, on the other hand, the measures to harmonise the national exceptions to these prohibitions came to take a variety of forms, depending on whether Community legislation intended, or not, to exhaustively occupy a certain field so as to pre-empt further action of the Member States except where permitted by the Community directives concerned.[6] As a result, different harmonisation methods came to be used: *total* harmonisation allowing no derogation in the pre-empted area except for safeguard measures or to the extent permitted in the directive; *optional* harmonisation allowing producers to apply national norms *or* Community norms, some directives allowing the Member States to exercise the option (opting-out); *partial* harmonisation regulating some aspects of the subject matter only (e.g. only rules for certain cross-border transactions); *minimum* harmonisation allowing Member States to provide for more stringent rules; *alternative* harmonisation allowing Member States to choose between alternative methods of harmonisation; mutual recognition of controls (whereby Member States are required to recognise each other's control).[7]

---

[3] Introduction to the book mentioned in n. 1, at xii.

[4] Case 120/78, *Rewe* v. *Bundesmonopolverwaltung für Branntwein* [1979] ECR 649, para. 13.

[5] On that evolution, see Craig and De Bùrca, *EU Law* (2nd edn, 1998), pp. 1124–1132; Lenaerts, Van Nuffel and Bray, *Constitutional Law of the European Union* (1999), pp. 205–211. For an analysis of the new approach (as developed in the Commission's White Paper of 1985) in a context of Contract law and its limited use in the future for harmonisation of mandatory rules of contract law, see J. Drexl, "Continuing Contract Law Harmonisation under the White Paper of 1985 – Partly with Alterations" lecture held at the SECOLA/CCLE colloquium in Leuven on 1 December 2001; see also below n. 30.

[6] P.J. Slot, "Harmonisation" (1996) *European Law Review* pp. 378–397, at 388–389. For a recent example, see ECJ judgment of 25 April 2002, Case C 52/00, *Commission* v. *France*, nyr, holding that the Product Liability directive 85/374/EEC aims at total harmonisation.

[7] For details, see P.J. Slot, l.c., at 382–388; also E. Vos, "Differentiation, Harmonisation and Governance" in *The Many Faces, op. cit.* n. 1, 145–179, where the models, somewhat differently categorized, are applied to the specific sector of food law and where the working of the standing committee on Foodstuffs is discussed.

In their book on the many faces of differentiation in EU law, the authors have drawn attention to many factors, other than the aforementioned methods of harmonisation, which have brought the prevailing paradigma to shift from uniformity towards diversity. Those factors are: the effect of the principle of subsidiarity (and proportionality), the use of soft law techniques, the implementation or modification of Community law undertaken by national courts and private actors, the conclusion of partial and parallel international agreements and differentiation accepted in the shaping of the EC's external relations. And, of course, also the flexibility clauses in the Treaty of Maastricht on EMU and social policy and the provisions on closer cooperation in the Treaty of Amsterdam (and Nice) have led, and will lead, to further differentiation. One should not see that necessarily as a retreat from the original European spirit: as already mentioned, enlargement and broadening, if it is not to go at the expense of further deepening of cooperation, will go hand in hand with differentiation; provided, however, that the decision-making process for flexibility to be accepted, will be made sufficiently flexible as well. Moreover, if subsidiarity is not exclusively understood as bringing the level of policy and law making "closer to the citizen", but also as allowing private organisations and individuals to participate in policy and law making, i.e. to bring "the citizen closer to the Union", then differentiation – as a result of allowing Member States, their Parliaments and private actors to participate in the Community's legislative activities – can be seen as an evolution towards participative or deliberative democracy.[8]

It is one thing to provide in uniform rules, another to provide in uniform *remedies* to stimulate compliance and to make judicial enforcement possible if need be. In that respect the ECJ has played a role which can hardly be overestimated. Thanks to the Court's bold interpretation of Article 12 EEC (now 25 EC) in *Van Gend & Loos*,[9] private enforcement was made possible, first of (precise and unconditional) Treaty provisions and then of regulations and directives as well (the first two eventually also against individuals). This saga has been told so often that it does not bear repetition. It has led to the shaping of specific remedies of restitution, compensation and interim relief, in addition to the (ever expanding) general remedy of setting aside national rules which are inconsistent with Community law.[10] All these remedies can be used in litigation before domestic courts by private parties who allege their rights to have been infringed. As a result, not only separate rules are set aside but whole sets of relatively uniform (remedial) rules are made available in the laws of the Member States.[11] Some have seen this evolution as evidence of activism on the part of the ECJ. However, seen in retrospect, that evolution is rather an illustration of the Court's determination to secure plaintiffs full access to court (as is required by Articles 6 and 13 ECHR to which the ECJ makes explicit reference). And indeed, if Community rules confer

---

[8] For an effort in that direction, see the Commission's White Paper on *European Governance* of 25 July 2001, COM(2001) 428 final.

[9] Case 26/62 [1963] ECR 1.

[10] For an overview, see W. van Gerven, "Of Rights, Remedies and Procedures" (2000) *Common Market Law Review* 501–536.

[11] W. van Gerven, "Bridging the gap between Community and National laws: towards a principle of homogeneity in the field of legal remedies?" (1995) *Common Market Law Review* 679–702.

uniform rights upon private parties, there must also be remedies in the laws of the Member States which allow those parties to be treated equally when it comes to enforce those rules against infringements by public authorities or, eventually, other private parties. So far the ECJ imposes only minimal harmonisation in that regard, i.e. by requiring Member States to eliminate restrictions which make judicial relief impossible or excessively difficult, provided that, where a Member State provides more extensive relief in national law matters, it must also grant such relief in similar issues of Community law.[12] It is to be hoped that the Court will be ready in the future to raise that standard to the level of *adequate* relief throughout the Community.[13]

As mentioned above, the new approach of harmonisation, as adopted by the Commission after *Cassis de Dijon*, has had for consequence that, for products, only basic health and safety standards were laid down by directive while it was left to standardisation committees to specify those standards in more technical rules. It also led to the instalment of information and notification procedures intended to forestall measures restricting trade,[14] as was the case of Directive 83/189[15] – now replaced by Directive 98/34 laying down a procedure for the provision of information in the field of technical standards and regulations and of rules on Information Society services.[16] Also in that respect, the ECJ lent its full support by providing in an efficient remedy, to be initiated by plaintiffs before a national court, in case of a Member State's failure to comply with the directive's notification requirement. Indeed, in *CIA Security International*, the Court ruled that non-compliance, by the Member State concerned, with a procedural rule of the sort provided in Directive 83/189, rendered the technical regulations involved inapplicable. As a further result, in that judgment the Court made another inroad on its established doctrine that directives can have no horizontal direct effect, by allowing plaintiffs to rely on the ineffectiveness of such national regulation in private litigation, and thus against other individuals (so-called "incidental" horizontal effect).[17]

Harmonisation Beyond the EU's Legal Framework

The book on harmonisation of European Private Law mentioned at the outset of this chapter has nothing in common with the book on differentiation referred to above. It is not about harmonisation in EU law nor is it about EU law at all. It deals with European law in the sense of an emerging *ius commune* in the area of private law, and is written by "comparative" lawyers, not by "Community" lawyers. Both areas of harmonisation are usually seen in isolation: as in many other legal fields lawyers specialised in one field tend to ignore those specialised in another field. As long as that happens, harmonisation in the EU remains too narrow in scope, as I explained

---

[12] See further T. Tridimas, *The General Principles of EC Law* (1999) at 279 ff.

[13] See my contribution in n. 10.

[14] Lenaerts, Van Nuffel and Bray, *op. cit.*, at 207.

[15] [1983] OJ L109/8.

[16] [1998] OJ L204/37, as amended by Directive 98/48 [1998] OJ L217/18.

[17] Craig and De Bùrca, at 206 ff. See further S. Weatherill, "Breach of Directives and Breach of Contract" (2001) *European Law Review* 177–186.

elsewhere[18] – and as I will repeat now briefly at the risk of boring those who already heard it.

Harmonisation in a context of European Community law has a bright side and a dark side. The *bright* side is that it brings the national laws of the Member States together (at a varying degree of approximation, as we have seen), however only in limited areas of the law. The latter is so because of the fundamental principle of EU law which is that Community institutions enjoy jurisdiction to the extent only that the Member States have transferred competences to the EC or the EU. As a result, and this is the *dark* side, harmonisation within the EU has a disruptive effect on the legal systems of the Member States because it cuts through areas of domestic law which, before Community harmonisation, were regulated in a coherent manner. The reason is that harmonisation through Community law, including case law, can only occur regarding those aspects of a Member State's internal law, mainly cross-border aspects, which fall within the Community legislature's jurisdiction, and accordingly must leave intact other aspects of domestic law, dealing with similar issues though, which remain outside Community jurisdiction. The only way to reduce the impact of this disruptive effect is for Community and national legislatures, and courts, (i) to take each others' legal systems into account when laying down own rules, or finding own solutions, and (ii) to base such rules and solutions as much as possible on principles which the legal systems of the Community and the Member States have in common. And, indeed, that is the method advocated in Article 288, para. 2, EC and in Article 6, para. 1, TEU, the first dealing with extra-contractual liability of Community institutions and the second with the basic principles on which the Union is founded. And that is also what the ECJ states to be its current practice.[19]

Obviously, national legislatures and especially courts will not be able to discover common principles or solutions – since, unlike the Community courts, they do not have an important research department composed of lawyers from all Member States. Consequently, they will need to rely on comparative law research carried out in universities or other research institutes. The book on harmonisation mentioned above is the result of such a research project, and it is particularly useful because it is concerned with differences in legal mentalities and methodology between the Member States' legal systems.

Fortunately, comparative law research in view of stimulating the emergence of a *ius commune europaeum* is not to start from scratch. Indeed, during the last 10 to 20 years many research groups have carried out a considerable amount of work and have produced quite a number of text and case books, edited legal periodicals in many languages, drafted principles of European law and set up codification projects in mainly patrimonial private law.[20] All these initiatives have in common that they

---

[18] See, e.g. my contribution to the *Liber Amicorum* in honour of Lord Slynn of Hadley on "Comparative Law in a texture of Communitarization of national law and Europeanization of Community Law" in David O'Keeffe (ed.), *Judicial Review in European Union Law* (2000) 433–445.

[19] In *Brasserie*, case C-46/93 [1996] ECR I-1029, para. 41.

[20] For an overview, see A. Hartkamp, "Perspectives for the Development of a European Civil Law" in M. Bussani and H. Matthei (eds), *Making European Law* (Trento, 2000), pp. 39–60, at 55–60.

intend, in varying degrees and with differences in methodology, to make European doctrinal writings and materials available to teachers and students, judges and other practitioners, legislators and administrators who want to look at their own law in a European perspective. All of them tend to show how convergence between the legal systems in the Union and its Member States takes place, and how the process can be encouraged and improved. However, not all of them wish to reach unification – not even within limited areas of the law – through the development of *binding* rules. For indeed, the ultimate purpose of convergence is "to strengthen the common legal heritage of Europe (and) not to strangle its diversity".[21] Casebooks, textbooks and *non-binding* restatements of principles are therefore often seen as the best instrument to reach convergence. However that be, living together in a context of European integration, and within the legal framework constituted by the EU and the European Convention of Human Rights, will unavoidably and increasingly promote commonalities between the national legal systems of the Member viz. the Contracting States.

To be sure, some argue that commonalities within legal families will necessarily remain superficial, and that it is an illusion to think that common principles can be uncovered. That, however, is to underestimate the dialectical process of interaction which takes place between domestic laws and Community law. Such interaction is most obvious, of course, in surroundings of the European institutions of the Union and of the Council of Europe, thus the Luxemburg and the Strassburg courts, where lawyers from different States are working closely together and where, in the preparation of legislative and judicial documents, the legal systems of the States are so to speak omnipresent in the minds of all those involved. The regulations and judgments which are the result of this decision-making process are published in all languages and implemented in all legal systems. They are extensively discussed in legal procedures before domestic courts and analysed in legal writings. Convergence of legal systems and legal mentalities is therefore unavoidable and, moreover, does not remain limited to European Community or Convention law as it spills over in other areas of domestic law. To quote by way of example the words of a common lawyer: "the principal distinction between common law and civil law styles of interpretation in terms of the contrast between simple literalism and purposivism ... has narrowed very considerably,"[22] just like the import of general principles developed in European law into the domestic legal systems has become a reality which cannot be disregarded. However, that should not be a one-way street: general principles of Community law should not be created out of the blue sky but must be founded on concepts and principles drawn from the domestic legal systems.[23] For Community law it is indeed

---

21 Thus the foreword in W. van Gerven, J. Lever and P. Larouche," *Cases, Materials and Text on National, Supranational and International Tort Law* (2nd and enlarged edn, Hart Publishing, 2000). Also H. Beale, A. Hartkamp, H. Kötz and D. Tallon, *Cases, Materials and Text on Contract Law* (1st edn, Hart Publishing, 2002), both published in the *Ius Commune casebooks for the common law of Europe* series.

22 Ian McLeod, *Legal Method*, (3rd edn, MacMillan, 1999), at 325. See more specifically the House of Lords' decision in *Pepper* v. *Hart* [1993] 1 All ER 42, discussed at 297.

23 For an example in the area of tort law, see W. van Gerven, "The Emergence of a Common European Law in the Area of Tort Law: the EU Contribution", text of a lecture held at the BIICL in London (publication forthcoming).

a matter of crucial importance that it does not evolve, "en vases clos", into a *Fremdkörper* which lacks credibility and legitimacy in the Member States.

For the EU Member States and the Community to promote such a larger approximation through comparative law research, may, to some extent, be seen as complying with the duty of cooperation which Article 10 EC imposes upon the Member States and, as set out in the ECJ's case law,[24] also upon the Community institutions. That would be so insofar as convergence between the law of the Community and the laws of the Member States is needed, in the words of Article 10 EC, to "facilitate the achievement of the Community's tasks". Thus, e.g. can it be seen as an obligation for the Member States to make their competition rules, and the interpretation thereof, converge as much as possible with the competition rules of the Community, that is insofar as there is no particular justification for maintaining differences; just as it is an obligation for the EC to assist the Member States, their administration and judiciary in developing homogeneous rules, and interpretations, as well as remedies to enforce competition rules (see *infra*, pp. 11ff).[25]

Harmonisation of Consumer Law and of Contract Law in General

On 11 July 2001 the Commission submitted a communication on European Contract Law to the Council and the European Parliament. It also asked reactions from "stakeholders" – by which it meant, among others, businesses, legal practitioners, academics and consumer groups. A few months later, i.e. on 2 October 2001, the Commission published its Green paper on EU Consumer Protection asking again for reactions from the public on the future direction of EU consumer protection. Remarkably enough, the two documents do not refer to each other, even although both concern contract law. As remarkably is it, that none of the papers examines whether there is such a legal basis in the EC Treaty to go ahead with comprehensive legislation. Whether there is such a legal basis, particularly for contract law in general but also for comprehensive consumer regulation (i.e. not limited to cross-border transactions) is a matter which needs careful analysis, especially now that the ECJ, in its *Tobacco*-judgment of 5 October 2000,[26] has given a strong warning that the issue of legal basis must be taken seriously by the Community legislature. According to that

---

[24] An extension which the ECJ has read into Article 10 EC: see Lenaerts and Van Nuffel, *op. cit.*, at pp. 421–424.

[25] In areas of domestic law where homogeneity is not required "to facilitate the achievement of the Community's tasks", it is a matter for the Member States' legal order itself to determine whether convergence must be brought about for reasons of good governance, that is to maintain coherence of the legal order in the Member State concerned and/or to secure equal treatment of plaintiffs and defendants in domestic litigation regardless of whether claims or defences are based, in similar issues, on Community law, in combination with implementing national law, or solely on national law. See e.g. House of Lords in *M.* v. *Home Office* [1994] AC 377 with regard to the remedy of interim relief against the Crown.

[26] Case C-376/98, *Germany* v. *Parliament and Council*, [2000] ECR I-8419. For an examination of the Commission's Communication in the broader context of codification of private law, see my article "Codifying European Private Law? Yes, if…!" (2002) *European Law Review* 156–174.

judgment, Article 95 EC will indeed no longer be seen to provide a sufficient legal basis on the basis of "a mere finding of disparities between national rules and the abstract risk of obstacles to the exercise of fundamental [economic] freedoms or of distortions of competition liable to result therefrom".[27] Actually, in the past such an abstract risk was often used in the preambles of directives, including consumer directives, to justify harmonisation measures.[28] As a result of this warning, the Commission, in both documents: the Communication and the Green Paper, makes an urgent request to all stakeholders to document the concrete need for harmonisation. That may be less of a problem for harmonisation of consumer law than it is for contract law in general, insofar as Article 153, para. 3, EC can be regarded to offer an autonomous legal basis, that is independent from the provisions of Article 95 EC.[29]

The Commission's *Green Paper on Consumer Protection* is a well-structured document which describes the *present* state of protection, outlines alternatives for the future direction and the issues involved and analyses the methods of enforcement. Its general purpose is to examine how consumer regulation can facilitate easy access of consumers to goods and services promoted, offered and sold across the borders (2.1). It observes that present Community legislation contains only a few generally applicable directives, in addition to numerous directives containing rules for specific sectors or selling methods. Accordingly, in important areas where no Community regulation exists so far – notably in the areas of marketing practices, practices linked to the contract, payment and after-sales services (2.2) – national regulation solely applies with considerable differences in substance and application. Surely, many Member States have a general legal principle, sometimes supported by specific laws, for regulating business-consumer commercial practices (2.3). But also in that respect there are important differences which tend to become even more important with the growth of "new economy" commercial practices unforeseen by existing specific rules but already caught by general principles and treated in different ways (*ibid., in fine*).

As for the *future* direction which consumer law should take and in line with the "away from detail and over-regulation" approach – which is the objective of "mutual recognition" for goods (*supra*, p. 2)[30] – the Commission now favours a so-called "mixed approach" of comprehensive (not piecemeal) regulation laid down in

[27] At para. 84 of the judgment.

[28] See S. Weatherill, "The European Commission's Green Paper on European Contract Law: Context, Content and Constitutionality" (2001) *Journal of Consumer Policy* 339–399, at 346 ff. (the text of the Commission's Communication of 11 July 2001 is reproduced in annex to the article).

[29] On that point, see W. van Gerven, *art. cit.* in n. 26, at 167, fn. 55 and 56. On the history of Article 153 EC, see J. Stuyck, "European Consumer Law after the Treaty of Amsterdam: Consumer Policy in or Beyond the Internal Market" (2000) *Common Market Law Review* 367–400, at 379 ff.

[30] The "mutual recognition approach" is typical for goods and relates more particularly to technical standards. It is based on the recognition of the rules in the country of origin of the goods. As such it cannot be applied to contract law where, according to a general principle of private international law, the contracting parties are free to choose their own law with regard to non-mandatory rules whereas for mandatory consumer contract rules the law of the country of the consumer's domicile is normally applicable (see Article 5(1) of the European Convention on Contract Law). See further J. Drexl, *art. cit.* n. 5, at pp. 6–8 of the manuscript.

a framework directive, supplemented by targeted directives where necessary, and leaving room for "formal stakeholder participation in the regulatory process" (3.4). The general framework directive would be based on a general clause drawing on existing legal models based on "fair commercial practices" or "good market behaviour" (4.1) or, in a more limited version, on a concept of "misleading and deceptive practices" (4.2). General obligations on information disclosure would be central to both alternatives (4.3). Self- and co-regulation, practical guidance in recommendations or indicative lists, and stakeholder participation are presented as useful devices (4.4, 4.5 and 4.6). Finally, proposals for adequate enforcement are submitted to consultation (5.1 and 5.2). In that regard, it is noteworthy that, according to the Commission, "although consumers and consumer associations, will continue to have an essential enforcement role to play, through the courts, a fully functioning consumer internal market will also depend on public consumer enforcement authorities acting in cooperation as 'enforcers of last resort'" (5.1). And indeed, the focus of the paper on public enforcement in cooperation is clearly more present in the many options presented under 5.2. than private enforcement, that is by (private) "public interest groups".[31]

The Commission's *Communication on European contract law* is of a different, namely more academic nature. It presents four options of which only the last is novel. The first option is doing nothing (hardly an alternative), the second is to encourage non-binding common principles in the area of general contract law (thus giving moral support to already existing sets of non-binding principles), the third is to improve the quality of existing legislation (which is self-evident) whilst the fourth is to adopt new comprehensive legislation at EU level, i.e. "an overall text comprising provisions on general questions of contract law as well as specific contracts. For this option, the choice of instrument and the binding nature of the measures need to be discussed" (4.4. under 61). In a recent article, I have examined the communication and put it in the perspective of codification of private (patrimonial) law generally.[32] For indeed, projects to regulate – in a binding Code – contract law, tort law, unjust enrichment and fiduciary relations, are well underway. In that article, I came to the conclusion "that, if codification of private law were to come about *beyond* the area of contract law on which the Communication focuses, it should, in the absence of an amendment of the EC Treaty [which is needed because of the actual lack of legal basis], be done by international agreement and in accordance with a procedure which complies as much as possible with the principle of participative democracy [and therefore with the participation of national parliaments]". If codification remains *limited to* contract law, then a combination of (non-binding) general principles with a review of existing sectoral Community law is to be recommended. However that is, codification at the European level should be preceded, and accompanied, by flanking measures: for indeed, as important as codification itself is it to educate lawyers who are able to work with it, and to provide them with knowledge and tools needed

---

[31] On enforcement initiated by public interests groups, see L.W. Gormley, "Public Interest Litigation in Community law" (2001) *European Public Law* at 51–62.s.

[32] See n. 26 above.

to apply the new codification. Amongst those flanking measures comparative research to uncover common foundations of the Member States' legal systems is crucial, as emphasized above (p. 5 ff.), to make sure that European codification is accepted in the Member States and effectively applied by the national authorities, mainly the domestic courts.

Codification of European contract law, and contract law alone – as envisaged in the Communication's fourth option – either by regulation or by international agreement, is not for the near future. The only realistic approach for the near future is to adopt a set of non-binding principles of contract law in combination with improving the existing Community legislation, mainly in the field of consumer law. And even that approach raises difficult problems where the second limb, improving existing legislation, is concerned. For indeed, in the area of consumer law the choice is then between unification or harmonisation only. The former – assuming that there is a legal basis for it in Article 95 or 153 EC – implies that both, the existing directives and the Member States' implementing legislation now in effect, be turned into one or several comprehensive *regulations*. But that may be a bridge too far, considering that national governments may not wish to achieve uniformity because they do not want to do away with the possibility of maintaining national preferences as much as possible.[33] If, contrariwise, the option is taken to achieve harmonisation through one or several comprehensive *directives*, the question then arises whether harmonisation should be minimal or maximal. In case of minimal harmonisation, the Member States would still be allowed to maintain stricter consumer laws with for consequence that differences in mandatory rules would continue to hinder free movement of goods and services.[34] But also maximum harmonisation may not be acceptable for political reasons as it would require Member States with stricter consumer laws to lower domestic standards of protection.[35]

Considering these difficulties the "mixed approach" advocated by the Commission in its Green paper seems indeed the most realistic approach. It consists in "develop(ing) a comprehensive ... EU framework directive to harmonise national fairness rules for business–consumer commercial practices. This would be based on similar models to those seen in certain Member States and third countries ... (It) would not override sector-specific directives such as the unfair contract terms directive ... (and) would amount to a safety net to cover practices where cross-border restrictions are identified and which fall outside the coordinated fields of sector-specific Directives. Where necessary, the framework directive would be accompanied in due course by a reform of existing consumer protection directives to ensure the overall

[33] See further G. Howells, "European Consumer Law – The minimal and maximal harmonisation debate," lecture held in Leuven at the SECOLA/CCLE Conference referred to in n. 5, at p. 7 of the manuscript.

[34] It is argued by some that after the ECJ's Tobacco-judgment referred to in n. 26 above, minimum harmonisation for mandatory rules is no longer acceptable: see J. Drexl, "Continuing Contract Law Harmonisation under the White Paper of 1985 – Partly with modifications", referred to in n. 5, at p. 12 of the manuscript.

[35] *Ibid.*, at p. 16 where some "second best" solutions are discussed.

coherence of the consumer protection system... once the framework directive has been established and experience has been gained of its operation in practice".[36]

The "mixed approach" of consumer law harmonisation should be combined, as advocated above, with a set of non-binding general contract rules. Contrary to the existing proposals, such set of principles should however be drafted having regard to the many areas of contract law (such as consumer, labour, financial services and public procurement law) where mandatory rules, of national or Community origin, are in effect. Indeed, codification of only non-mandatory contract law (for which contracting parties may choose their own law) is in itself too academic because it remains abstracted from the bulk of daily life situations where the doctrine of party autonomy and party equality is no longer fully applicable. At the very least, a set of general contract principles should contain references to existing Community rules in the aforementioned areas of mandatory law, and give indications as to the impact which those rules would have on the application of the general rules. In that same context, an effort should be undertaken to draft mandatory rules, particularly consumer laws, from a *neutral* consumer protection point of view, i.e. not – or not exclusively – in a perspective of internal market integration. For indeed, as was correctly pointed out, "(t)he Community claims to favour a high level of protection, but the need for internal market justifications means that Community laws often only deal with part of the problem".[37] In that regard inspiration could be drawn from modern codifications, such as the recent Dutch Code, which is not only comprehensive from a viewpoint of subjects and areas covered (including consumer and labour law for instance) but also from a viewpoint of weighing interests globally, that is having regard also, in areas where mandatory rules apply, to the particular interest of classes of persons who are regarded to be weaker parties.[38]

Private and Public Enforcement

Rules remain dead letter when their compliance cannot be enforced, just like individual rights deriving from such rules remain dead letter when they cannot be enforced through remedies before courts of law. Public and private enforcement are therefore essential. When rules, and therefore rights, are involved which are intended to achieve uniformity, or at least harmonization, throughout the Community, public and private enforcement must be made sufficiently uniform, or harmonized, as well.

Public authorities rely primarily on public enforcement through administrative or penal sanctions. A prime example thereof is EC competition law. The enforcement of the prohibitions of Articles 81 and 82 EC, as laid down in Regulation nr. 17, is

---

36 At 3.4., first paragraph of the Green Paper.

37 G. Howells, *art. cit.*, at p. 9 of the manuscript.

38 See further my article referred to in n. 24, at pp. 161 and 170–171.

indeed in the hands of the Commission which is empowered to institute administrative proceedings, at its own initiative or following a complaint from a private party. It is also empowered, where an infringement is established, to impose administrative penalties, including fines (which are not penal in name but very much equivalent to penal sanctions as to substance). Private enforcement before national courts (that is enforcement undertaken by private individuals with the help of civil law remedies) also exists in the area of EC competition law, but is not complete since the domestic courts cannot monitor compliance with the full Article 81 EC, i.e. including granting an exemption under Article 81(3). That will change when the decentralisation proposal of the EC Commission is approved by the Council and the European Parliament.

According to that proposal, also called modernization proposal,[39] the competition authorities in the Member States and the national courts will bear prime and full responsibility for the application and (public respectively private) enforcement of Article 81, including para. 3, and Article 82 EC. Private enforcement before national courts resulting in nullity of cartel agreements and, more importantly, in compensation for damage sustained by contracting or third parties, including consumers, should then play a more important role. That is particularly so now that the ECJ stated, in its *Courage/Crehan* judgment,[40] that "[t]he full effectiveness of Article 8[1] of the Treaty and, in particular, the practical effect of the prohibition laid down in Article 8[1] would be put at risk if it were not open to any individual to claim damages for loss caused to him by contract or by conduct liable to restrict or distort competition".[41] As a result of this judgment, it is most likely that the ECJ will be called upon in later litigation to flesh out the conditions under which liability for infringements of competition rules by private enterprises will arise; as it was led to do in its "Francovich" case law with respect to liability of public authorities for infringements of Community law. However, that process of harmonisation through *case law* will take years and, moreover, will not necessarily result in remedial and procedural rules which would make private enforcement really and equally effective in all Member States. For indeed, it is the Court's religion to refer to domestic law when it comes to determine the *extent* of the remedy of compensation. To make private enforcement really and equally effective, it will therefore be necessary for the Community *legislature* to issue a regulation on the basis of Article 83 EC by which effective remedies are put at the disposal of the national courts. With regard to the remedy of compensation, such regulation should also provide rules concerning the plaintiff's burden of proof, in view of facilitating it, both with regard to causation and the existence of damage, as well as rules enumerating the heads of damage for which

---

39 For an overview, see C.D. Ehlermann, "The Modernization of EC Antitrust Policy: A Legal and Cultural Revolution" (2000) *Common Market Law Review* 537–590.

40 Case C-453/99 [2001] ECR I-6297.

41 Para. 26 of the judgment.

compensation can be obtained. Such a regulation should also deal with the remedies of nullity, interim relief and collective claims.[42]

As already mentioned (p. 8), the Green Paper on Consumer Protection contains proposals with regard to what it calls "adequate enforcement structures" mainly, however, in relation with *public* enforcement; for which it relies very much on cooperation between public bodies in different Member States in order "to combat traders acting cross-border in a fraudulent, dishonest or unfair way" (5.1). It focuses particularly on the necessity to develop a framework and practical tools allowing the systematic exchange of information between Member States and with third countries. It points out that the need for the Commission to monitor equally effective national enforcement policies will become even more crucial with enlargement and the accession of countries without a long history of consumer protection enforcement (*ibid.*). The establishment of common databases and communication networks that respect confidentiality requirements and the possibility for Member States to carry out coordinated enforcement actions (simultaneous investigations, injunctions) are amongst the tools which the Commission wants to install (5.2).

As for *private* enforcement, the Green Paper refers to the essential role which consumers and consumer associations will continue to play through the courts in which connection it mentions the "Injunctions Directive",[43] however without submitting any proposals to extend or improve the impact of the directive and, regrettably, without monitoring its usefulness in the past. It would seem therefore that, except for lip service, the Commission does not really believe in private enforcement, at least not in this area of Community law. In its present state, the Injunctions Directive harmonises national rules relating to actions for an injunction aimed at the protection of collective consumer interests. It intends, in instances covered by directives listed in the Annex (which have to be transposed into the Member State's internal law!), to facilitate injunctions in cross-border situations, that is in the event of an infringement in one Member State which has effects in another. It provides in independent public bodies and/or private consumer protection organisations (possibly to include professional organisations) to be designated by a Member State, in accordance with requirements laid down in its own law, as a competent authority to bring actions for injunctions. It obliges Member States to allow designated consumer associations from another Member State to bring actions before its courts. The directive does not cover actions for monetary compensation; it only provides in injunctions, publication of a judgment and/or of a corrective statement. Periodic penalty payments are

---

[42] I have made an attempt to make this proposal concrete by presenting a draft regulation in annex to my contribution to the 2001 *Annual EC Competition Law and Policy Workshop* organised by the European University Institute in Florence. The subject of my contribution was "Substantive remedies for the private enforcement of EC antitrust rules before national courts". The contribution will be published in the Institute Annual 2001 and has in the meantime been published in [J. Stuyck and H. Gilliams (eds)] *Modernisation of European Competition Law*, Leuven Centre for a Common law of Europe (CCLE), Intersentia, 2002, at 93–136.

[43] Directive 98/27 of 19 May 1998 on Injunctions for the Protection of Consumer Interests, OJ 1998 L166/51.

allowed insofar as the Member State's legal system so permits. It has been rightly pointed out that the directive is much too limitative in scope and content of harmonisation (particularly as regards *ius standi* and sanctions) and that it is moreover insufficiently clear as to whether it goes beyond the situation of cross-border situations.[44] It is therefore regrettable that the Green Paper does not envisage any progress in respect of private enforcement. The fact that the protection of diffuse interests through collective claims (to be distinguished from class actions) is not popular in all Member States and differently regulated in the Member States certainly helps to explain the Commission's reluctance to take a further step forward.[45]

To Conclude

Whilst the paradigm of harmonisation in the EU has clearly shifted from uniformity towards differentiation, time has come to do something about the incoherence which differentiation entails. The paradigm of differentiation must therefore go hand in hand with the paradigm of *homogeneity*. Homogeneity means that legislatures and judges, particularly at the Community level, must be ready to systematically aim to achieve a large degree of coherence between the instruments of harmonisation, or unification, within the same area of Community law as well as between the different areas of Community law. It also means that legislatures and judges at the Community and the national level must strive for homogeneity between Community law and the legal systems of the Member States. In that connection, particular attention must be given to homogeneity as to remedies which must enable private parties to see their rights adequately enforced before Community and national courts.

---

44 G. Betlem, "Cross-border Private Enforcement of Community Law" in J.A.E. Vervaele a.o. (ed.), *Compliance and Enforcement of European Community Law* (Kluwer, 1999) 391–418, at 412–416. On the Injunctions Directive see also M. Bogdan, " Some Reflections Regarding the New EU Directive on Injunctions for the Protection of Consumer Interests" (1998) *Consumer Law Journal* 369 ff.

45 On collective claims in a comparative law context and distinguished from class actions, see W.van Gerven a.o., book on *Tort Law* referred to in n. 21, at pp. 248–277.

Chapter 2

The Principle of Non-Discrimination and EC Social Policy

*Síofra O'Leary**

Introduction

The purpose of this Chapter is to highlight some key EC legislative developments over the last 50 years relating to the principle of non-discrimination as well as those in the field of social policy, keeping in mind the underlying theme of the conference on the quality of legal harmonisation in the European Union. I take as the intended meaning and scope of harmonisation the definition provided by Professor van Gerven, drawn presumably from Article 94 EC, namely the approximation of laws by way of directives.

Anyone who is even vaguely acquainted with the panoply of legislation adopted by the Community legislature in the field of social policy and with the wide-ranging application of the non-discrimination principle will understand that it is well-nigh impossible in such a short space to examine the development of the law in these areas comprehensively. In addition, it is questionable whether the optic of harmonisation is the ideal one with which to examine either field. The provisions of the EC Treaty on the free movement of persons and services, for example, which contain a specific expression of the general principle of non-discrimination on grounds of nationality, do not seek harmonisation of the substantive provisions of national employment and social law. Rather they seek to create a new form of administration of the market in labour and services: an internal market whereby access is undistorted by discriminatory or restrictive national rules and practices.[1]

Similarly, although in the early 1970s the Community legislature embarked on the drafting and adoption of a whole range of social and employment legislation covering anything from the rights of workers in the event of insolvency to equal pay for male and female workers, this legislation incorporated, for legal and political reasons, only minimum harmonisation. The legal reasons for the choice of this level of harmonisation lay in the limited nature of the legal bases available in the existing Treaties for the adoption of EC legislation in those fields. Essentially, the original EEC Treaty seemed to empower the Council to harmonise or, in the words of the

---

* Legal Secretary, European Court of Justice.

[1] See B. Hepple, "Harmonisation of Labour Law in the European Communities" in J. Adams (ed.), *Essays for Clive Schmitthoff* (Abingdon, Professional Books Ltd, 1983) pp. 14–28, 15.

M. van Empel (ed.), "From Paris to Nice": Fifty Years of Legal Integration in Europe, 15–32.

Treaty, approximate, national laws only if this was justified on economic grounds and not for the purpose of achieving social progress *per se*. Politically, there was and still is considerable reluctance in, indeed opposition from, certain Member States to EC interference with the regulation of national systems of labour law, industrial relations and social policy generally.[2] This has been most notably exemplified in recent years by the United Kingdom's attempts to annul the working time Directive, which had been adopted by qualified majority on the basis of the health and safety provisions of the EC Treaty, and by its refusal to be bound by the Social Chapter attached to the Maastricht Treaty.[3] Proposals for legislation on the protection of pregnant workers, on information and consultation of employees,[4] on the establishment of a European Company,[5] to name but a few, languished before the Council for many years due to Member States' inability to reach agreement on their content and scope. The objective of the Community legislature in the field of social policy has generally not been to seek uniformity but instead to establish a minimum floor of common rights. Even in more recent years when several more far-reaching legal bases for the adoption of social legislation have been added to the EC Treaty, the tendency remains the introduction of minimum or alternative harmonisation. The use of directives in the field of social policy has thus permitted the Member States flexibility in achieving the objectives of EC law while allowing them alternative methods of achieving those objectives and, in some cases, alternative levels of protection.[6]

The next section of this chapter is devoted to the vast and amorphous field of social policy. The jury is still out on what EU social policy actually covers or seeks to achieve. As some commentators have remarked: "It could be a debate about the place in economic and commercial development of social equity, of the fair distribution of resources, and of rights at work; or it could be about economic efficiency, and the degree to which this can be furthered through the manipulation of social conditions; or it could be about the search for a 'level playing field' in the Single Market, so that market distortions caused by what has become known as 'social dumping' can be

---

[2] In the particular context of labour law see also Hepple, *ibid.*, p. 22: "There has not been, and is unlikely to be, a systematic harmonisation of all or even major aspects of labour law. This is because labour law, perhaps more than any other branch of law with which the EC is concerned, is so closely linked to the peculiarities of national industrial and political traditions." See also S. Simitis and A. Lyon-Caen, "Community Labour Law: A Critical Introduction to its History," in P. Davies *et al.* (eds), *European Community Labour Law: Principles and Perspectives; Liber Amicorum Lord Wedderburn* (Oxford, Clarendon Press, 1996) pp. 1–22, 5, who argue that the approximation of national laws to the extent that the regulatory structure of the EC resembles that of a single state is not necessary.

[3] See Case C-84/94 *United Kingdom* v. *Council* [1996] ECR I-5755.

[4] Finally adopted as Directive 2002/14/EC of the European Parliament and of the Council of 11 March 2002 establishing a general framework for informing and consulting employees in the European Community – Joint Declaration of the European Parliament, the Council and the Commission on employee representation, OJ 2002 L80/29.

[5] Finally adopted as Council Regulation (EC) No. 2157/2001 of 8 October 2001 on the Statute for a European Company (SE), OJ 2001 L294/1.

[6] See, e.g. Council Directive 2001/23/EC of 12 March 2001 on the approximation of the laws of the Member States relating to the safeguarding of employees' rights in the event of transfers of undertakings, businesses or parts of undertakings or businesses, OJ 2001 L 82/16.

avoided; or it could be about a new Community dimension focusing on social affairs as an area deserving attention in its own right."[7]

EC employment legislation at least can be divided roughly into the following principal categories: the free movement of persons, equal treatment and equal opportunities for men and women, employment protection legislation specifically geared to (minimum) protection of the rights of employees in the event of the restructuring of undertakings, legislation on information, consultation and worker participation and health and safety legislation addressing employees' working environment. Other primary and secondary EC law concerning, variously, competition law, state aids, or public procurement, also have a potential effect on domestic employment and social policies.[8] Indeed given the primacy accorded the requirements of competition and free markets, at least in the early days of European integration, some authors regard national social law as having been "eroded" in the name of the demands of competition.[9] This, as Professor van Gerven has pointed out in Chapter 1, reflects the potentially disruptive effect of EC harmonisation on the legal systems of the Member States, with EC law cutting through areas of domestic law which before Community harmonisation were regulated in a coherent way.[10]

Given the breadth of EC social policy, the discussion in the section "EC Social Policy" is limited to two specific areas of EC law where the Community legislature has attempted to introduce a minimum degree of harmonisation – namely the 1992 Directive relating to the protection of pregnant workers and those on maternity leave and the Directive, recently amended, on transfers of undertakings – with a view to getting a clearer picture of the level and quality of harmonisation achieved in this field. This discussion is preceded by an overview of the available legal bases in the EC Treaty for the adoption of social policy legislation.

The third section first outlines the principle of non-discrimination on grounds of nationality contained in Article 12 EC and those provisions of the Treaty relating to the free movement of persons and services. Although specific expressions of this principle are contained in other Treaty provisions concerning agriculture, competition and tax, they are omitted from the discussion in this section due to time constraints, as is EC law on the prohibition of discrimination on grounds of sex. The third section focuses instead on recent legislation, adopted following the introduction of Article 13 EC by the Amsterdam Treaty, establishing a general framework for equal treatment in employment and occupation. Expanding and concretising the non-discrimination

---

[7] See F. von Prondzynski and A. Kewley, "Social Law in the European Union: The Search for a Philosophy" (1995/96) 2 *Columbia Journal of European Law* 265–275, 266.

[8] See, e.g. Cases 31/87 *Beentjes* [1988] ECR 4635 (public procurement); or C-67/96 *Albany* [1999] ECR I-5751 (competition).

[9] See Simitis and Lyon-Caen, *op. cit.*, p. 11.

[10] An excellent example of the disruptive effect of EC law can be found, in the context of the free provision of services, in the case-law of the Court on the application to the employees of providers of services working in a Member State other than that where the provider is established (posted workers) of host Member State social security and minimum wage legislation, e.g. in Case C-39/98 *Finalarte Sociedade de Construçao* [2001] ECR I-7831.

principle previously limited to grounds of nationality in Article 12 EC, Article 13 EC now provides: "Without prejudice to the other provisions of this Treaty and within the limits of the powers conferred by it upon the Community, the Council, acting unanimously on a proposal from the Commission and after consulting the European Parliament, may take appropriate action to combat discrimination based on sex, racial or ethnic origin, religion or belief, disability, age or sexual orientation."

EC Social Policy

The legal basis constraints on the development of EC social policy

The commitment of the original EEC Treaty to social and employment matters was limited. Prior to the landmark decisions of the Court of Justice in a trilogy of cases brought by a Belgian air hostess who complained of sex discrimination by her employers contrary to what was then Article 119 EEC (now 141 EC),[11] it seemed that no direct rights were conferred by the Treaty on employees or Community nationals generally by the Treaty's social provisions. The latter were in any case underscored by an ambivalent commitment to the pursuit of both economic and social objectives. The former Articles 117 and 118 EEC may have contained some high-sounding objectives – *inter alia*, the promotion of improved working conditions and a raised standard of living – but these provisions were, in the words of the Court of Justice,[12] of a purely programmatic nature.

The reason for the limited commitment to social policy in the original Treaty was simple: there was relatively little support at the time it was being negotiated for the view that fair competition and transnational social policy and labour law were closely interconnected and it was thought, in the main, that the economic integration sought by the establishment of a common market did not require a social counterpart. Regulatory action by the Community was envisaged only where necessary to remedy specific distortions of competition. Thus, Article 119 was included in the original EEC Treaty precisely because it was believed that lower pay for female workers in some Member States might give them a competitive advantage and therefore distort competition.[13] Generally, however, Member States regarded labour law and social policy as domestic issues and, as Barnard points out "at a time of unprecedented activity at national level, there was little pressure for harmonisation at Community level."[14] In subsequent years, the adoption of a series of social action

[11] See Cases 80/70 *Gabrielle Defrenne* v. *Belgium* [1970] ECR 445; 43/75 *Gabrielle Defrenne* [1976] ECR 455; and 149/77 *Gabrielle Defrenne* v. *Société Anonyme Belge de Navigation Aérienne Sabena* [1978] ECR 1365.

[12] See Case 149/77 *Defrenne III*, paras 19 and 31; Case 126/86 *Fernando Roberto Giménez Zaera* v. *Instituto Nacional de la Seguridad Social* [1987] ECR 3697, paras 11 and 13; and Case C-72/91 *Firma Sloman Neptun Schiffarts AG* v. *Seebetriebsrat Bodo Ziesemer* [1993] ECR I-887.

[13] See further C. Barnard, *EC Employment Law*, 2nd ed. (Oxford, Oxford University Press, 2000) Chapter 1, for further background.

[14] *Ibid.*, p. 5.

programmes from the early 1970s, the Single European Act (SEA, 1986), the Community Social Charter (1989), the Maastricht and Amsterdam Treaties (1992 and 1998), not to mention the jurisprudence of the Court of Justice, have all contributed to the coming of age of the social dimension of EC law.

Economic recession and industrial unrest in the 1970s indicated that the economic neo-liberalism which underpinned the Treaties was failing on its own to protect working and living standards in the Communities.[15] In a series of meetings of what was the equivalent of today's European Council, held in The Hague in 1969, the Member States committed themselves to attributing the same importance to energetic proceedings in the field of social policy as to the realisation of an economic and financial union and charged the Community institutions with the task of drawing up social action programmes. Following on the adoption of the 1974 Social action programme, the Council adopted its first three equality Directives on equal pay, equal treatment with regard to access to employment, vocational training, promotion and working conditions and equal treatment with regard to statutory social security schemes.[16] These Directives were adopted on the basis of Articles 94 and 308 EC. The former provides that the Council shall, unanimously, issue directives for the approximation of such laws, regulations or administrative provisions of the Member States *as directly affect the establishment or functioning of the common market*. The latter, which has been described as an *ultima ratio*, to be used only if other measures fail, allowed the Council, once again acting unanimously, to take measures *necessary to attain the objectives of the Treaty*, where the Treaty itself has not provided the necessary powers. The dominant model in this field has undoubtedly been that of minimum harmonisation.

The 1972–74 social action programme was also the starting point for legislation designed to afford employees limited employment protection in the event of the restructuring of the undertaking which employed them. A Directive on collective redundancies was adopted in 1975 with a view to ensuring that greater protection was afforded to workers in the event of collective redundancies, while taking into account the need for balanced economic and social development within the Community.[17] The Directive also sought to promote the approximation of Member State legislation on collective redundancies while ensuring that the improvement of living and working conditions was maintained within the meaning of the former Article 117 EEC. The limited protection afforded by the collective redundancies

---

15 Thus failing to achieve an accelerated raising of the standard of living in the Communities as required by Article 2 EEC.

16 Council Directive 75/117/EEC of 10 February 1975 on the approximation of the laws of the Member States relating to the application of the principle of equal pay for men and women, OJ 1975 L45/19; Council Directive 76/207/EEC of 9 February 1976 on the implementation of the principle of equal treatment for men and women as regards access to employment, vocational training and promotion, and working conditions, OJ 1976 L39/40; and Council Directive 79/7/EEC of 19 December 1979 on the progressive implementation of the principle of equal treatment for men and women in matters of social security, OJ 1979 L6/24. The Equal Treatment Directive was amended by Directive 2002/73/EC of the European Parliament and of the Council of 23 September 2002, OJ 2002 L269/115.

17 Council Directive 75/129/EEC of 17 February 1975 on the approximation of the laws of the Member States relating to collective redundancies, OJ 1975 L48/29.

Directive is emphasised by the fact that it did not intend to interfere with employers' freedom to bring about collective redundancies. Instead, this partial harmonisation measure set minimum standards for undertakings to ensure that they consulted with workers' representatives properly when contemplating collective redundancies and notified the competent public authorities of their plans. Article 5 specifically provided that the Directive "shall not affect the right of Member States to apply or to introduce laws, regulations or administrative practices which are more favourable to workers or to promote or to allow the application of collective agreements more favourable to workers." The 1975 Directive has since been amended by Directive 92/56 and in turn consolidated by Directive 98/59.[18] Another partial harmonisation Directive was adopted in 1977, providing protection for employees in the event of a change in their employer by ensuring that their rights are safeguarded.[19] The Acquired Rights Directive is discussed in more detail below.

Finally, a third piece of employment protection legislation adopted in the wake of the first social action programme was the insolvency Directive adopted in 1980.[20] Also adopted on the basis of Article 94 EC, this Directive sought to promote the approximation of the laws of the Member States relating to insolvency while improving the living and working conditions of those employees by offering them the following limited protection in the event of insolvency. The Directive required Member States to establish guarantee institutions to guarantee payment of employees' outstanding claims resulting from contracts of employment or employment relationships. It also provided that the employer's non-payment of compulsory contributions to insurance institutions under the State social security scheme must not adversely affect employees' benefit entitlements. Finally, Member States were also obliged to ensure that the rights of former employees no longer employed at the time of the employer's insolvency were protected, particularly in respect of old-age benefits, including survivors' benefits, under occupational or supplementary schemes which fall outside the national social security system.

Most importantly, the SEA extended qualified majority voting in Council to the field of health and safety. The importance of this amendment cannot be underestimated.

---

[18] Council Directive 92/56/EEC of 24 June 1992, OJ 1992 L245/3, consolidated by Council Directive 98/59/EC of 20 July 1998 on the approximation of the laws of the Member States relating to collective redundancies, OJ 1998 L225/16.

[19] Council Directive 77/187/EEC of 14 February 1977 on the approximation of the laws of the Member States relating to the safeguarding of employees' rights in the event of transfers of undertakings, businesses or parts of businesses, OJ 1977 L61/126, subsequently amended by Council Directive 98/50/EC of 29 June 1998, OJ 1998 L201/88 and consolidated by Directive 2001/23. See also the decisions of the Court in Cases C-382/92 *Commission* v. *United Kingdom* [1994] ECR I-2345; and Case C-383/92 *Commission* v. *United Kingdom* [1994] ECR I-2479, relating to the directives on collective redundancies and acquired rights: "the Community legislature intended both to ensure comparable protection of workers' rights in the different Member States and to harmonise the costs which such protective rules entail for Community undertakings."

[20] Council Directive 80/987/EEC of 20 October 1980 on the approximation of the laws of the Member States relating to the protection of employees in the event of insolvency of their employer, OJ 1980 L283/23; subsequently amended by Council Directive 87/164/EEC of 2 March 1987, OJ 1987 L66/11.

The adoption of at least some social policy legislation no longer required unanimous Member State approval. Although qualified majority voting would undoubtedly be accompanied by protracted negotiation of sensitive proposals (and with the United Kingdom in particular increasingly entrenched in its opposition to labour market regulation almost all proposals would henceforth be considered sensitive), the chances of legislation being adopted were much higher than before. The former article 118a EC provided that the Council could adopt in a number of different fields, by means of directives, *minimum* requirements for gradual implementation, having regard to the conditions and technical rules obtaining in each of the Member States. Clearly this was recognition that the EC objective was not to harmonise all labour standards but merely to provide for a floor of basic rights. On the basis of this new legal basis, a whole range of new directives were adopted, including the Directive on working time and a Directive providing special protection for pregnant workers and those on maternity leave, which is also discussed below. The Court has held that where a directive laying down minimum requirements is adopted under Article 136 EC (the former Article 118a), the Member States remain free to introduce more stringent measures for the protection of working conditions.[21]

The Maastricht Treaty signalled not only the introduction of further more far-reaching social provisions, but also the prospect of a two or multi-speed Europe. With one Member State in particular refusing originally to be bound by the Social Policy Agreement (SPA) and protocol included therein, diversity or flexibility rather than harmonisation were now the new leitmotifs of EC social policy. Qualified majority voting was once again extended in the SPA so that other measures relating, for example, to working conditions, information and consultation of workers, equality between men and women with regard to labour market opportunities, were no longer to be subject to the unanimity rule in Council. In addition, the SPA envisaged a far greater role for the social partners – they would be consulted on the content of future legislative proposals but they could also negotiate agreements which would thereafter be given *erga omnes* effect by a Council decision. A number of Directives on the burden of proof in sex discrimination cases,[22] European works councils,[23] part-time work[24] and parental leave[25] were adopted following the introduction of the

---

[21] See the former Article 118a(2) and Case C-2/97 *Borsana* [1998] ECR I-8597.

[22] Council Directive 97/80/EC of 15 December 1997 on the burden of proof in cases of discrimination based on sex, OJ 1998 L14/6. Following the United Kingdom's acceptance of the Social Chapter, Directives which had been adopted on the basis of the SPA were readopted on the basis of Article 94 EC and now apply to all Member States.

[23] Council Directive 94/45/EC of 22 September 1994 on the establishment of a European Works Council or a procedure in Community-scale undertakings and Community-scale groups of undertakings for the purposes of informing and consulting employees, OJ 1994 L254/64; extended to the United Kingdom by Council Directive 97/74/EC of 15 December 1997, OJ 1997 L10/22.

[24] Council Directive 97/81/EC of 15 December 1997 concerning the Framework Agreement on part-time work concluded by UNICE, CEEP and the ETUC – Annex: Framework agreement on part-time work, OJ 1997 L14/9.

[25] Council Directive 96/34/EC of 3 June 1996 on the framework agreement on parental leave concluded by UNICE, CEEP and the ETUC, OJ 1996 L145/4.

SPA by the Maastricht Treaty. The Directives on parental leave and part-time work transposed framework agreements concluded by the social partners at European level (UNICE, CEEP and ETUC).

Finally, the Amsterdam Treaty also introduced amendments to the Treaty's social provisions, the principal amendment being to the text of the former Article 119 EC. Article 141 EC now includes a legal basis for the adoption of legislation by the Council pursuant to the co-decision procedure to ensure the application of the principle of equal opportunities and equal treatment of men and women in matters of employment and occupation, including the principle of equal pay for equal work or work of equal value.[26]

Legislative protection of pregnant workers and those on maternity leave: Directive 92/85

As we have seen, EC sex equality law developed on the basis of a patchwork of Treaty provisions, essentially the principle of equal pay in Article 141 EC and the provisions of the so-called equality Directives adopted on the basis of Articles 94 and 308 EC. These Directives were conceived not simply as a means to achieve equality between male and female workers in terms of pay, working conditions, social security provision and equal access to employment and vocational training, but also, if not principally, in terms of their effect on the establishment and functioning of the common market. Until the adoption of Directive 92/85,[27] provision for pregnancy and maternity in the equality directives was scant and formulated essentially in negative terms. Specifically, Article 2(3) of Directive 76/207 provided that "This directive shall be without prejudice to provisions concerning the protection of women, particularly as regards pregnancy and maternity." When cases began arriving at the Court in the late 1980s, the latter was forced to address, within the existing, partial legal framework, whether the protection of the employment rights and working conditions of women during specific periods of their working lives which are unique to their sex could be reconciled with the fundamentals of the principle of equality.[28]

---

[26] Article 141(3) EC. In addition, Articles 2 and 3 EC now include the principle of equality between men and women as one of the tasks of the EC as well as one of its activities and Article 137 EC provides that the EC shall complement and support the activities of the Member States in the field of equality between men and women with regard to labour market opportunities and treatment at work.

[27] Council Directive 92/85/EEC of 19 October 1992 on the introduction of measures to encourage improvements in the safety and health at work of pregnant workers and workers who have recently given birth or are breast-feeding (tenth individual Directive within the meaning of Article 16(1) of Directive 89/391/EEC) OJ 1992 L348/1.

[28] For discussion of the sometimes unsatisfactory, sometimes incoherent nature of the Court's jurisprudence prior to the introduction of directive 92/85 see C. McGlynn, "Ideologies of Motherhood in European Community Sex Equality Law" (2000) 6 *European Law Journal* 29–44; E. Caracciolo di Torella and A. Masselot, "Pregnancy, Maternity and the Organisation of Family Life" (2001) 26 *European Law Review* 239–260; and S. O'Leary, *The Employment Case-law of the European Court of Justice. Judicial Policy, Structures and Processes* (Oxford, Hart Publishing, 2002), Chapter 5.

Unlike Directive 76/207, which was adopted on the basis of Article 308 EC and which seeks to achieve equal treatment for men and women in a variety of fields, Directive 92/85 was adopted on the basis of the health and safety provisions of the former Article 118a EC and is concerned specifically with the protection of pregnant women, those who have recently given birth and those who are breastfeeding.[29] The preamble of Directive 92/85 reflects the need to place this piece of legislation within the context of the Treaty's health and safety legal provisions to secure adoption and the concern that the protection of pregnant women, those on maternity leave and those breastfeeding should not result in unfavourable treatment or work to the detriment of directives concerning equal treatment for men and women.[30]

The Directive applies to pregnant workers who inform their employers of their condition, workers who have recently given birth and workers who are breastfeeding. The definitions of worker and breastfeeding worker, as well as the requirements on informing employers, are governed by national law, with the result that the personal scope of the Directive may vary substantially depending on the Member State concerned. Articles 3–6 of the Directive deal with the hazards (chemical, physical, biological) which may be encountered by pregnant workers or those who have recently given birth, while Article 7 covers night work. Article 8 of the Directive provides that Member States shall take the necessary measures to ensure that pregnant workers are entitled to a continuous period of maternity leave of at least 14 weeks allocated before and/or after confinement in accordance with national legislation and/or practice. This leave must include compulsory maternity leave of at least 2 weeks allocated before and/or after confinement. Pregnant workers are also entitled to time off, without loss of pay, in order to attend ante-natal examinations. Article 10, which partly codifies the jurisprudence of the Court, deals with protection from dismissal. It is prohibited to dismiss pregnant workers from the beginning of their pregnancy to the end of the 14 weeks (minimum) maternity leave, save in exceptional cases unconnected with their condition which are permitted under national legislation and/or practice. It is up to the employer to explain, with reference to duly substantiated grounds, the reasons why a pregnant employee has been dismissed during this protected period. Member States are to take the necessary measures to protect pregnant workers from dismissal which is unlawful by virtue of Article 10. During the course of maternity leave, Article 11(2) provides that the rights connected with the employment contract must be ensured, as must the maintenance of the worker's pay or payment of an adequate allowance. The latter shall be deemed adequate if, according to Article 11(3),

---

[29] For discussion of the legislative background to Directive 92/85 as well as its content and effect see variously N. Burrows, "Maternity Rights in Europe – An Embryonic Legal Regime" (1991) 11 *Yearbook of European Law* 273–293; E. Ellis, "Protection of Pregnancy and Maternity" (1993) 22 *Industrial Law Journal* 63–67; and V. Cromack, "The E.C. Pregnancy Directive – Principle or Pragmatism" (1993) *Journal of Social Welfare and Family Law* 261–272.

[30] Opposition to the use of the former Article 118a EC as the legal basis for legislation with social and employment protection objectives was voiced by the House of Lords Select Committee on the European Communities, *Protection at work of pregnant women and women who have recently given birth and child care*, Session 1991–1992, 2nd report, p. 12; see also the memorandum by the Confederation of British Industry annexed to the House of Lords' Report, p. 12.

it guarantees income at least equivalent to that which the worker concerned would receive in the event of a break in her activities on grounds connected with her state of health, subject to any ceiling laid down under national legislation. Pursuant to Article 11(4), Member States may make entitlement to pay or to the allowance described above conditional upon the worker concerned fulfilling the conditions of eligibility for such benefits laid down under national legislation, but a period of employment in excess of twelve months immediately prior to the presumed date of confinement cannot be required. Member States are obliged to introduce into their national legal systems such measures as are necessary to enable all workers who should themselves be wronged by failure to comply with the obligations arising from this Directive to pursue their claims by judicial process and/or by recourse to other competent authorities.

It is far from clear whether Directive 92/85 brings about improvements in the safety and health at work of pregnant workers and workers who have recently given birth or are breastfeeding. The Report from the Commission on the implementation of the Directive reveals that very few Member States actually benefited from its adoption.[31] However, its adoption at least means that the Court need no longer wrestle to find solutions in the equal treatment/non-discrimination tools which were at its disposal in an area where comparisons of male and female are often if not always untenable. It remains to be seen, of course, whether Directive 92/85 is any more successful than the principle of equal treatment in protecting pregnant workers before and after the birth of their children. Of interest in terms of the discussion of harmonisation at EC level is the extent to which the more stringent protection sought by some Member States had to be sacrificed on the altar of compromise in order for its adoption to be secured.[32] As Ellis explains, although qualified majority voting in relation to health and safety may make it easier for legislation ultimately to be adopted, there is plenty of room for an opponent of such legislation to minimise the substantive content of such harmonisation measures.

This is not the place to detail the deficiencies in the Directive, of which there are many. Suffice it to say that even this special protection instrument is not free from the difficulties which dogged the Court's pregnancy and maternity jurisprudence in the past. Thus, only mothers benefit from maternity leave pursuant to the Directive and Member States are not obliged to provide them with their full pay, or a high percentage thereof, during this period. They may simply receive an income equivalent to the standard rate of national sick pay. The directive, though it guarantees a *minimum period of maternity leave*, may leave the most vulnerable employees with little if any protection in terms of *maternity pay* as, if they do not qualify under national law for statutory sick pay, they may be entitled to, at most, a one off compensation payment during their maternity leave. As a result, they will inevitably be forced back to work before their fourteen weeks entitlement has expired out of sheer economic necessity.[33] In the United Kingdom, women who earn less than £57 a week do not

---

[31] COM (99) 100 final.

[32] See Ellis, *loc. cit.*

[33] *Ibid.*, 67.

enjoy the protection afforded by the Directive and it is estimated that approximately 20% of women fall below this threshold. Furthermore, many part-timers do not earn more than the national insurance threshold for eligibility for such payments.

The minimalist regime introduced by the Directive – in terms of the protected period of maternity leave and the maternity pay or allowance payable to female workers on leave – may have been an improvement on the existing statutory position in some Member States such as the United Kingdom, but it has been greeted with distinct disappointment in other Member States such as Italy or France where far more generous statutory provisions were already in operation.[34] The minimum period of 14 weeks leave is now respected in all Member States, but while some Member States restrict statutory legal entitlement to this minimum, others provide for 28 weeks statutory protected leave. Similarly, while women in some Member States are entitled to 100% of their salaries when on maternity leave, in other Member States they are entitled to only a percentage of their salary for a number of weeks of the protected leave period, followed by a payment in line with statutory sick pay thereafter. All Member States subject entitlement to maternity pay or compensation to conditions linked to length of service, residence and insurance and these conditions vary from one Member State to the next. The disappointing nature of the Directive's provisions on maternity pay are emphasised by the ILO Maternity Convention 2000, which provided that, where a ratifying state is "insufficiently developed", it may pay cash benefits during maternity leave at a level no less than sickness or temporary disability benefits. Otherwise, ratifying States should provide not less than two thirds of the woman's previous income. Not surprisingly, the Member States of the European Union were not those the ILO had in mind when referring to insufficiently developed States.

The minimum nature of the protection afforded by the 1992 Directive is also emphasised in the first case to come before the Court on the interpretation of the directive's provisions. In the *Boyle* case, the applicants argued that aspects of the maternity scheme of the UK's Equal Opportunities Commission were incompatible with the directive.[35] The Court disagreed – the minimum obligations imposed on Member States by Directive 92/85, in particular by Article 8, do not cover supplemental periods of maternity leave afforded by an employer to a pregnant employee. The rights conferred by the Directive on pregnant workers and those who have recently given birth thus constitute a special protection regime, which may undermine any attempt by female workers to claim that legislative provisions, because of the disproportionate effect they have on female workers, give rise to discrimination. Although pregnant workers may still rely on the equality Directives, it is clear that their legal rights once on maternity leave are governed by the special protection regime in Directive 92/85. The minimalist nature of the provisions of this compromise text will not always work in their favour.[36]

---

[34] See, e.g. the details provided in the House of Lords Select Committee Report, *op. cit.*, p. 7.

[35] Case C-411/96 Boyle v. Equal Opportunities Commission [1998] ECRI-6401.

[36] See also A. Masselot and K. Berthou, "La CJCE, le droit de la maternité et le principe de non discrimination – vers une clarification?" (2000) *Cahiers de droit européen* 637–656.

Transfers of undertakings: Directive 77/187 as amended

The Preamble of Directive 77/187 made clear the reasons for the introduction, as early as 1977, of such a relatively advanced employment protection measure with the potential to fundamentally affect Member State labour laws.[37] Although the Directive did not concern the substantive level and scope of national employment terms and conditions, it was of fundamental importance in ensuring that employees did not lose the enjoyment of the terms and conditions applicable to their contracts as a result of the reorganisation and transfer of their employer's business. According to the first recital, economic trends were resulting, at both national and EC level, in changes to the structure of undertakings as a result of legal transfers and mergers. The purpose of the Directive was to ensure that the rights of employees, in the event of a change of employer, were safeguarded. However, the preamble also made clear that one of the principal reasons for the introduction of a minimum level of employment protection at EC level was the fear that disparities in employment protection legislation between Member States might have a deleterious effect on the transfers and mergers which it was in the common market's interest to bring about as a result of greater economic integration. Thus, the Directive reflected the dual economic and social aims that characterised much of the Community's social action programme.[38] Directive 77/187 reflected both the Community's attempts to ameliorate "the unacceptable by-products of growth"[39] and its intention to eliminate distortions of competition. Traces of the tension between the Directive's social and economic facets can be found throughout the case-law of the Court of Justice which has been called upon, essentially, to balance the employment protection objectives of the Directive with the need to ensure that there are no untoward disincentives to transferring business in an

---

[37] On Directive 77/187 generally see M.C. Rodríguez-Piñero Royo, "Transmisión de empresas y derecho europeo" in *La transmisión de empresas en Europa*, Collana di diritto comparato e comunitario del lavoro e della sicurezza sociale (Cacucci Editor, 1999); F. Vandamme, "Concentrations d'entreprises et protection des travailleurs" (1977) 13 *Cahiers de droit européen* pp. 25–48; M.F.G.M. Legnier, "Transferts d'entreprises et protection des travailleurs dans le cadre communautaire" (1977) *Revue du marché commun* 473–482; Report of the House of Lords Select Committee on the European Communities, *Transfer of Undertakings: Acquired Rights*, Session 1995–1996, 5th Report.

[38] See, however, the Opinion of Advocate General Cosmas (para 15) in Case C-472/93 *Luigi Spano and Others* v. *Fiat Geotech SpA and Fiat Hitachi Excavators SpA* (*formerly Fiat Hitachi Construction Equipment SpA*) [1995] ECR I-4321, where he stated that the Directive pursues a manifestly social objective. See further G. More, "The concept of 'undertaking' in the Acquired Rights Directive: the Court of Justice under pressure (again)" (1995) 15 *Yearbook of European Law* 135–155, at 136–137, where she points out that the social focus of the Commission's original proposal, namely ensuring that employees did not forfeit essential rights and advantages acquired prior to a change of employer (COM (74) 351 Final/2, para. 7), was diluted during the process of adoption, with the need to safeguard the functioning of the common market gaining strength. She questions whether this change in emphasis was deliberate or merely a means of shaping the Directive to fit its Article 94 EC legal basis. Closely related to the Acquired Rights Directive were Directive 75/129 (collective redundancies) and Directive 80/987 (insolvency). All three Directives were intended to ensure appropriate protection for the employee in situations associated with company restructuring and long-term economic difficulties.

[39] See the 1974 Social Action Programme, Bull. EC. Supp. 2/74, 13 and the discussion in M. Shanks, *European Social Policy, Today and Tomorrow* (Oxford, Pergamon, 1977).

increasingly integrated and globalised European market. Professor van Gerven comments correctly that the smaller number of Member States in the original Communities allowed uniformity to be the prevailing paradigm, with the result that harmonising directives were often as precise and detailed as regulations. It must be said that Directive 77/187 was perhaps one of the exceptions to this rule. The Directive's provisions were minimalist to say the least, with central concepts such as legal transfer and what constitutes a transfer of an undertaking left undefined, despite substantial differences at Member State level as regards what such concepts entail. Unsurprisingly, this has led to a not inconsiderable number of references from national courts seeking guidance as to how best to interpret the Directive.

Article 1(1) indicated to which transfers Directive 77/187 would apply. It provided that the Directive should apply to the transfer of an undertaking, business or part of a business to another employer as a result of a legal transfer or merger. The Directive provided employees essentially with three forms of protection. In the first place, Article 3 provided that the transferor's rights and obligations arising from a contract of employment or from an employment relationship existing on the date of a transfer would, by reason of such transfer, be transferred to the transferee.[40] Following the transfer, the transferee was bound to observe the terms and conditions agreed in any collective agreement on the same terms applicable to the transferor under that agreement, albeit Member States could limit the period for observing such terms and conditions (Article 3(2)). Article 3(3) stated, however, that the preceding paragraphs would not cover employees' rights to old-age, invalidity or survivors' benefits under supplementary company or inter-company pension schemes outside the statutory social security schemes in Member States. As Davies points out, when adopting the 1977 Directive, the Member States opted for a narrow form of acquired rights: transferred employees were entitled to the same level of employment protection *vis-à-vis* the transferee as they had been *vis-à-vis* the transferor. The purpose of the Directive was not to demand a harmonised level of employment protection but simply to ensure that the level of protection that pertained prior to the transfer continued to be guaranteed thereafter.[41] The second form of protection afforded by Directive 77/187 referred to the fact that the transfer of an undertaking did not in itself constitute grounds for dismissal of employees by the transferor or the transferee. Dismissal of employees was, however, in accordance with Article 4(1), permissible for economic, technical or organisational reasons entailing changes in the workforce; a provision which underlined the compromise inherent in the Directive between the need to protect employees and the need to recognise the hard realities of business life. Article 4(2) of the Directive provided that, if the contract of employment or the employment relationship were terminated because the transfer involved a substantial

---

40 Article 3(1) of Directive 77/187 also provides that Member States may provide that, after the date of transfer and in addition to the transferee, the transferor shall continue to be liable in respect of obligations which arose from a contract of employment or an employment relationship.

41 See P. Davies, "Acquired Rights, Creditors' Rights, Freedom of Contract, and Industrial Democracy" (1989) 9 *Yearbook of European Law* 21–53, 21; and R. Upex, "The Acquired Rights Directive and its Effect upon Consensual Variation of Employees' Contracts" (1999) 24 *European Law Review* 293–299.

change in working conditions to the detriment of the employee, the employer was to be regarded as having been responsible for termination of the contract of employment or of the employment relationship. Finally, Article 6 of Directive 77/187 required that employees' representatives be informed by the transferor and the transferee of the reasons for the transfer, the legal, economic and social implications of the transfer for the employees and of the measures envisaged in relation to the employees. This information was to be provided in good time before the transfer was carried out.[42] Directive 77/187 did not affect the right of Member States to apply or introduce laws, regulations or administrative provisions which were more favourable to employees (Article 7).

Twenty four years later, an amended (Directive 98/50) and consolidated (Directive 2001/23) version of the 1977 directive seems to confirm a shift from a quest for harmonisation (albeit minimum), to greater explicit recognition of the need for flexibility. The amended Directive refers to employees as any person who, in the Member State concerned, is protected as an employee under national law, the Commission having failed to incorporate an EC definition of employee. The Directive is without prejudice to national laws as regards the definition of contract of employment or employment relationship (Article 2(2)). Member States *may* provide that, after the date of transfer, the transferor and the transferee shall be jointly and severally liable in respect of obligations which arose before the date of transfer from a contract of employment or employment relationship existing on the date of transfer (Article 3(1)). Member States *may* limit the time-frame in which transferees are obliged to observe the terms and conditions of collective agreements by which they are bound by virtue of the transfer (Article 3(3)). An essential aspect of the Acquired Rights Directive is that a transfer does not constitute a valid ground for dismissal. However, Member States remain free not to apply the provisions of the Directive to categories of employees who do not enjoy protection against dismissal at national level. Article 5 also provides that, *unless Member States provide otherwise*, certain employment protection provisions in the Directive shall not apply to a transfer where the transferor is the subject of bankruptcy or analogous insolvency proceedings. Member States may also limit the obligations on businesses deriving from the information and consultation provisions of the Directive to businesses with a certain number of employees (Article 7(5)). Clearly, the amended Directive continues to provide employees with a basic floor of rights in the event of a transfer but it also permits Member States a considerable degree of flexibility in the transposition of its provisions.

THE PRINCIPLE OF NON-DISCRIMINATION IN EC LAW

The principle of non-discrimination on grounds of nationality

Article 12 EC provides that "Within the scope of application of this Treaty, and without prejudice to any special provisions contained therein, any discrimination on

---

[42] See further Davies (1989), *loc. cit.*, 27–29, for discussion of how and why the original proposals for the 1977 Directive relating to consultation were watered down during the course of the adoption process.

grounds of nationality shall be prohibited."[43] Specific expression of this general principle can be found in Articles 39, 43 and 49 EC which concern the free movement of persons and services in the internal market. Article 39 EC provides that the free movement of workers shall entail the abolition of any discrimination based on nationality between workers of the Member States as regards employment, remuneration and other conditions of work and employment.[44] Freedom of establishment entails, pursuant to Article 43 EC, the right to take up and pursue activities as self-employed persons and to set up and manage undertakings in a Member State other than one's Member State of origin, under the conditions laid down by that Member State for its own nationals.[45] Finally, Article 49 EC seeks to secure equal access for nationals of Member States to the market for the provision of services in a Member State other than that where the provider of services is established.[46] The principle of non-discrimination is not restricted to clear incidences of discrimination founded on nationality or establishment. The Court of Justice has held that EC law prohibits all forms of disguised discrimination which, although applying other criteria of distinction, lead, in fact, to the same result. This is known as indirect or covert discrimination.[47]

The provisions of EC secondary legislation on the free movement of persons and services are well known and there is no need to reproduce them or the debates which have accompanied their development – whether legislative or judicial – in detail here.[48] The guarantees of non-discrimination and free movement in the Treaty were translated into secondary legislation during the course of the late 1960s and early 1970s. Principally this legislation addresses the free movement and residence rights of economically active EC nationals, the rights of migrant workers and their families when resident in a Member State other than their Member State of origin and the co-ordination of Member State social security rules for those EC nationals who have availed of their free movement rights.[49] The Court has played a central role in the development of EC law relating to the free movement of persons and services.

---

[43] Article 12 also provides that the Council may adopt rules designed to prohibit such discrimination. Little use has been made of this legal basis, the Council preferring to adopt legislation on the basis of the more general provisions on approximation and the internal market and common market later in the Treaty.

[44] See, e.g. Case 131/85 *Gül* [1986] ECR 1573, on access to employment.

[45] See, e.g. Case 90/76 *Van Ameyde* [1977] ECR 1091.

[46] In Case 33/74 *Van Binsbergen* [1974] ECR 1299, para 10, the Court regarded Article 49 EC as a means of abolishing "any discrimination against a person providing a service by reason of his nationality or of the fact that he resides in a Member State other than that in which the service is to be provided".

[47] See Case 352/85 *Bond van Adverteerders* v. *Netherlands* [1988] ECR 2085; and the definition of overt and covert discrimination of Advocate General Jacobs in Case C-76/90 *Säger* v. *Dennemeyer* [1991] ECR I-4221, para 19.

[48] See E. Guild and D. Martin, *The Free Movement of Persons in the European Union* (London, Butterworths, 1996); J. Handoll, *The Free Movement of Persons in the European Union* (Chichester, Wiley, 1995); S. O'Leary, *The Evolving Concept of Community Citizenship: From the Free Movement of Persons to Union Citizenship* (London, Kluwer, 1996); S. O'Leary, "The Free Movement of Persons and Services", in P. Craig and G. De Búrca (eds), *The Evolution of EU Law* (Oxford, OUP, 1999) pp. 377–416; and Barnard, *op. cit.*, pp. 111–196.

[49] See, in particular, Council Directive 64/221/EEC of 25 February 1964 on the co-ordination of special measures concerning the movement and residence of foreign nationals which are justified on

For the purposes of our discussion, it should perhaps be noted, as I mentioned at the outset, that "harmonisation" as such is not an ideal perspective from which to view the development of EC law in this field. In the main, the EC's anti-discrimination model means that it is up to the legislature, whether at national or EC level, to determine the substantive content of the rights to be enjoyed. The courts simply determine whether individuals belonging to a particular group (migrant workers, students, service providers, female workers) have been adversely affected in the distribution of certain advantages or disadvantages, without considering the justice or consistency, in absolute terms, of decisions made by the legislature. As Barbera points out: "[I]n the realm of private relations, such as labour relations, the anti-discrimination model embodies a notion of procedural justice which does not guarantee any particular outcome in distributive terms, in the sense that it does not establish a positive duty to remove the social disadvantage suffered by the individuals belonging to the protected groups [...] nor does it ensure a fair distribution of benefits."[50] Thus, a migrant worker may claim entitlement to a child-care allowance on the basis that national workers are entitled thereto, but the actual decision regarding the provision of such an allowance is one taken by the national legislature. In the absence of harmonisation, EC law seeks to ensure that the internal market operates effectively by ensuring that goods, persons, services and capital circulating within it are not subject to discriminatory or restrictive national rules and practices. Member States can only justify such measures with reference to the express derogations provided in the Treaty or with reference to a series of judicially-created mandatory or imperative requirements. Where the question of harmonisation has arisen time and again is in the field of social security for migrant workers and self-employed persons, where the Court has consistently emphasised that EC law seeks to co-ordinate rather than harmonise provisions of national law.[51]

---

grounds of public policy, public security or public health, OJ Eng. Sp. Ed., Series-I (63–64) p. 117; Regulation (EEC) No. 1612/68 of the Council of 15 October 1968 on freedom of movement for workers within the Community, OJ Eng. Sp. Ed. 1968 L275/2 (amended by Regulation (EEC) 312/76, OJ 1976 L3/2 and Council Regulation (EEC) 2434/92, OJ 1992 L25/1); Council Directive 68/360/EEC of 15 October 1968 on the abolition of restrictions on movement and residence within the Community for workers of Member States and their families, OJ Sp. Ed. 1968 L257/13; Regulation (EEC) No. 1251/70 of the Commission of 29 June 1970 on the right of workers to remain in the territory of a Member State after having been employed in that State, OJ Sp. Ed. 1970 L142/24; Regulation (EEC) No. 1408/71 of the Council of 14 June 1971 on the application of social security schemes to employed persons and their families moving within the Community, OJ Eng Sp. Ed., Series-I 71(II) p. 416; Council Directive 73/148/EEC of 21 May 1973 on the abolition of restrictions on movement and residence within the Community for nationals of Member States with regard to establishment and the provision of services, OJ 1973 L172/14; Council Directive 75/34/EEC of 17 December 1974 concerning the right of nationals of a Member State to remain in the territory of another Member State after having pursued therein an activity in a self-employed capacity, OJ 1975 L14/10.

[50] M. Barbera, "Not the Same? The Judicial Role in the New Community Anti-Discrimination Law Context" (2002) *Industrial Law Journal* 82–91, 84.

[51] See Article 42 EC and, in particular, Regulation (EEC) no. 1408/71 of the Council of 14 June 1971 on the application of social security schemes to employed persons and their families moving within the Community (OJ 1971 L323/38).

Beyond nationality – the general non-discrimination provision introduced by the Amsterdam Treaty

The introduction of a general anti-discrimination clause in Article 13 EC has meant that the Court of Justice should no longer, as it has on occasion in the past, have to grapple with references from national courts in which applicants have sought to extend the scope of say EC law on sex equality to cover complaints of discrimination on grounds of sexual orientation not explicitly provided for in the EC Treaty or secondary legislation.[52] Article 13 empowers Member States to adopt measures to combat various forms of discrimination and a number of anti-discrimination Directives have been adopted on this basis.[53] Directive 2000/78 establishes a general framework for equal treatment in employment and occupation aimed at combatting discrimination on the grounds of religion or belief, disability, age or sexual orientation as regards employment and occupation.[54] The Directive applies to all persons, as regards both the public and private sectors, including public bodies, in relation to conditions for access to employment, to self-employment or to occupation, employment and working conditions, including dismissals and pay (Article 3(1)(a) and (c)). It applies to both direct and indirect discrimination and the definition of the latter is broader than that previously found in EC legislation on the burden of proof. Another innovation in the Directive is the inclusion of harassment within its scope as a form of discrimination, albeit what constitutes harassment is to be defined in accordance with national laws and practices (Article 2(3)). Directive 2000/78 also contains a number of important innovations in EC non-discrimination law. Barbera observes that the development of EC anti-discrimination law to date has been the subject of four essential conditions – the prohibitions were enumerated; the Court of Justice operated on a comparative basis; the rights in question were mainly negative; and the concept of equality chosen as a reference was generally formal rather than substantive. In contrast, this new Directive reflects what can only be regarded as a general non-discrimination principle[55] and it contains explicit attributions of positive rights.

---

[52] See Cases C-13/94 *P.* v. *S. and Cornwall County Council* [1996] ECR I-2143; and C-249/96 *Lisa Jacqueline Grant* v. *South West Trains* [1998] ECR I-621.

[53] See Council Directive 2000/43/EC of 29 June 2000 implementing the principle of equal treatment between persons irrespective of racial or ethnic origin, OJ 2000 L180/22. See also Council Decision of 27 November 2000 establishing a Community action programme to combat discrimination (2001 to 2006), OJ 2000 L303/23; and the Commission's proposal for a Council Framework Decision on combatting racism and xenophobia, COM (2001) 664 final. See also the discussion in M. Bell, "Article 13 EC: The European Commission's Anti-Discrimination Proposals" (2000) *Industrial Law Journal* 79–84; and P. Skidmore, "EC Framework Directive on Equal Treatment in Employment: Towards a Comprehensive Community Anti-Discrimination Policy?" (2001) *Industrial Law Journal* 126–132.

[54] Council Directive 2000/78/EC of 27 November 2000, OJ 2000 L303/16. For discussion of the difficulties in reaching agreement on this text see the House of Lords Select Committee on the European Communities, *The EU Framework Directive on Discrimination*, Session 2000–01, 4th report.

[55] Admittedly, the Court has, on occasion, relied on such a principle (see Joined Cases 75 and 117/82 *Razzouk and Beydoun* [1984] ECR 1509 and C-13/94 *P*), but it was arguably the compartmentalisation of EC non-discrimination law in the past which hindered the applicants' claim in Case C-249/96 *Grant*.

Article 5, e.g. concerning disability, creates a freestanding obligation on employers to provide reasonable accommodation.

Unsurprisingly, the Directive also contains a number of derogations. It includes an exemption for measures undertaken in order to protect public security, order or health (Article 2(5)). It does not apply to payments of any kind made by State schemes or similar, including State social security or social protection schemes (Article 3(3)). Special exemptions are provided in relation to particular occupational activities, particularly those within churches or other religious organisations (Article 4(1) and (2)). There is also a reinforced exemption from age provisions for entitlement to pensions (Articles 3(3) and 6(2)) and the provisions of the Directive relating to age and disability do not apply to the armed forces (Article 3(4)). Member States may also maintain or adopt specific measures designed to prevent or compensate for disadvantages linked to any of the grounds covered by the directive (Article 7). They may provide for a higher level of protection than that laid down in the Directive but they cannot reduce the level of protection against discrimination which they already afford (Article 8).

Chapter 3

Corporate Law

*Jan Wouters**

1. Introduction

More than 35 years ago – on 9 March 1968, to be precise – the Council of the EEC adopted the first harmonization directive in the field of company law.[1] The First Directive took the lead for a whole procession of Community initiatives in the area of company and accounting law. Between 1968 and today, nine (main) Directives were enacted, covering a variety of topics (see Section 2.1), and two Regulations, one on European economic interest groupings (EEIGs)[2] and the other, quite recently, on the European Company.[3] This impressive result does not alter the fact that it is now more than 13 years since the most recent Directive (the Twelfth Directive on single-member private companies[4]) saw the light of the day and European harmonization seems currently to have lost much of its dynamism.

After four decades of Community action in the area of company and accounting law, this seems a good moment to take stock.[5] First, we will briefly explore what the EU has achieved in the field, what EU plans are still in the pipeline, and what impact

---

* Professor of International Law and the Law of International Organizations, Leuven University; *of counsel*, Linklaters De Bandt. This chapter is an update of an article which appeared in (2000) 37 *Common Market Law Review* 257–307. No account could be taken any more of the Report of the High Level Group of Company Law Experts on "A Modern Regulatory Framework for Company Law in Europe" of 4 November 2002.

[1] First Council Directive of 9 March 1968 on coordination of the safeguards which, for the protection of the interests of members and others, are required by Member States of companies within the meaning of the second paragraph of Article 58 of the Treaty, with a view to making such safeguards equivalent throughout the Community, OJ 1968, L 65/8.

[2] Council Regulation 85/2137/EEC, of 25 July 1985 on the European Economic Interest Grouping (EEIG), OJ 1985, L 199/1.

[3] Council Regulation 2157/2001/EC, of 8 October 2001 on the Statute for a European Company (SE), OJ 2001, L 294/1. This Regulation has been simultaneously adopted with Council Directive 2001/86/EC, of 8 October 2001 supplementing the Statute for a European company with regard to the involvement of employees, OJ 2001, L 294/22.

[4] Twelfth Council Company Law Directive of 21 December 1989 on single-member private limited-liability companies, OJ 1989, L 395/40.

[5] For a critical evaluation after 25 years of harmonization, see De Kluiver, "Disparities and Similarities in European and American Company Law. What about Living Apart Together?" in Wouters and Schneider (eds), *Current Issues of Cross-Border Establishment of Companies in the European Union* (Antwerp, Maklu, 1995), pp. 287–315. The literature on EU company law is particularly extensive. For the most

M. van Empel (ed.), "From Paris to Nice": Fifty Years of Legal Integration in Europe, 33–74.

the European initiatives have had on national law (Section 2). Then, we will focus on the essential question: why does the EU intervene in company law (Section 3)? Here, we take a critical look at the objectives the European Commission has sought to achieve, in order to reach our own conclusions about the appropriate role for "Europe" in the area of company and accounting law – bearing in mind the present political-legal and economic context in the EU. Finally, we present a number of remarks on the challenges facing the EU in the areas of company, accounting and securities law, also in the light of EMU and the globalization of economies and financial markets (Section 4).

2. What is, and What may Come

2.1. The "acquis"

As noted above, what has been realized by the Community in the field of company and accounting law is impressive. It includes the following measures:

- the First Directive[6] (1968) harmonized the national rules on disclosure of company documents, the legal validity of contracts entered into by the company and the nullity of companies. Its sphere of application covers limited liability companies and limited partnerships;

---

recent overviews and commentaries see, e.g. Blaurock, "Europäisches und deutsches Gesellschaftsrecht: Bilanz und Perspektiven eines Anpassungsprozesses" (1998) *Zeitschrift für Europäisches Privatrecht* 460–483; *Id.*, "Steps Toward a Uniform Corporate Law in the European Union" (1998) 31 *Cornell International Law Journal* 377–393; Boucourechliev, "Die Harmonisierung des Gesellschaftsrechts in der Europäischen Union: Erreichtes und Perspektiven" (1999) RIW 1–6; Bovis, *Business Law in the European Union* (London, Sweet & Maxwell, 1997); De Pasquale and Fringo, *Diritto comunitario delle societa* (Padua, CEDAM, 1997); Dorresteijn, Kuiper, and Morse, *European Corporate Law* (Deventer, Kluwer Law and Taxation, 1994); V. Edwards, *EC Company Law* (Oxford, OUP, 1999); Hohloch and Albracht, *EU-Handbuch Gesellschaftsrecht* (Berlin, Herne, 1997); Hopt, *Company Law in the European Union: Harmonization or Subsidiarity*, Rome, Centro di studi e ricerche di diritto comparato e straniero, No. 31, 1998; *Id.*, "Europäisches Gesellschaftsrecht – Krise und neue Anlaüfe" (1998) ZIP 96–106; Kolvenbach, "Neue Initiative zur Weiterentwicklung des Europäischen Gesellschaftsrechts?" (1996) EuZW 229–234; Maitland-Walker, *Guide to European Company Laws* (2nd edn. Sweet & Maxwell, 1997); Santa Maria, *EC Commercial Law* (London, Kluwer, 1996); Schutte-Veenstra, *Europese Richtlijnen Vennootschapsrecht* (Deventer, Kluwer, 1997); Villiers, *European Company Law – Towards Democracy?* (Aldershot, Ashgate, 1998); *Id.*, "Harmonisation of Company Laws in Europe – With an Introduction to Some Comparative Issues", in Howells (ed.), *European Business Law* (Aldershot, Dartmouth, 19XX), pp. 169–195; Werlauff, *EC Company Law: The Common Denominator for Business Undertakings in 12 States* (Copenhagen, Jurist-og Okonomforbundets, 1993); *Id.*, "Common European Company Law: Status 1998" (1998) *European Business Law Review* 169–175, 210–216, 274–280; Wiesner, "Europäisches Unternehmensrecht im Umbruch" (1996) AG 390–395; *Id.*, "Überblick über den Stand des Europäischen Unternehmensrechts" (1998) EuZW 619–635; Wymeersch, "Unternehmensrecht in Europa – Perspektiven einer Harmonisierung", in *40 Jahre Römische Verträge*, Schriften des Rechtszentrum für europäische und internationale Zussamenarbeit (Vol. 9, 1998), pp. 187–203.

6 *Supra* n. 1. See *inter alia* the standard work by E. Stein, *Harmonization of European Company Laws. National Reform and Transnational Coordination* (New York, Bobbs-Merrill Company, 1970); Lutter, "Die erste Angleichungs-Richtlinie zu Art. 54 Abs. 3 lit. g) EWGV und ihre Bedeutung für das geltende

- the Second Directive[7] (1976) harmonized the rules for capital formation and protection with respect to public limited liability companies. It was supplemented by Directive 92/101/EEC[8] (1992);
- the Third Directive[9] (1978) harmonized the rules concerning (domestic) mergers of public limited liability companies, while the Sixth Directive[10] (1982) did this for (domestic) divisions of public limited liability companies;
- the Fourth Directive[11] (1978) harmonized the rules on annual accounts, while the Seventh Directive[12] (1983) approximated the rules on consolidated

---

Deutsche Unternehmensrecht" (1969) EuR 1–9; Van Ommeslaghe, "La première directive du Conseil du 9 mars 1968 en matière de sociétés", (1969) CDE 495–563, 619–665; Maeijer, "De eerste E.E.G. richtlijn en de rechtsgeldigheid van de verbintenissen van de Belgische en Nederlandse vennootschap" (1969) TPR 27–47. See also, on the Draft First Directive, the reports by van Maeyens and Heenen, *Europees vennootschapsrecht. Le régime juridique des sociétés dans la C.E.E.*, postdoctoral courses 1966–67 K.U.L., (Antwerpen, Standaard, 1968), 85–108 resp. 109–124; Fikentscher and Groβfeld, "The proposed directive on company law" (1964) *Common Market Law Review* 259–270.

[7] Second Council Directive 77/91/EEC of 13 December 1976 on coordination of safeguards which, for the protection of the interests of members and other, are required by Member States of companies within the meaning of the second paragraph of Article 58 of the Treaty, in respect of the formation of public limited liability companies and the maintenance and alteration of their capital, with a view to making such safeguards equivalent, OJ 1977, L 26/1. See, e.g. Houin, "Droit des sociétés. La deuxième directive du 13 décembre 1976: constitution de la S.A., maintien et modification du capital social", (1978) RTDE 728–735; Keutgen, "La deuxième directive en matière de sociétés" (1977) RPS 1–30; Masschaupt, and Storm, *De Tweede EEG-Richtlijn inzake vennootschapsrecht* (Zwolle, Tjeenk Willink, 1978); Morse, "The Second Directive: Raising and Maintenance of Capital" (1977) *European Law Review* 126–132; Schmitthoff, "The Second EEC Directive on company law" (1978) *Common Market Law Review* 43–54.

[8] Council Directive 92/101/EEC of 23 November 1992, OJ 1992, L 347/64.

[9] Third Council Directive 78/855/EEC of 9 October 1978 based on Article 54(3)(g) of the Treaty concerning mergers of public limited liability companies, OJ 1978, L 295/36. See, e.g. Heenen, "La directive sur les fusions internes" (1981) CDE 15–25; Keutgen, "La directive européenne sur les fusions nationales" (1979) RPS 98–120; Sanders, "De derde richtlijn" (1979) TVVS 41–47, 77–84.

[10] Sixth Council Directive 82/891/EEC of 17 December 1982 based on Article 54(3)(g) of the Treaty concerning the division of public limited liability companies, OJ 1982, L 378/47. See, e.g. Barbaso, "The harmonisation of company law with regard to mergers and divisions" (1984) *Journal of Business Law* 176–184.

[11] Fourth Council Directive 78/660/EEC of 25 July 1978 based on Article 54(3)(g) of the Treaty on the annual accounts of certain types of companies, OJ 1978, L 222/11. The most important amendments to this Directive and the Seventh Directive were effected by: Council Directive 90/605/EEC of 8 November 1990 amending the Fourth and Seventh Directives as regards the scope of those Directives, OJ 1990, L 317/60; Council Directive 94/8/EC of 21 March 1994 amending the Fourth Directive as regards the revision of amounts expressed in ecus, OJ 1994, L 82/33; Council Directive 1999/60/EC of 17 June 1999 amending Directive 78/660/EC as regards the revision of amounts expressed in ecus, OJ 1999, L 162/65; and, most recently, Directive 2001/65/EC of the European Parliament and the Council of 27 September 2001, OJ 2001, L 283/28.

[12] Seventh Council Directive 83/349/EEC of 13 June 1983 based on the Article 54(3)(g) of the Treaty on consolidated accounts OJ 1983, L 193/1; most recently amended by Directive 2001/65/EC, *supra*, previous note. See *inter alia*, both on the Fourth and Seventh Directive, Niessen, "Zur Angleichung des Bilanzrechts in der Europäischen Gemeinschaft" (1984) *Rebels Zeitschrift* 81–122. On the Seventh Directive in particular, see, e.g. Cooke, "The Seventh Directive – An Accountant's Perspective" (1984) *European Law Review* 143–160; Petite, "The conditions for consolidation under the 7th Company Law Directive" (1984) *Common Market Law Review* 81–121.

accounts. The two Directives necessitated the adoption of the Eighth Directive[13] (1984), which harmonized a number of rules concerning the requirements to be met by the statutory auditors of accounting documents;
- the Eleventh Directive[14] (1989) harmonized the disclosure requirements for branches;
- the Twelfth Directive[15] (1989), lastly, obliged the Member States to make the form of private limited company which exists in their legal systems open to one single shareholder, and harmonized a number of rules concerning these single-member limited companies.

The Regulations on EEIGs[16] and on the European Company (SE) mentioned above are the result of the EC's efforts to provide businesses with instruments under European law (and therefore not under diverging national legal rules) for transnational cooperation or concentration. Both instruments have their shortcomings, though. Instead of providing a full-fledged European legislative framework, both Regulations frequently refer back to the national law of the Member State in which the EEIG[17] or the SE has its seat. The EEIG suffers moreover from its restricted objectives (to facilitate the economic activities of its members; the purpose may not be to make profits for itself[18]), its limitation – due to German worries about *Mitbestimmung* – to 500 employees at most,[19] the unlimited joint and several liability of its members,[20] and its fiscal transparency.[21] Although the number of EEIGs has

[13] Eighth Council Directive 84/253/EEC of 10 April 1984 based on Article 54(3)(g) of the Treaty on the approval of persons responsible for carrying out the statutory audits of accounting documents, OJ 1984, L 126/20. See, e.g. Feuillet, "La huitième directive du Conseil des Communautés européennes et le commissariat aux comptes" (1984) Rev Soc 709–721; Olivier, "Perspectives du contrôle légal des comptes dans la Communauté européenne" (1989) Rev Dr Int Comp 209–229.

[14] Eleventh Council Directive 89/666/EEC of 21 December 1989 concerning disclosure requirements in respect of branches opened in a Member State by certain types of company governed by the law of another State, OJ 1989, L 395/36.

[15] *Supra* n. 4.

[16] It is hardly possible to give an overview of the literature on the EEIG. See, e.g. Centre Jean Renauld (ed.), *Les groupements d'intérêt économique* (Brussels, Academia-Bruylant, 1991); *De Europese en Belgische Economische Samenwerkingsverbanden (EESV en ESV)*, (1989) TRV special number; Ganske, "Die Europäische wirtschaftliche Interessenvereinigung (EWIV) – eine neue "supranationale" Unternehmensform als Kooperationsinstrument in der Europäischen Gemeinschaft" (1985) DB Supp. 20/85; *Id., Das Recht der Europäischen wirtschaftlichen Interessenvereinigung (EWIV)* (Bundesanzeiger, 1988); Israel, "The EEIG – A major step forward for Community law" 9 *Company Lawyer* 14–22; Lentner, *Das Gesellschaftsrecht der Europäischen wirtschaftlichen Interessevereinigung (EWIV)* (Baden-Baden, Nomos, 1994); Van Gerven and Aalders (eds), *European Economic Interest Groupings. The EEC Regulation and its Application in the Member States of the European Community* (Deventer, Kluwer, 1990); von der Heydt and von Rechenberg (eds), *Die Europäische Wirtschaftliche Interessenvereinigung* (Stuttgart, Poeschel, 1991).

[17] An example is Article 5(a) EEIG Regulation, concerning the name of an EEIG: see Case C-402/96, *European Information Technology Observatory*, ECR [1997] I-7515.

[18] Article 3(1) EEIG Regulation. See in this context the important restrictions in Article 3(2), to prevent an EEIG being used for mergers or the formation of holding companies.

[19] Article 3(2)(c) EEIG Regulation.

[20] Article 24(1) EEIG Regulation.

[21] Article 40 EEIG Regulation.

grown over the years (at present there are a good 900 in total), one cannot really speak of an overwhelming success.[22] Whether the SE will become a success story only future can tell: the Regulation will only enter into force on 8 October 2004[23] and it is doubtful that, without accompanying fiscal measures,[24] companies will want to make use of it on a large scale.

2.1. Past and pending projects

The above-mentioned achievements should not make us forget that in the field of company law there have been almost as many initiatives taken by the Commission which have *not* led to results, at least as yet. These concern the following problem children:

- A Fifth Directive[25] on the structure of public limited liability companies, and the powers and obligations of their organs, and employee participation had been in preparation for nearly 30 years, but its chances of being adopted got less and less real over the years. The Commission ingloriously withdrew its proposal in the autumn of 2001. In the meantime, the proposal has exerted some influence on new company legislation in various Member States.[26]
- A draft for a Ninth Directive on corporate groups[27] has never even officially been proposed by the Commission, and has led a rather phantom existence ever since the mid 1980s.

---

[22] The figures reveal large differences in the use of EEIGs per Member States. For instance, Belgium has almost a quarter of all EEIGs (242), while Finland has only one, and Denmark 3. After Belgium come France (194), UK (114), Netherlands (91), Germany (85) and Italy and Spain (52 each): Commission, *G.E.I.E. Groupements Européens d'Intérêt Economique. Liste des constitutions*, Brussels, 3 July 1998, 2.

[23] Article 70.

[24] See in this respect Commission, *Towards an Internal Market without tax obstacles. A strategy providing companies with a consolidated corporate tax basis for their EU-wide activities*, Communication to the Council, the European Parliament and the Economic and Social Committee, 23 October 2001, COM(2001) 582, pp. 18–19.

[25] Proposal for a Fifth Directive founded on Article 54(3)(g) of the Treaty concerning the structure of public limited companies and the powers and obligations of their organs (original proposal OJ 1972, C 131/49; amended proposal, OJ 1983, C 240/2; further amendments in OJ 1991, C 7/4 and OJ 1991, C 321/9). See at the time of the original proposal, e.g. Keutgen, "La proposition de directive européenne sur la structure des sociétés anonymes" (1973) RPS 1–22; Scholten, "Medezeggenschap van werknemers en structuur van de vennootschap in Europees verband" (1978) SEW 706–736; Van der Haegen, and Knops, "La proposition de cinquième directive CEE relative à la structure des sociétés anonymes ainsi qu'aux pouvoirs et obligations de leurs organes" (1976) JT 397–407. On the revised 1983 proposal see, e.g. Dine, "The Fifth Draft Directive – a False Dawn?" (1983) *European Law Review* 83–102. See recently Du Plessis and Dine, "The fate of the draft fifth directive on company law: accommodation instead of harmonisation" (1997) *Journal of Business Law* 23–47.

[26] See, e.g. for Belgium, the rules on public requests for the granting of authorizations (Articles 74 §§ 2 and 3 Companies Act) and shareholders meetings (Article 74ter Companies Act), as well as the influence of the "one share, one vote" principle in Article 33(1) revised Draft Fifth Directive on the amendment, by Law of 18 July 1991, of the voting limitation of Article 76 Companies Act: *Doc. parl.*, Senate, 1990–91, No 1107/1, 90.

[27] The draft has never been published officially: for a French version from the mid 1980s, with explanations, see, e.g. CDVA (ed.), *Modes de rapprochement structurel des entreprises. Tendances*

- The proposal presented in 1985 for a Tenth Directive[28] which would enable cross-border mergers between public limited liability companies – originally drafted in order to break through the impasse affecting a draft treaty of 1972,[29] based on Article 293 (ex 220) EC – never even reached the Council, due to the problems around rules on worker participation, but stranded on the first reading in the European Parliament.[30]
- The history of the proposed Thirteenth Directive on public takeover bids[31] is just as tortuous: a first draft was proposed in 1989, when public bids were coming thick and fast and the political will for harmonization seemed to be present in the context of completing the internal market (1992 project), but it soon got bogged down.[32] Since then, the Commission has subjected the Thirteenth Directive to a drastic shot of subsidiarity therapy. In 1996, a new, much-slimmed down, draft Directive was published, which in the meantime again been revised, in November 1997.[33] After much haggling, including a Spanish–UK rift on

---

actuelles endroit des affaires (Brussels, Story, 1986), pp. 223–263. For a German version, see Lutter, *Europäisches Unternehmensrecht. Grundlagen, Stand und Entwicklung nebst Texten und Materialien zur Rechtsangleichung* (4th edn, Berlin, De Gruyter, 1996), p. 244.

[28] Proposal for a Tenth Council Directive based on Article 54(3)(g) of the Treaty concerning cross-border mergers of public limited companies, OJ 1985, C 23/11. See esp. Farmery, "Removing legal obstacles to cross-border mergers: EEC proposal for a tenth directive" (1987/2) *Business Law Review* 35–36 and 53; Van Solinge, *Grensoverschrijdende juridische fusie. Beschouwingen aan de hand van de derde en tiende EEG-richtlijn inzake het vennootschapsrecht* (Deventer, Kluwer, 1994).

[29] See for this draft treaty and the associated *Goldman Report*, Bull. EC, supp. 13/73. In a statement of 17 December 1973 on the removal of legal barriers to the linking-up of undertakings, the government representatives from the Member States had declared that they would "do their utmost to complete promptly the work on the Agreement on transnational mergers" (OJ 1973, C 117/15), but in fact nothing came of this. See for comments, e.g. Goldman, "Rapport concernant le projet de convention sur la fusion internationale des sociétés anonymes" (1974) RTDE 464–570; *Id.*, "La fusion des sociétés et le projet de convention sur la fusion internationale des sociétés anonymes" (1981) CDE 4–14; Koppensteiner, "Grundlagenkritische Bemerkungen zum EWG-Entwurf eines Übereinkommens über die internationale Verschmelzung von Aktiengesellschaften" (1975) *Rebels Zeitschrift* 418–443; Loussouarn, "La concentration des entreprises dans la Communauté économique européenne" (1974) Rev Crit Dr Int Privé 235, at 246–259; Luzzatto, "La convenzione CEE sulla fusione delle società", in *Il diritto delle società nella Comunità economica europea* (Padua, Cedam, 1975), pp. 101–115; Scholten, "Fusies binnen de EEG" (1974) SEW 661, at 669–683; L. Timmerman, "De internationale juridische fusie. Een beschouwing over het ontwerpverdrag inzake de internationale juridische fusie" (1976) TPR 289–327.

[30] See the negative opinion in the so-called *Fontaine report*: report of 28 October 1987 of the Committee on legal affairs and rights of citizens, *EP Session*, 1987–88, doc. A2–0186/87, PE 113.303/def. The parliament did not approve this report, but sent it back to the relevant committee: Acts *EP*, 16 November 1987, No. 2-358/20.

[31] Original proposal, OJ 1989, C 64/8; amended proposal, OJ 1990, C 240/7; entirely new proposal, OJ 1996, C 162/5; since then amended proposal of November 1997, OJ 1997, C 378/10; newest proposal of 2 October 2002, OJ 2003, C 45 E/1.

[32] See, e.g. as well as numerous other commentaries, Wouters, "Towards a level playing field for takeovers in the European Community? An analysis of the proposed thirteenth directive in light of American experiences" (1993) *Common Market Law Review* 267–310.

[33] The 1996 version was again revised in November 1997. For comments on the 1996 version, see, e.g. Krause, "Der revidierte Vorschlag einer Takeover-Richtlinie" (1996) AG 209–217; C. Peter, "Revidierter Vorschlag für eine 13. gesellschaftsrechtliche EU-Richtlinie über Übernahmeangebote" (1996) SZW 177–179; Raaijmakers, "Herziening Fusiecode en nieuw ontwerp Dertiende Richtlijn" (1996) TVVS

Gibraltar, the Council managed to adopt a common position in 2000.[34] However, matters went all but smooth in the European Parliament, which proposed important changes to the text of the common position. With much pain a joint text was adopted by a Conciliation Committee on 6 June 2001 but it was unexpectedly voted down by the Parliament on 4 July 2001: 273 members voted in favor and 273 members voted against the compromise text. The Commission soon announced its intention to come up with a new proposal. For this purpose, it decided to set up a High Level Working Group of Company Law chaired by Prof. Jaap Winter, which delivered its first report on 10 January 2002.[35]

– After the final adoption of the European Company Statute, the Commission could re-activate its efforts concerning, in particular, the Tenth Directive on cross-border mergers, a Fourteenth Directive on cross-border transfer of seat (although the proposals have as yet not even officially been submitted),[36] as well as three pending "socio-economic" proposals, that is, the draft statutes for a European Association (EA), a European Cooperative Society (ECS) and a European Mutual Society (EMS) and the associated arrangements for employees.[37]

2.3. Impact on national law

The precise impact of European harmonization on national company law and accounting law and – even more – the practice in these areas in the Member States, is extremely difficult to estimate. This should perhaps be done for each Member State

---

65–69; and the national reports in Wymeersch, "The proposal for a 13th company law directive on takeovers: a multi-jurisdiction survey" (1996) *European Financial Services Law* 301–307, 1997, 2–7. Analyses of the 1997 proposal can be found in Steins Bisschop, "Gewijzigd Voorstel Dertiende Richtlijn van 11 november 1997" (1998) TVVS 80–82; M. Weber, "Der geänderte Vorschlag der Kommission für eine Takeover-Richtlinie von 10.11.1997" (1998) EuZW 464–469; Witt, "Der neue Vorschlag für eine EG-Richtlinie über Übernahmeangebote" (1998) EWS 318–323.

[34] OJ 2001, C 23/1.

[35] *Report of the High Level Group of Company Law Experts on Issues Related to Takeover Bids*, Brussels, 10 January 2002. For the newest Commission proposal, see *supra* note 31.

[36] The draft has been in circulation since 1997; for a German version, see (1999) ZGR 157. In the same issue of ZGR (1–2/1999), the contributions of a symposium recently held in Bonn on the Fourteenth Directive and its probable impact on national law are published. See Di Marco, "Der Vorschlag der Kommission für eine 14. Richtlinie. Stand und Perspektiven" (1999) ZGR 3–12; K. Schmidt, "Sitzverlegungsrichtlinie, Freizügigkeit und Gesellschaftsrechtspraxis" (1999) ZGR 20–35; Priester, "EU-Sitzverlegung – Verfahrensablauf" (1999) ZGR 36–50; Rajak, "Britisches Recht und der Vorschlag einer 14. Richtlinie" (1999) ZGR 111–125; Wymeersch, "Die Sitzverlegung nach belgischem Recht" (1999) ZGR 126–146; L. Timmerman, "Sitzverlegung von Kapitalgesellschaften nach niederländischem Recht und die 14. EU-Richtlinie" (1999) ZGR 147–156.

[37] For the original proposals of 5 March 1992, see resp. OJ 1992, C 99/1, 17 and 40. Amended proposals date from 6 July 1993: see respectively OJ 1993, C 236/1, 17 and 40. Each of the draft regulations is accompanied by a (since then also amended) draft directive on the involvement of employees: original proposals in resp. OJ 1992, C 99/14, 36 and 46; amended proposals in resp. OJ 1993, C 236/14, 36 and 56. For comments on the ECS, see, e.g. Bacher, "Alternative 'Europäische Genossenschaft (SCE)'?", in Henssler, Kolbeck, Moritz and Rehm, (eds), *Europäische Integration und globaler Wettbewerb* (Heidelberg, Recht und Wirtschaft, 1994), pp. 457–473; Galle, "Naar een Europees coöperatierecht", in *Ondernemingsrecht in internationaal perspectief. Opstellen van bedrijfsjuristen bij gelegenheid van het 65-jarig bestaan van het nederlands Genootschap van de Bedrijfsjuristen* (Deventer, Kluwer, 1995),

separately, and even research for one country requires a lot of effort. In general, it is hard to deny that over the last three decades, European measures have had the effect of thoroughly ploughing up company and accounting law in the Member States, and have worked as a catalyst. The Directives have time and again required more or less fundamental changes in national company legislation;[38] in addition, many national legislatures – for instance in Belgium, the Netherlands[39] and France[40] – have voluntarily applied many of the European rules to other forms of company not covered by the Directives, either straight away, or in the course of time.

The European Directives, above all the First, Second and Fourth, have at the time considerably modernized national company and accounting laws, in the fields covered by them. There has been a fear that, as a result of the Directives' fragmentary character (since they are restricted to particular topics, and only affect certain forms of company[41]), they would lead to a loss of coherence in national company law. This

---

pp. 43–54; Luttermann, "Die Europäische Genossenschaft. Zum Verordnungsvorschlag der EG-Kommission vom 6.3.1992 in der geänderten Fassung vom 6.7.1993" (1994) ZVglRWiss 1–37; Schaffland, "Die Europäische Genossenschaft – Eine neue Rechtsform" (1991/1) DWiR 18–21. On the EMS proposal, see Maleville, "Vers un statut de la mutualité européenne" (1993) RGAT 741–753; Von Maydell, "Die geplante europäische Gegenseitigkeitsgesellschaft – Gesellschaftsrecht als Instrument für eine grenzüberschreitende Krankenversicherung", in Schmidt and Schwark (eds), *Unternehmen, Recht und Wirtschaftsordnung. Festschrift für Peter Raisch zum 70. Geburtstag* (Cologne, Heymann, 1995), pp. 433–440; on the EA proposal, see Vollmer, "Der Europäische Verein" (1993) ZHR 373–399. For all three revised proposals together, see Roest, "Wijzigingsvoorstellen Europese vereniging, coöperatieve vennootschap en onderlinge maatschappij" (1993) *Stichting & Vereniging* 170–172. See on the mechanisms provided in the amended EA proposals to combat abuse of the charitable status, answer by Mr. Papoutsis, on behalf of the Commission, of 31 July 1995, in reply to written question No. E-2055/95 by I. Read, of 12 July 1995 ("Organizations miss-using (sic) cover of charitable status"), OJ 1995, C 273/52.

38 See, e.g. for Belgium the overview from 1970 to the beginning of the 1990s: Tilquin and Simonart, *Traité des sociétés*, I (Diegem, Kluwer, 1996), pp. 50–68, Nos. 64–92.

39 For the Netherlands, reference may be made to the rules on capital protection, which (leaving aside some differences on minimum capital, issuing competence and purchase rules) are generally parallel to those of the NV: see Maeijer, *Vertegenwoordiging en Rechtspersoon. De naamloze en de besloten vennootschap*, in *Asser's Handleiding tot de beoefening van het Nederlands burgerlijk recht* (Zwolle, Tjeenk Willink, 1994), p. 11, para. 6; Van Schilfgaarde, *Van de BV en de NV* (10th edn., Arnhem, Gouda Quint, 1995), 68. Also with respect to mergers, the Dutch legislation goes further than the Third Directive: mergers are possible for all legal persons mentioned in Book 2 of the Civil Code, except for associations without full legal personality ("verenigingen zonder volledige rechtspersoonlijkheid"): Van der Heijden, *Handboek voor de naamloze en de besloten vennootschap* (Zwolle, Tjeenk Willink, 1992), 12th edn revised by Van der Grinten, p. 704, para. 404.

40 See examples mentioned in Guyon, "L'influence communautaire sur le droit français des sociétés", in Henssler *et al.*, *op. cit.*, pp. 425, 434–436.

41 The Commission has had a number of studies carried out into the possible extension of the sphere of application of directives which to date only cover public limited liability companies: see Commission, *Study on Second Directive's extension to other types of companies* (Luxembourg, Office of Official Publications EC, 1993), which examines the extension of the scope of the Second Directive to (in UK terms) limited partnerships and private limited companies, and more or less equivalent forms in other Member States; *Id.*, *Study on extension of scope of the Third and Sixth company law directives*, Luxembourg, Office of Official Publications EC, 1993. See, on the former study, Schutte-Veenstra, "Mogelijke uitbreiding van de werkingssfeer van de tweede richtlijn inzake kapitaalbescherming tot andere rechtsvormen" (1994) TVVS 95–97.

fear was certainly plausible,[42] but seems to be at least partly compensated by the Directives' "spillover"[43] or "reflex"[44] effect, i.e. the above-mentioned tendency on the part of national legislatures to make (certain of) the rules in question applicable to other company forms. For Member States such as Belgium and the Netherlands,[45] the Directives seem in general to have been of benefit to the quality of their company law. The restrictive rules on nullity, the *prokura* system for representation of the company *vis-à-vis* third parties, the system of rules on capital formation and maintenance (but see Section 4.1 on more problematic provisions of the Second Directive), the principle of a "true and fair view" in the area of company accounts, the coherent set of rules on mergers and divisions: all these are achievements which are to a great extent thanks to the European Directives.

But these innovations are already not so new anymore. For instance, the system of disclosure for companies dates in most Member States from the implementation of the First Directive. In the era of Internet and far-reaching digitalization, the question squarely arises of a global modernization of this system, not just under national law, but also in the framework of the First Directive (Sections 3.3.2 and 4.1).

In addition, one cannot help noticing that the implementation of the European Directives has led in some aspects to a heavier burden of rules and a greater rigidity of national company laws.[46] On the whole, this is not so much due to the directives themselves, but more to the relevant national legislature, which has often gone much further than the European rules[47] and/or has not made use of a number of possibilities for

---

[42] See W. Van Gerven, "Foreword", in *The European Private Company*, 7. See already at the time the First Directive was being implemented in the Netherlands, the reservations of Löwensteyn, according to whom the relevant implementing legislation "creates an arbitrary enclave of foreign norms in our domestic company law, as a result of which that law has certainly lost some of its clarity and manageability" (our transl.): "De wet tot aanpassing van het Nederlandse vennootschapsrecht aan de 'Eerste Richtlijn'" (1971) TVVS 335, 379, 385.

[43] Wymeersch, *op. cit.*, 188.

[44] Bouwes, "De voortgang van de harmonisatie van het vennootschapsrecht", in *Grensoverschrijdend privaatrecht. Een bundel opstellen over privaatrecht in internationaal verband. Aangeboden aan Mr. J. van Rijn van Alkemade bij zijn afscheid als raadsadviseur bij het Ministerie van Justitie* (Deventer, Kluwer, 1993), pp. 27, 39.

[45] See for the Netherlands, Timmerman, "Wat hebben de Europese Richtlijnen in ons vennootschapsrecht aangericht?" (1996) AA 309–314, according to whom, the harmonization has done more good than harm to the system of Dutch company law.

[46] *Cf.* for the Belgian law, Tilquin, "La société privée et la société faisant ou ayant fait publiquement appel à l'épargne – Evolutions récentes" (1993) TBH 92, 708, pp. 744, No. 71, according to whom "le droit belge a hérité, à l'intermédiaire des directives européennes, de la structure rigide 'externe' du droit allemand alors que l'on considère généralement, pour le surplus, que dans la structure interne de la majorité des formes sociétaires, ce droit est fort souple."

[47] For a number of provisions of the Company law Directives, their minimal, maximal or exhaustive character is open to question, e.g. on the exclusivity of the rule on the right of pre-emption in cases of capital increase as set out in Article 29 Second Directive, *cf.* Case C-42/95, *Siemens* v. *Nold*, [1996] ECR I-6017, and (1997) V&F, 30, note by Byttebier and François, "Voorkeurrecht in geval van inbreng in natura en de tweede richtlijn", (1997) SEW, 247, note by Schutte-Veenstra. On this problem in German law see earlier, e.g. Hirte, "Vereinbarkeit der Inhaltskontrolle des Bezugsrechtsauschlusses bei Sacheinlagen mit europäischen Recht?" (1995) DB 1113–1116; Kindler, "Die sachliche Rechtfertigung des aktienrechtlichen Bezugsrechtsausschlusses im Lichte der Zweiten Gesellschaftsrechtlichen Richtlinie der Europäischen

simplification offered by the relevant Directive;[48] or else has allowed the system of rules which previously existed to continue alongside the implementation of rules from a Directive (resulting in an undesirable measure of complexity).[49] For instance, in implementing the rules contained in the Second Directive on the right of pre-emption of existing shareholders when new shares are issued and on a company's acquiring its own shares ("share buybacks"), a number of Member States have been very restrictive, and have ignored various possibilities and exceptions which were allowed for in the Directive.[50] The tendency in recent years in a number of countries to make the regime governing share buybacks more flexible[51] indicates that national legislatures have undergone a change of mentality since the 1970s as far as company law is concerned.

It would be interesting to test national company legislation against the potential for flexibility allowed within the European framework. Nevertheless, the European rules themselves should be critically examined as to their desirability and efficacy; as will become evident, part of the challenge facing the EU is to test its company and accounting law *acquis* on this basis, and to prevent a *Sperrwirkung* or risk of petrification of national law (Section 4.1).

Gemeinschaft" (1994) ZHR 339–370; Meilicke, "Vereinbarkeit der Inhaltskontrolle des Bezugsrechtsauschlusses mit europäischem Recht" (1996) D.B., 513–517. In connection with the final judgment by the BGH in the *Siemens* case, see Volhard, "'Siemens/Nold': Die Quittung" (1998) AG 397–404.

48 One example is the possibilities for simplification which Articles 27 and 28 Third Directive offer, where for instance the Belgian legislature only made very partial use of these in the context of Articles 174/24 and 174/25 Belgian Companies Act.

49 A rather unattractive example of this is the special regime which exists in Belgium for cross participations between a parent limited liability company and its subsidiaries, introduced by Law of 13 April 1995 in implementation of Directive 92/101/EEC.

50 See the comparative data in Schutte-Veenstra, *Harmonisatie van het kapitaalbeschermingsrecht in de EEG* (Deventer, Kluwer, 1991), pp. 180–190 resp. 114–131.

51 See "Inkoop van eigen aandelen verovert Europa", *Financieele Dagblad*, 31 March 1998. For an analysis of the question why share buybacks were hitherto so rare in Europe, see Vermaelen, *Share Buybacks in Europe* (Brussels, CEPS Research Report No. 21, 1997). See, for the recent German reform of the regime governing share buybacks in the *Gesetz zur Kontrolle und Transparenz im Unternehmensbereicht (KonTraG)* of 5 March 1998, Lingemann and Wasmann, "Mehr Kontrolle und Transparenz im Aktienrecht: Das KonTraG tritt in Kraft" (1998) BB 853, at 860–861; Escher-Weingart and Kübler, "Erwerb eigener Aktien" (1998) ZHR 537–562. For France see "Le régime juridique et fiscal des rachats de leurs propres actions par les entreprises va être réformé", *Les Echos*, 23 February 1998; "Rachat par les sociétés de leurs actions propres: rapport Esambert", *Lamy Droit du Financement*, March 1998, 1–2. For a short comparative overview of the legal and fiscal treatment of share buybacks in the EU Member States, and the planned reforms in various Member States, see Shrimpton and Millerschip, "Share buybacks", (March 1998) *European Counsel*, 15–21; see also Skog, "Der Erwerb eigener Aktien: Reformsbestrebungen in den EU-Mitgliedstaaten" (1997) ZGR 306–333. For a comparison between the UK and Germany, with attention paid to the abuse which can be made of share buybacks, see Stawowy, "The Repurchase of Own Shares by Public Companies and Aktiengesellschaften" (1996) *The ELSA Law Review* 58–83.

3. Why European Company Law?

3.1. Aims of the Commission

An innocent company lawyer could ask why the EU has anything to do with company law in any case. Isn't this an area of the law which can better be dealt with at national level? Strangely enough, this existential question has never been answered completely satisfactorily, right up to today. This is partly due to the somewhat fuzzy mandate given to the Commission and the Council in Article 44(3)(g) (ex 54) – the traditional legal basis of harmonization directives in the area of company and accounting law: this provision obliges the institutions to attain freedom of establishment "by coordinating to the necessary extent the safeguards which, for the protection of the interests of members and others, are required of Member States of companies and firms within the meaning of the second paragraph of Article 48 [ex 58] with a view to making such safeguards equivalent throughout the Community". Despite this "piling up of vague legal terms",[52] one would expect that, in the 40 years or more that the Treaty has been in effect, the European Commission might have formed a coherent view of what EU action was necessary in the field of company law. However, this is not, or no longer, the case. The initiatives taken and opinions adopted by the Commission over the years seem to be ruled by the needs of the day.

3.1.1. The Eu(ro)phoric 1960s: the Berkhouwer report

If the Commission ever had a global vision of European company law, then it was evident in the *Berkhouwer report* of 1966. It appears from this and from the explanatory memorandum accompanying the draft First Directive, that the Commission initially saw in Article 44(3)(g) an extremely broad mandate: harmonization had to cover "all provisions concerning structure and organs of companies, formation and maintenance of its capital, the composition of the profit and loss account, the issue of securities, mergers, conversions, liquidations, guarantees required in cases of company concentrations, etc."[53]

---

[52] C.W.A. Timmermans, "De harmonisatie van nationale voorschriften op het gebied van het vennootschapsrecht" (1971) SEW 608, at 610 (our translation).

[53] Our translation. See the opinion of the Commission as given in the report drawn up by C. Berkhouwer on behalf of the Commission for the internal market regarding the proposal of the Commission of the EEC to the Council (document 10/1964–1965) for a directive concerning the coordination of the safeguards which, for the protection of the interests of members and others, are required by Member States of companies within the meaning of Article 48(2) ex 58(2) of the Treaty, with a view to making such safeguards equivalent, European Parliament Session (1966–67), 9 May 1966, doc. 53, p. 7, nr. 13, with, subsequently, strong criticism from the rapporteur on this broad interpretation, pp. 22–26, nrs. 11–26. See further the explanatory memorandum by the Commission accompanying the proposal for a First Directive, Bull. EC, supp. 3/64, 18, in which it gives its opinion that the freedom of establishment and freedom to provide services in relation to companies is only feasible if legal certainty is guaranteed in all circumstances and for all forms of company: a task of extremely great importance, which covers the whole area of company law; see also the memorandum of 22 April 1966 concerning the introduction of a European trading company, Bull. EC, supp. 9–10/66, 8–9.

The Commission justified that broad interpretation by reading three aims into Article 44(3)(g): (i) facilitating freedom of establishment of companies, insofar as statutes of the various company forms needed harmonizing, so that companies from one Member State who establish themselves in another Member State could have easier access to the means of credit and financing in the latter State which are necessary for the activities of their agencies and branches; (ii) avoiding a situation whereby the freedom of establishment in effect entailed movements of capital and activities on the basis of the more stringent or more lax character of national legislation; and (iii) guaranteeing legal certainty in intra-Community operations.

The first aim, facilitating freedom of establishment, offers in our view the most appropriate justification for EU action on company law (see Section 3.3.1). The link between company law harmonization and access to means of credit and financing in the host State seems, on the other hand, rather tenuous.[54] In a EU where capital movements have been free, since 1990,[55] and the euro is rapidly causing the financial markets to integrate, this argument has no practical value at all.

The second aim is in essence a "negative" one, and amounts to the prevention of a Delaware effect in the EC. Historically, this seems in fact to be the most important motive for including Article 44(3)(g) in the EC Treaty chapter on right of establishment: a number of delegations (in particular, the French) insisted on harmonization at the time the Treaty was being negotiated, as a *quid pro quo* for the liberal grant of a right of establishment to companies. They were determined that the Netherlands, which was famous at the time for the flexibility of its company law, should not become a European "Delaware", with companies being established there because of the low burden of legal rules, and then setting up agencies and branches throughout the whole EC with virtually no protection for local creditors.[56] This view too seems in need of some adjustment today; we will return to it below (Section 3.2.3).

---

[54] One could argue, in theory, that by harmonization of the rules on capital protection the credit institutions in the host State will be more easily inclined to grant credit to agencies and branches of EU companies. Whether this reasoning corresponds to reality is, to say the least, uncertain. As far as means of financing are concerned, the Commission apparently intended the rules concerning emission of securities, but here too, the link between harmonization and facilitation of the exercise of the right to establishment is tenuous: see the critical remarks in the *Berkhouwer report*, para. 22, p. 25.

[55] Pursuant to Council Directive 88/361/EEC of 24 June 1988, OJ 1988, L 178/5, movement of capital throughout the EC was liberalized by 1 July 1990; only for Greece, Ireland, Portugal and Spain there was a temporary postponement: see on this, e.g. Wouters, "La libération des mouvements de capitaux au sein de la Communauté européenne" (1989) RIDE 303–350.

[56] See C.W.A. Timmermans, *op. cit.*, (1971) SEW, para. 9, 614; see, more explicitly on the "quid pro quo" character of company law harmonization; *Id.*, *op. cit.*, (1983) TVVS 166; *Id.*, "Die Europäische Rechtsangleichung im Gesellschaftsrecht" (1984) *Rebels Zeitschrift* (1), 12–13; *Id.*, "Methods and Tools for Integration", in Buxbaum, Hertig, Hirsch, and Hopt (eds), *European Business Law. Legal and Economic Analyses on Integration and Harmonization* (Berlin/New York, De Gruyter, 1991), pp. 129, 132. See already for this view Krekeler, *Wirtschaftliche Integration und Gesellschaftsrecht – amerikanische Erfahrungen und europäische Irrwege*, PhD diss. München, 1973, 192. See, in the same line, Abeltshauser, "Towards a European Constitution of the Firm: Problems and Perspectives" (1990) 11 *Michigan Journal of International Law* 1235, 1246; Conard, "The European Alternative to Uniformity in Corporation Laws" (1991) 89 *Michigan Law Review* 2150, 2156 and 2158; Houin, "Le régime juridique des sociétés dans la Communauté Economique Européenne" (1965) RTDE 11, 16; Séché, in *Commentaire Mégret*, III, 2nd ed. (Brussels, Ed. Université Libre de Bruxelles, 1990), Section 25, p. 47; Stein, *Harmonization of European Company Laws*, 37.

In the third policy aim, harmonization fulfils a supplementary function alongside free movement, which also seems tenable today, i.e. promoting legal certainty in intra-Community commercial relations. This aim is handled most systematically in the First Directive: in harmonizing rules on disclosure of essential company information, the authorization to represent the company *vis-à-vis* third parties (rejection of the *ultra vires* doctrine, in favor of the German *prokura* system), and rules on nullity, the EC followed the "basic thesis that it is necessary to ensure smooth functioning of and legal certainty in international transactions".[57] But the subsequent harmonization initiatives, especially the Second (capital[58]), Third (mergers) and Fourth (annual accounts) Directives, reveal how autonomous the harmonization programme had become. Any link they have with the realization of freedom of establishment for companies is at best indirect; the emphasis is entirely on legislative policy aims of equivalent protection for shareholders and creditors in the common market.[59]

3.1.2. The 1970s: industrial policy

As if the Commission had not got enough on its plate, since the beginning of the 1970s it elaborated another theme in the development of Community company law. Now, the impulse came from industrial policy: according to the Colonna memorandum of 1970,[60] unification or harmonization of company law rules should contribute to making European companies more competitive, by offering them instruments and rules facilitating cross-border mergers and cooperation, in order to form "transnational European companies". Initiatives such as the SE, the EEIG and the creation of a law on groups fitted in with this perspective.[61] Moreover, in its 1975 Green paper on Employee participation and company structure, the Commission considered a strengthened role for employees in the decision-making structures of companies necessary, in order to facilitate cross-border company restructuring *and* to give a more

---

[57] See the explanatory memorandum accompanying the proposal for a First Directive, Bull. EC, supp. 3/64, 18. See also the judgment of the Court of Justice in Case 32/74, *Haaga*, [1974] 1201, para. 6, where the Court stated that it is the objective of the First Directive "to guarantee legal certainty in dealings between companies and third parties in view of the intensification of trade between Member States following the creation of the Common Market".

[58] Articles 2 and 3 of the Second Directive can be seen as following on from the disclosure rules of the First Directive (there however only applying to public limited companies), while Articles 4 and 5 build on the liability (Article 7) and nullity rules of the First Directive (Articles 11 and 12), both inspired by legal certainty and protection of legitimate interests of third parties. In the same way, the theme of legal certainty plays a role in the nullity rules concerning mergers and divisions of public limited companies (Articles 22 and 23 Third Directive and Articles 19 and 22 Sixth Directive).

[59] See second consideration Preamble to the Third Directive; first consideration Preamble to the Fourth directive; fifth consideration Preamble to the Sixth Directive.

[60] Commission, "De industriepolitiek van de Gemeenschap. Memorandum van de Commissie aan de Raad", Brussels, 18 March 1970, of which the document with the principles and general policy lines is included in Bull. EC, supp. 4/70. The memorandum got its name from the then Commissioner G. Colonna di Paliano. See also Colonna di Paliano, Bull. EC, 5-1970, 7–10.

[61] See Colonna memorandum, Bull. EC, supp. 4/70, 17. On this industrial policy foundation for Community company law harmonization see above all C.W.A. Timmermans, *op. cit.*, (1983) TVVS 166–169; *Id.*, *op. cit.*, (1984) *Rabels Zeitschrift* 15–20.

forward-looking, democratic content to company institutions at European level: this was how it justified the rules on employee participation and structure in the proposals for a Fifth Directive and for the SE.[62]

The blockages which followed with respect to the SE and the Draft Fifth Directive, and the laborious nature of work on the draft on groups of companies took a lot of the shine off this "grand design" and the élan of the Commission. After the successes of the 1970s (Second, Third and Fourth Directives), harmonization degenerated into a kind of muddling through.[63]

3.1.3. The 1980s: pragmatism and the White Paper

Since the 1980s, it seems as though the Commission has swapped its original ambitious visions for an imposed pragmatism. In the White Paper on Completing the Internal Market, it did – true enough – refer to the above-mentioned industrial policy objectives in order to revive the measures proposed in that context (SE, Tenth Directive, groups[64]), but without much success. Since then, there is hardly any trace of an over-arching vision in the harmonization process:[65] sometimes a company law Directive has enterprise policy aims, such as the Twelfth Directive on single-member private companies, which is part of the EC's SME policy;[66] sometimes protection of (minority) shareholders' interests, such as the Thirteenth Directive on public takeover bids; and sometimes the facilitation of companies' exercise of the right of establishment (Eleventh Directive on branches).[67]

---

62 Commission, "Employee participation and company structure in the European Community", Bull. EC, supp. 8/75, 9–10.

63 C.W.A. Timmermans, *op. cit.*, in *European Business Law*, 129.

64 Commission, *Completing the Internal Market. White Paper of the European Commission for the European Council (Milan, 28–29 June 1985)*, Brussels, 14 June 1985, COM(85) 310, pp. 35–37, paras. 136–144. In fact there is some inconsistency between the text of the White Paper and the timetable annexed: mention is made, *inter alia*, of a planned proposal in 1987 or 1988, respectively, for a directive on liquidation of companies. The draft on this never led to an official proposal by the Commission: see the text in Lutter, *Europäisches Unternehmensrecht*, 299.

65 A good analysis of the conceptual ambiguities of the harmonization programme can be found in Buxbaum and Hopt, *Legal Harmonization and the Business Enterprise. Corporate and Capital Market Law Harmonization Policy in Europe and the U.S.A.* (Berlin/New York, De Gruyter, 1988). This book and the insights developed in it were part of a more recent discussion with various specialists: see *European Business Law. Legal and Economic Analyses on Integration and Harmonization*. See also Dine, "The Harmonization of Company Law in the European Community" (1989) 9 YEL (93), 97–99.

66 See third and fifth considerations Preamble. A direct link between freedom of establishment and the compulsory introduction of single-member private companies is hard to find. Indirectly, the Directive means that, insofar as this could still be a problem, non-recognition of private companies on the basis that there is only one shareholder is at present out of the question.

67 See first consideration Preamble Eleventh Directive and the Commission's explanatory memorandum accompanying its original proposal for an Eleventh Directive of 23 July 1986, COM(86) 397, p. 1, para. 1 and pp. 3–4, para. 7. This shows that the main aim of the Directive is to remove obstacles to the creation of branches which result from divergences in the rules on disclosure in the Member States.

3.1.4. The 1990s: upheaval and (cautious) new start

In the 1990s, the "spirit of subsidiarity" which overcame the Commission's activities in the wake of the Maastricht Treaty[68] strengthened the doubts about the need for Community action in the field of company law. Despite the attempt to recapitulate the policy aims in the strategic programme at the end of 1993,[69] it seems that right up to today there has been no question of an overall reconsideration and review. The initiatives which have appeared since the end of 1995[70] are notable for their pragmatism and lavish references to subsidiarity. They do not exactly reveal a unified vision.

3.1.5. A fourfold crisis

The piecemeal and pragmatic approach of the last two decades has not been to the benefit of the EU's activity in company law. An atmosphere of crisis has been apparent for years; as Behrens has remarked, company law harmonization is currently undergoing a crisis on all fronts: conceptually (e.g. participation versus consultation of employees), in relation to competence (subsidiarity[71]), legitimacy (new preference

---

[68] On the impact of the principle of subsidiarity on company law activities of the EC, see e.g. Buck, "Subsidiaritätsprinzip und Europäisierung des Gesellschaftsrechts", in *Das Subsidiaritätsprinzip in der Europäischen Union* (1995), pp. 73–86; Raaijmakers, "De ontwikkeling van het Europees vennootschapsrecht tussen federalisme en subsidiariteit", in Bekkers, Van den Hurk and Leenknegt (eds), *Subsidiariteit en Europese integratie* (Zwolle, Tjeenk Willink, 1995), pp. 125–145; Schön, "Gesellschaftsrecht nach Maastricht – Art. 3b EGV und das europäische Gesellschaftsrecht" (1995) ZGR 1–38; *Id.*, "Mindestharmonisierung im europäischen Gesellschaftsrecht" (1996) ZHR 221–249. See also Van der Grinten, "Harmonisatie van het vennootschapsrecht" (1993) NV 311–313, according to whom company law can, in conformity with the principle of subsidiarity, be left to the Member States, and the EU should stop further efforts at harmonization.

[69] See Commission, *Making the most of the internal market: Strategic programme*, Communication to the Council of 22 December 1993, COM(93) 632, 33–34. The *objectives* of Community action in the field of company law and accounting mentioned here by the Commission are (i) the mobility of firms in order to allow them to benefit from the advantages of a unified market (ii) the equality of the conditions of competition between firms established in different Member States (iii) the promotion of commercial links between the Member States (iv) the stimulation of cooperation between firms across frontiers and (v) the facilitation of cross-border mergers and acquisitions. The *action points* which the Commission then enumerates can, however, hardly be called "strategic". Rather, there is a vague suggestion that a "fundamental reflection" on the legal framework for firms in the single market is intended, which had never materialized, right up to today. For the rest, the Commission announced "reflection on", but hardly concrete initiatives for, (i) accounting problems and comparability of financial information published by companies, (ii) the role, position and responsibility of the statutory auditor (weakly justified in order to improve the reliability of published financial information), and (iii) the affiliations between subsidiaries and parent companies established in different Member States.

[70] In passing, reference can be made to the (not strictly company law) Council Recommendation 92/443/EEC of 27 July 1992 concerning the promotion of participation by employed persons in profits and enterprise results (including equity participation), OJ 1992, L 245/53. On the impact of this recommendation on the practice of financial participation of employees, see the contributions in the "Dossier financiële participatie" (1997) *Bank Fin.* 127–227.

[71] See also Van Hulle, "Het beleid van de Europese Unie inzake boekhoudrecht", in *Het boekhoudrecht in de samenleving*, C.B.N. Colloquium 8–9 October 1996 (Brussels, Ced. Samson, 1997), pp. 249, 250: "The European reality of today is characterized by euroscepticism, by subsidiarity, by questions about the role of the Commission and by deregulation" (our transl.). See also *id.*, "Respons", in Jan Ronse Instituut (ed.), *Knelpunten van dertig jaar vennootschapsrecht* (Kalmthout, Biblo, 1999), 359, 364–365.

for decentralized development of the law), and loyalty (Member States' resistance to implementation).[72] It seems, in all honesty, far from certain that the recent adoption of the European Company Statute will solve this crisis. It may as well reveal the fact that today the Commission does not have (or no longer has) any coherent vision or agenda in the field of company law.

3.2. Changes in the political–legal and economic context

The present crisis atmosphere in European company law is linked with the fundamental changes in the political–legal and economic context which have taken place, compared with the 1960s, 1970s and even 1980s.

3.2.1. Political–legal context

On the institutional–legal level, the Commission nowadays has to take into account – much more than it used to – constraints in the EC Treaty itself. As far as the competence of the EC to undertake harmonizing activities is concerned, mention must be made above all of Article 5 (ex 3b) EC, introduced by the Maastricht Treaty. This provision makes it clear, first of all, that the Community does not enjoy a full competence, but may only act within the system of attributed competences and objectives (first paragraph: so called "attribution principle"[73]); this means that for Community action there must always be an appropriate legal basis in the EC Treaty.[74] That this is not always evidently so is apparent from the struggles which have been going on for years about the legal basis for the SE Regulation.[75]

---

[72] Behrens, "Krisensymptome in der Gesellschaftsrechtsangleichung" (1996) EuZW 193; *Id.*, "Krisensymptome in der Gesellschaftsrechtsangleichung", in Immenga, Möschel and Reuter (eds), *Festschrift für Ernst-Joachim Mestmäcker zum siebzigsten Geburtstag* (Baden-Baden, Nomos, 1996), pp. 831–849.

[73] For a further analysis of this provision see, e.g. Devroe and Wouters, *De Europese Unie*, pp. 125–128, paras 145–147; Lenaerts and Van Nuffel, *Europees recht in hoofdlijnen* (2nd edn, Antwerpen, Maklu, 1999), pp. 135–140, paras 95–101. See on the significance of the attribution principle, e.g. Opinion 2/94 of the Court of Justice, of 28 March 1996 ("accession to ECHR), [1996] ECR I-1759, para. 23.

[74] The case law of the Court on legal basis requirements stems from the judgment in Case 45/86, *Commission* v. *Council* ("General tariff preferences") [1987] ECR 1493, para. 11. Since then it has been confirmed frequently; see e.g. Case C-209/97, *Commission* v. *Council*, [1999] ECR I-8067. In its Opinion 2/94 at para. 25, the Court of Justice confirmed that the EC can also act on the basis of implied powers, i.e. competences which flow implicitly from the EC Treaty.

[75] The European Parliament and the Commission have been arguing for years that the correct legal basis is Article 95 (ex 100a) EC, given that the SE is considered an essential instrument for the realization of the internal market; most Member States, on the other hand, believe that the SE should be based on the general provision, Article 308 (ex 235) EC. The practical significance is great: in the former case, the Parliament is co-legislator with the Council, and only a qualified majority is required in the latter; in the latter case, the Parliament only has an advisory role, and unanimity is required in the Council. Remarkably, the SE Regulation adopted on 8 October 2001 uses Article 308 EC as legal basis.

In addition, the subsidiarity principle, as expressed in Article 5, second para., EC, means that in areas which do not fall within the exclusive competence of the EC – such as company law[76] – the Community may only legislate "if and in so far as the objectives of the proposed action cannot be sufficiently achieved by the Member States and can therefore, by reason of the scale or effects of the proposed action, be better achieved by the Community". The Commission will therefore have to examine in each case whether – and convince the Member States in the framework of the Council that – (certain) Community action in a particular subdivision of company law is better than purely national action.

Finally, under the proportionality principle expressed in Article 5, third para., EC, Community action may "not go beyond what is necessary to achieve the objectives of the Treaty".

Since 1992, under heavy political pressure, the Commission has embarked on a reconsideration of its legislative proposals in the light of these principles. At the Edinburgh European Council (11–12 December 1992), this led the Commission to promise to review its proposal for a Thirteenth Directive, taking into account the principle of subsidiarity.[77] In the new 1996 and 1997 proposals, there is indeed generous reference to subsidiarity[78] and the Commission stresses that it is merely a "framework Directive" – which Hopt has rightly called a tautology.[79]

The Amsterdam Treaty, in force since 1 May 1999, continues this development with the Protocol on the application of the principles of subsidiarity and proportionality, annexed to the EC Treaty. This Protocol is inspired to a great extent by the guidelines of the Edinburgh European Council on subsidiarity.[80] Unlike these guidelines, however, the Protocol has treaty status.[81] It is hard not to see in this the

---

[76] The Commission has developed an earlier, disputable, interpretation of this concept as far as internal market legislation is concerned, whereby it claims exclusive competence in the area of harmonization measures concerning the internal market. See the criticism in Devroe and Wouters, *De Europese Unie*, para. 148, pp. 129–131; see also arguing against the Commission's claim, Schwartz, "EG-Kompetenzen für den Binnenmarkt: Exklusiv oder konkurrierend/subsidiär?" in Due, Lutter and Schwarze (eds), *Festschrift für Ulrich Everling*, vol. II (Baden-Baden, Nomos, 1995), pp. 1331–1354.

[77] See Bull. EC, 12-1992, point I.23, p. 18, where the Commission admitted that certain of its proposals "tend to go into excessive detail in relation to the objective pursued" and announced its intention to "revise a number of them so that they establish general principles to be given more detailed form by the Member States". The first case then mentioned in which this would be applied was public takeover bids.

[78] See esp. Preamble of the proposals dating from 1996 and 1997, 3rd and 4th considerations, as well as the Commission's explanatory memorandum.

[79] Hopt, *Company Law in the European Union: Harmonization or Subsidiarity*, 11–12: "This is hardly an innovation, for it is already implicit in the instrument of the directive ... 'Framework directive' is therefore a kind of tautology, meaning a 'directive-like directive'." Timmermans replied to this, in "Community Directives Revisited" (1998) 17 YEL 1, 6, that the concept "framework directive" "may nevertheless constitute a useful shorthand to emphasize that Community institutions, and the Commission particularly, will subject draft directives to a serious analysis of what is necessary."

[80] See Presidency conclusions of the Edinburgh European Council on "Overall approach to the application by the Council of the subsidiarity principle and Article 3b of the treaty on European Union (sic)", Bull. EC, 12-1992, point. I.15.

[81] Article 311 (ex 239) EC. The Court of Justice has never ruled on the Edinburgh guidelines, but did not seem very impressed as to their legal status; see judgment in Case C-233/94, *Germany* v. *Parliament and Council*, [1997] ECR, I-2405, para. 80.

intention that the Community institutions comply more strictly with the subsidiarity and proportionality principles. The impact of the Protocol on the content of future harmonization action on company law is hard to estimate. The Protocol is a two-edged sword: it emphasizes that subsidiarity is a dynamic concept, which has to be applied in the light of the Treaty aims, and which allows "Community action within the limits of its powers to be expanded where circumstances so require, and, conversely, to be restricted or discontinued where it is no longer justified."[82] That could lead one in any direction: on the one hand it can be argued that substantial parts of company law need to be harmonized so that companies can reap the benefits of the unified European market and the euro to the full; others will argue that company law rules can be enacted and adapted to new developments more efficiently at the national level, and that a certain competition between legal rules is healthy for the single market, so that new EU initiatives are superfluous, and even certain (parts of) Company law Directives already in force could be called into question (see Section 3.2.2).[83]

In themselves, the above-mentioned principles do not explain the faltering in European company law. In other areas of legislation (e.g. harmonization of technical requirements, consumer law, environmental law) the EU has not become any less industrious, although the same principles apply here too.[84] In particular, the altered political and economic context (Section 3.2.2) seems to be at the root of the standstill. In the area of company law, Member States these days are less sympathetic towards harmonization than they were in the 1960s and 1970s. The increased complexity implied by harmonization for an EU with 15, and even 25 or 30, Member States is one factor. The search for a common denominator, and reaching legislative policy choices, is much more difficult than it used to be – and will become even more so – especially bearing in mind that even in the past complaints were made that harmonization proposals showed too much German (Fifth and Ninth Directives) or too much English (Thirteenth Directive) influence.[85] On this point, too, the question

[82] Point (3), Subsidiarity Protocol.

[83] These two opposing points of view are eloquently expressed by Blanquet, *op. cit.*, pp. 15–16.

[84] See Rimanque and Wouters, *De betekenis van de grondwet voor de Europese rechtsorde* (Deventer, Tjeenk Willink, 1998), p. 65, para. 45. Although the Court of Justice ensures the application of these principles, practice has already shown that the Court will not put itself in the place of a political EU institution once a particular measure has been taken: it confines itself to a marginal review which focuses mainly on compliance with the requirement to give reasons and the proportionality test as far as legislation by the Council or Council and Parliament is concerned: see esp. judgment in Case C-84/94, *United Kingdom* v. *Council*, [1996] ECR I-5755, para. 47. This approach by the ECJ was expected and advocated at the time: see esp. Emiliou, "Subsidiarity: an effective barrier against the enterprise of ambition?" (1992) *European Law Review* 383 at 405; Van Gerven, "De beginselen subsidiariteit, evenredigheid en samenwerking in het Europese gemeenschapsrecht" (1991–92) RW 1241 at 1245, para. 11.

[85] On the evolution from what was originally strong German (and, but less, French) influence, to a predominantly English influence in the harmonization programme, see Hopt, *op. cit.*, pp. 6–8. In fact, this view should not be seen absolutely. For instance, the Second Directive certainly reveals a strong German influence in the area of capital protection in a number of provisions, but, e.g. its controversial Article 23(1) (i.e. prohibition for a company to advance funds, make loans or provide security with a view to acquisition of its shares by a third party) is distinctly British in origin, namely Section 54 Companies Act 1948: Schutte-Veenstra, *op. cit.*, p. 151.

arises why harmonization makes progress in other areas, and not here. If necessary, harmonization could take place on the basis of a qualified majority in the Council, surely?[86] The explanation is probably to a great extent that in the area of company law, Member States have deeply-rooted national traditions which are closely linked to the organization of the national economy and – insofar as the position of employees is concerned – of their collective labor relations; that is not so – or at least less so – for relatively new branches of the law such as consumer law or environmental law, or for technical matters such as product requirements. Really strong arguments are needed in order to convince Member States of the need to harmonize such provisions. This is even more true given the increasing doubts which have arisen in various Member States since the 1990s about the intensity of regulation; here and there initiatives have been taken for de-regulation, such as in France with the introduction of the *société par actions simplifiée* (SAS)[87] and Germany with the *kleine AG-Gesetz*.[88]

3.2.2. Economic context

The changes in the economic context compared with the early years of the common market are no less important. The internationalization of business and of financial markets means that the question of European harmonization of company law and

---

[86] Except when issues concerning "representation and collective defence of the interests of workers and employers, including co-determination" are concerned, in which case the EC can only harmonize one the basis of unanimity; see Article 137, third para., EC, inserted by the Amsterdam Treaty in place of Article 2(3) of the Agreement on Social Policy (which the said Treaty repealed). It must also be recalled that since the Maastricht Treaty, the co-decision procedure applies for Directives based on Article 44 (ex 54) EC, which in practice means that as well as a qualified majority in the Council, there should also be an absolute majority of votes cast in the European Parliament in support of the draft Directive in question.

[87] Loi no 94–1 du 3 janvier 1994 instituant la société par actions simplifiée, as modified in important respects by Loi no 99–586 du 12 juillet 1999. It should be noted that the SAS is not a "société anonyme": although this was the original intention of the French legislature, the fear that it would be subject to the European Directives, in particular the Second Directive, led it to opt for a new form of company: see e.g. Guyon, "Présentation générale de la société par actions simplifiée" (1994) Rev Soc 207, 209. Nevertheless, the working rules of the SAS do conform to the principles of Community company law: Guyon, "La société par actions simplifiée et le droit communautaire", in *Société par actions simplifiée*, (Paris, GLN-Joly, 1994), 147–154, who even ends with the wish that the Community legislature would create a "société par actions simplifiée européenne", just as at the time the French *groupement d'intérêt économique* provided the model for the EESV. On the changes brought forward to the SAS in 1999, see Y. Guyon, "L'élargissement du domaine des sociétés par actions simplifiées (loi du 12 juillet 1999, Article 3), (1999) Rev Soc 505–509.

[88] Gesetz von 2.8.1994 für kleine Aktiengesellschaften und zur Deregulierung des Aktienrechts (*BGBl.*, 1994, I, 1961). See for an overview, e.g. Lutter, "Das neue 'Gesetz für kleine Aktiengesellschaften und zur Deregulierung des Aktienrechts" (1994) AG 429–447. The German deregulation was much more limited than the SAS however: *cf.* the comments of Weil and Kutscher-Puis, "Vague de débureaucratisation des Sociétés Anonymes allemandes: naissance d'une Société par Actions Simplifiée à l'Allemande?" (1994) DPCI 401, 409, that "A côté d'elle [i.e. the SAS], la petite société anonyme du droit allemand fait pâle figure ... En réalité, il ne s'agit que de corrections presque formelles du droit allemand des sociétés par actions, et rien de plus." See, nevertheless, on the usefulness of the "kleine AG" for family businesses, D. Bihr, "Die kleine AG – 'Rechtsform' für den Mittelstand?" (1999) BB 920–923.

accounting can no longer be viewed in an exclusively European framework. Standards are set at the international level, based on the dominance of the American securities market and on globally active institutional investors,[89] which means that, particularly in the area of corporate governance and law of company accounts, the EU should steer a very open course, if it does not want to hamper its own companies.

In the area of corporate governance in particular, the lack of a European position is painfully evident, especially now the work on a code on corporate governance at OECD level has progressed so quickly.[90] The newest study commissioned by the Commission on corporate governance, delivered by Weil, Gotshal & Manges in January 2002[91] notes this point too and rather than having the EU repeat the OECD's exercise in order to establish a voluntary EU-wide code on corporate governance standards, it suggests the Commission to focus its efforts on the reduction of legal and regulatory barriers to shareholder engagement in cross-border voting (so-called "participation barriers") as well as on the reduction of barriers to shareholders' (and potential investors') ability to evaluate the governance of companies (so-called "information barriers"). In fact, these are areas which the Commission has already included within the mandate of the aforementioned High Level Group of Company Law Experts.

3.2.3. Competition between regulatory systems as new paradigm?

Together with these political–legal and economic developments, the last 10 years have witnessed a shift in the underlying mentality. Whereas previously, harmonization of national law could rely on a kind of permissive consensus, and a Delaware phenomenon in Europe was considered undesirable,[92] academics, in particular, have started to wonder more and more whether competition between national regulatory orders might in fact lead to more efficient results. This is partly in the light of American experiences – where the fifty states compete with one another on the level of company law in order to attract "corporate charters", and whereby Delaware has

---

[89] See, e.g. the results of the study by Russell Reynolds, from which it transpires that the large European companies are increasingly adopting Anglo-American corporate governance standards: "European companies open up", *Financial Times*, 9 April 1999. See also, on the efforts by American institutional investors to impose Anglo-American corporate governance rules on German companies, Andre, "Cultural Hegemony: The Exportation of Anglo-Saxon Corporate Governance Ideologies to Germany" (1998) 73 *Tulane Law Review* 69–171.

[90] See *OECD Principles of Corporate Governance*, published on http://www.oecd.org/daf/governance/principles.htm.

[91] Weil, Gotshal & Manges, *Comparative Study of Corporate Governance Codes Relevant to the European Union and its Member States*, Final Report & Annexes I–III, January 2002.

[92] See, e.g. Kolvenbach, "EEC Company Law Harmonization and Worker Participation", (1990) 11 *University of Pennsylvania Journal of International Business Law* 709, 712; Schmitthoff, "The Future of the European Company Law Scene", in Schmitthoff (ed.), *The Harmonization of European Company Law*, (London, UK National Committee of Comparative Law, 1973), pp. 3, 9; Van Hulle, "De harmonisatie van het vennootschapsrecht in de Europese Gemeenschap", in *Harmonisatie van vennootschaps-en effectenrecht. Ervaringen en vooruitzichten in Europa en de Verenigde Staten* (Deventer, Kluwer, 1988), 35, 36–37.

traditionally played a pioneering role.[93] The new approach to harmonization since the Commission's Internal Market White Paper – i.e. minimum harmonization combined with mutual recognition and the principle of "home country control" – and the fact that the company law harmonization process has been bogged down for years, have convinced many people that better results can be expected from competition between legislatures (at least to some extent) as a mechanism for convergence of rules ("bottom-up" harmonization), than from forced, centralized efforts at uniformity ("top-down" harmonization).[94] This change of direction is all the more

---

[93] For a long time, this Delaware phenomenon has been a subject of controversy in the US itself: in outright opposition to this so-called "race of laxity" (the expression used by Justice Brandeis in his dissenting opinion in *Liggett Co.* v. *Lee*, 288 US 517, 558–559 (1933)) was W.L. Cary, "Federalism and Corporate Law: Reflections upon Delaware" (1974) 83 Yale L.J. 663, 668. Shortly afterwards, he was opposed by R.K. Winter, "State Law, Shareholder Protection and the Theory of the Corporation" (1977) 6 *Journal of Legal Studies* 251, 252, who argued that this phenomenon on the contrary led to a "rush to the top", i.e. in more efficient company law rules. The position adopted by Winter was widely supported on empirical basis in the 1980s and 1990s, albeit with some nuances, in writings by R. Romano: see, e.g. Romano, "Law as a Product: Some Pieces of the Incorporation Puzzle" (1985) 1 *Journal of Law, Economics & Organization* 225–283; *Id.*, "The State Competition Debate in Corporate Law" (1987) 8 *Cardozo Law Review* 709–757; *Id.*, *The Genius of American Corporate Law* (Washington, AEI Press, 1993); *Id.*, "Explaining American Exceptionalism in Corporate Law", in Bratton, McCahery, Picciotto and Scott (eds), *International Regulatory Competition and Coordination. Perspectives on Economic Regulation in Europe and the United States* (Oxford, Clarendon Press, 1996), pp. 127–152. The same view was supported by Butler, "Nineteenth-Century Jurisdictional Competition in the Granting of Corporate Privileges" (1985) 14 *Journal of Legal Studies* 129–166; see also Macey and Miller, "Toward an Interest-Group Theory of Delaware Corporate Law" (1987) 65 *Texas Law Review* 469–523. For an overview of proponents and opponents of the American Delaware phenomenon see Trachtman, "International Regulatory Competition, Externalization, and Jurisdiction" (1993) 34 *Harvard International Law Journal* 47, 61–63. The comparison between American and European experiences has already been carried out a number of times: see e.g. the study by Leleux, "Corporation Law in the United States and in the E.E.C. Some Comments on the Present Situation and Future Prospects" (1968–69) *Common Market Law Review* 133–176, which is still worth reading; Krekeler, *Wirtschaftliche Integration und Gesellschaftsrecht – amerikanische Erfahrungen und europäische Irrwege*; Buxbaum and Hopt, *Legal Harmonization and the Business Enterprise*. See more recently Carney, "The Political Economy of Competition for Corporate Charters", in *Current Issues of Cross-Border Establishment of Companies in the European Union*, 249–285; Charny, "Competition among Jurisdictions in Formulating Corporate Law Rules: An American Perspective on the 'Race to the Bottom' in the European Communities" (1991) 33 *Harvard International Law Journal* 423–456; De Kluiver, "European and American Company Law. A Comparison after 25 Years of EC Harmonization" (1994) *MJ* 139–165; *Id.*, *op. cit.*, in *Current Issues of Cross-Border Establishment of Companies in the European Union*, 287–315 (with reaction to the above-mentioned contribution by Carney); Reher, *Gesellschaftsrecht in gemeinsamen Märkten* (Baden-Baden, Nomos, 1997).

[94] See in general, e.g. Dreher, "Wettbewerb oder Vereinheitlichung der Rechtsordnungen in Europa?" (1999) JZ 105–112; Ehlermann, "Ökonomische Aspekte des Subsidiaritätsprinzips: Harmonisierung versus Wettbewerb der Systeme" (1995) *Integration* 11–21; Hauser, "Harmonisierung oder Wettbewerb nationaler Regulierungssysteme in einem integrierten Wirtschaftsraum" (1993) *Aussenwirtschaft* 459–476; Hauser and Hösli, "Harmonisation or Regulatory Competition in the EC (and the EEA)?" (1991) *Aussenwirtschaft* 497–512; Koopmans, "Concurrentie tussen rechtsstelsels" (1992) SEW 446–450; Reich, "Competition between legal orders: a new paradigm of EC law?", 29 *Common Market Law Review* 861–896; Siebert and Koop, "Institutional Competition. A Concept for Europe?" (1990) *Aussenwirtschaft* 439–459; Streit and Mussler, "Wettbewerb der Systeme und das Binnenmarktprogramm der Europäischen Union", in Gerken (ed.), *Europa zwischen Ordnungswettbewerb und Harmonisierung.*

remarkable given that combating the Delaware effect was one of the most powerful original motives for the company law harmonization programme (see Section 3.1.1).

In our view, too, a system whereby there is a certain competition between national company law rules as far as quality and efficiency are concerned, has much to be said for it. Such a competition in terms of quality will however only be possible in reality under certain circumstances, and these do not seem to be present in the EU for the time being (see the following text). However that may be, whether or not there is more competition between jurisdictions, it seems in our view that there is a not negligible role for EU harmonization, both in facilitating cross-border establishment and mergers of companies, and in combating certain external factors (see Section 3.3).

A fundamental precondition for effective competition between regulatory orders is that companies enjoy a real freedom of choice and movement in order to accept jurisdiction from any particular Member State. As is well known, there is an important distinction between the US and the EU – even leaving aside all other relevant economic, social and cultural differences[95] – in that the majority of the EU Member States adhere to the "real seat" theory (*siège réel*), or some variation thereof. The number of Member States that applies the "incorporation" theory has, it is true, increased with the successive accessions, but the ratio *siège réel* to incorporation countries is still, roughly, nine to six.[96] In the US, on the other hand, application of the incorporation

Europäische Ordnungspolitik im Zeichen der Subsidiarität (Springer, 1995), 75–107; Sun and Pelkmans, "Regulatory Competition in the Single Market" (1995) JCMS 67–89; Woolcock, *The Single European Market. Centralization of Competition among National Rules?* (London, Royal Institute of International Affairs, 1994); *Id.*, "Competition among rules in the single European market", in *International Regulatory Competition and Coordination. Perspectives on Economic Regulation in Europe and the United States*, 289–321. See, strongly against the idea of competition between legal orders, Everling, "Europäische Integration und Wettbewerb der Rechtsordnungen in der Rechtsprechung des Gerichtshofes der Europäischen Gemeinschaften", in Hopt (ed.), *Europäische Integration als Herausforderung des Rechts: Mehr Markrecht – weniger Einzelgesetze?* (Hanns Martin Schleyer Stiftung, 1991), 41–51. In the field of European company law, see, e.g. in favor competition, although with the necessary reservations, Hopt, "Europäisches und deutsches Übernahmerecht" (1997) ZHR 368, 381–384, with numerous references; *Id.*, *op. cit.*, (1998) ZIP 98–99; Wymeersch, "Harmoniser le droit des groupes de sociétés en Europe?", in Due, Lutter and Schwarze (eds), *Festschrift für Ulrich Everling* (Baden-Baden, Nomos, 1995), 1699, p. 1708, nr. 9 (in connection with the law on groups); see also Geens, "Tien jaar T.R.V. Ten geleide" (1998) TRV 547, 550. As for the question of transposability of US experiences on company law to the EU, see Merkt, "Das Europäische Gesellschaftsrecht und die Idee des 'Wettbewerbs der Gesetzgeber' " (1995) *Rabels Zeitschrift* 545–568.

[95] See our caveats for such a transatlantic comparison, in Wouters, *op. cit.*, (1993) *Common Market Law Review* 269–279. *Cf.* also Kohl, "Federalism and corporate law", in Pernice (ed.), *Harmonization of Legislation in Federal Systems: Constitutional, Federal and Subsidiarity Aspects – the European Union and the United States compared* (Baden-Baden, Nomos, 1996), 129, 135.

[96] See, with numerous references to relevant national choice of law rules, Wouters, "Private International Law and Companies' Freedom of Establishment" (2001) *European Business Organization Law Review* 101–139.

theory is – partly on the basis of federal constitutional principles[97] – self-evident.[98] This means, in actual fact, that the law of the state of incorporation regulates the "internal affairs" of a company, no matter where that company is situated or has its headquarters. American companies can therefore choose between 50 state company laws, and obviously fierce competition between the jurisdictions has resulted from this, also in connection with the collection of franchise taxes by the states.[99]

Although it is an interesting idea in theory, it does not seem feasible for the time being to introduce the incorporation theory for the whole of the EU. The troubles around the Treaty for the mutual recognition of companies of 1968 should be recalled, that Treaty being now consigned (and rightly so) to the annals of history.[100]

---

[97] On the significance in this context of the "full faith and credit clause" of the federal constitution, see, e.g. Reese and Kaufman, "The Law Governing Corporate Affairs: Choice of Law and the Impact of Full Faith and Credit" (1958) 58 *Columbia Law Review* 1118–1145; Weintraub, *Commentary on the Conflict of Laws* (3rd edn, Mineola, Foundation Press, 1986), 533. See however, with emphasis on the importance of the "Commerce Clause", Butler and Ribstein, *The Corporation and the Constitution* (Washington DC, AEI Press, 1995), 132–138.

[98] This "internal affairs rule" (pursuant to which the law applicable to the internal affairs of a company is that of the state of incorporation) is confirmed in various provisions of the Restatement (Second) of Conflict of Laws (1971): see, with note, Sections 296, 297, 302(2), 304, 305 and 307. See also Reese, Rosenberg and Hay, *Cases and Materials on Conflict of Laws* (Westbury, Foundation Press, 1990), 9th edn, 981; Scoles and Hay, *Conflict of Laws* (St-Paul, West Publishing, 1982), p. 885, Section 23.2. On the background to this rule, see, e.g. Buxbaum, "The Origins of the American 'Internal Affairs' Rule in the Corporate Conflict of Laws", in Musielak and Schurig (eds), *Festschrift für Gerhard Kegel zum 75. Geburtstag 26. Juni 1987* (Stuttgart, Kohlhammer, 1987), 75–94. All this does not detract from the fact that states sometimes claim the right to apply their own company law legislation, particularly when the company in question has only a very tenuous connection with its state of incorporation. In connection with the controversy around these "pseudo-foreign corporations", see, e.g. Kaplan, "Foreign Corporations and Local Corporate Policy" (1968) 21 *Vanderbilt Law Review* 433–481; Latty, "Pseudo-Foreign Corporations" (1955) 65 *Yale Law Journal* 137–173; R.E. Smith, "Choice of Law and the Corporation: The United States Supreme Court Expands the Doctrine of Public Policy", (1984) 10 *University of Dayton Law Review* 97–116. See more in general on the application by states of their company law to the "internal affairs" of companies incorporated under the law of other states: Demott, "Perspectives on Choice of Law for Corporate Internal Affairs" (1985) 48 *Law and Contemporary Problems* 161–198.

[99] See Alva, "Delaware and the Market for Corporate Charters: History and Agency" (1990) 15 *Delaware Journal of Corporate Law* 885, 887–888; Cary, *op. cit.*, (1974) 83 *Yale Law Journal* 664–669; Romano, *op. cit.*, (1987) *8 Cardozo Law Review* 709. Also in this area the US and the EU reveal an important distinction, given that periodic franchise (i.e. concession) taxes are not levied in the EU, and the capital taxes which are levied in several Member States have been partially harmonized by Council Directive 69/335/EEC of 17 July 1969 on indirect taxes on the raising of capital, OJ 1969, L 249/25, as repeatedly amended; *cf.* Merkt, *op. cit.*, (1995) *Rabels Zeitschrift* 564–565.

[100] Treaty of 28 February 1968 concerning the mutual recognition of companies and legal persons (Bull. EC, suppl. 2/69). Five of the original six Member States ratified this treaty, but the Netherlands never approved it, and in November 1993, the bill which had been introduced in 1972 to that end was formally withdrawn: Vlas, "Doek valt voor het EEG-Erkenningsverdrag" (1994) TVVS 16. Amongst the many commentaries see, e.g. Fredericq, "De onderlinge erkenning van vennootschappen en rechtspersonen in de Europese Economische Gemeenschap", in *Recht in beweging. Opstellen aangeboden aan Prof. Mr. Ridder R. Victor*, I (Antwerpen, Kluwer, 1973), 501–517; Renauld, "La reconnaissance mutuelle des sociétés dans le marché commun" (1968) RPS 207–243; Timmermans, "Het Verdrag van 29 februari 1968 inzake de onderlinge erkenning van vennootschappen en rechtspersonen. Enkele europeesrechtelijke

Conversion to the incorporation theory will not occur voluntarily – although for instance in Belgium this very step has been pleaded only recently[101] – and there seems to be insufficient political will for a harmonization of conflict-of-law rules concerning companies and legal persons,[102] even though the EC Treaty now contains a firmer basis for Community action in the field of convergence of private international law since the Amsterdam Treaty.[103] Obviously, application of the real seat theory largely (though not entirely[104]) prevents competition between jurisdictions in the field of company law: companies are obliged to be (re-)incorporated under the legal system of the State where they have their actual headquarters (i.e. their "real seat"). The arguments against the real seat theory may be numerous, but thus far the Court of Justice

kanttekeningen", in *Mededelingen van de Nederlandse Vereniging voor Internationaal Recht*, No. 81, (1980), 33–93; Van Hecke, "Erkenning, zetelverplaatsing en fusie", in *Europees vennootschapsrecht. Le régime juridique des sociétés dans la C.E.E.*, postdoctoral courses 1966–67 KUL, (Antwerpen, Standaard, 1968), 149–169. It is fortunate that the Treaty has remained a dead letter: not only is the question of "recognition" of a foreign company outdated (these days, in conflict of laws the prevailing view is that for the existence and capacity of a legal person to be established, application of the conflicts rule is sufficient), but also the Treaty gave the possibility to renounce the application of the incorporation theory (which was formally adhered to) by means of a declaration – and all five remaining Member States had made use of this possibility. Moreover, given the present state of European integration (especially taking account of the case law of the Court of Justice and the harmonization achieved thus far in company law) there is no need for a Treaty on recognition. See on this Wouters, *Het Europese vestigingsrecht voor ondernemingen*, paras 571–592.

[101] See Tilquin, "L'incorporation comme facteur de rattachement de la *lex societatis*" (1998) RPS 5–56. See already our criticism of the "real seat theory": Wouters, "Over vennootschappen, verwijzingsregels en vrijheid van vestiging" (1991) TRV 456, 460–464, paras 5–7.

[102] An idea which has been pleaded by Timmermans in the past: *op. cit.* (1984) *Rabels Zeitschrift* 39; *Id., op. cit.*, in *European Business Law*, 141; see also Geens, "Toespraak bij het afscheid van professor W.C.L. van der Grinten als voorzitter van de Commissie Vennootschapsrecht" (1993) NV 3, 5; Wouters, *op. cit.*, (1991) TRV 478, para. 25.

[103] See the new Article 65, sub b, EC, according to which "measures in the field of judicial cooperation in civil matters having cross-border implications" may be taken "insofar as necessary for the proper functioning of the internal market" "promoting the compatibility of the rules applicable in the Member States concerning the conflict of laws and jurisdiction". Although for the first five years after entry into force of the Treaty of Amsterdam unanimity is required for such measures, various important initiatives have already been taken, either by the Commission or by Member States, on the basis of this provision. On these initiatives and the various problems which Article 65 raises, see *inter alia* Basedow, "Die Harmonisierung des Kollisionsrechts nach dem Vertrag von Amsterdam" (1997) EuZW 609; Kohler, "Interrogations sur les sources du droit international privé européen après le traité d'Amsterdam" (1999) Rev Crit Dr Int Privé 1; Jayme and Kohler, "Europäisches Kollisionsrecht 1999 – Die Abentstunde der Staatsverträge" (1999) IPRax 401–413.

[104] There does remain a certain competition insofar as legislatures sometimes observe with some jealousy the interest in foreign company forms and, in order to attract foreign direct investment, introduce more attractive company forms or company law rules: *cf.* the introduction of the SAS in France, which was partly a reaction to the success of the Netherlands "B.V." (private limited company). There is also competition to the extent that EU nationals or companies can choose a less intensely regulated Member State in order to set up a company, and can then carry out activities in other Member States via agencies and branches, sometimes without the company in the home State carrying out any activities: for examples in case law of the Court of Justice, see Case 79/85, *Segers*, [1986] ECR, 2375 and Case C-212/97, *Centros*, [1999] ECR I-1459.

has not found it to be incompatible with the freedom of establishment. On the contrary, the *Daily Mail* judgment has validated it,[105] though the question arises to what extent this case still presents the prevailing view of the Court after *Centros*[106] and *Überseering*.[107] However that may be, as long as the majority of Member States adhere to the "seat theory", the only way to step up competition between jurisdictions is by easing rules on cross-border seat transfers. The fact that companies can change their personal statute with no hindrances does increase the pressure, in any case, on national legislatures to offer an attractive company law (and fiscal law) framework. In that respect, the plans for a Fourteenth Directive (Section 2.2) are to be greeted enthusiastically, even if the Commission still urgently needs to get to work on the fiscal component[108]

---

[105] Case 81/87, *Daily Mail*, [1988] ECR 5483; note by Stuyck, (1989) TRV 194, "Zetelverplaatsing en vrije vestiging van vennootschappen in de EEG". For an extensive analysis, including the question whether *Daily Mail* has been overtaken by later case law of the Court of Justice, see Wouters, *Het Europese vestigingsrecht voor ondernemingen*, paras 334–346.

[106] *Supra* n. 104. The case concerned the refusal by the Danish Ministry of Trade to register a branch of an English limited company (Centros), particularly as a result of the company's total lack of any capital (which is not required for private limited companies under English law). The Court of Justice considered this refusal to be in breach of Articles 43 (ex 52) and 48 (ex 58) EC. In conformity with its earlier *Segers* case law (*supra* n. 104), the Court found that the fact that the company in question carried out its activities solely via the branch did not form any obstacle: that an EU national establishes a company in a Member State where the company law rules are less stringent, is considered by the Court not to be an abuse of the right of establishment, but precisely an inherent element thereof (para. 27). Of interest to us is also the *obiter dictum* that the incomplete state of harmonization of relevant company law is "is of little consequence" and that "[m]oreover, it is always open to the Council, on the basis of the powers conferred upon it by Article [44 (ex 54)] (3)(g) of the EC Treaty, to achieve complete harmonization" (para. 28). A full assessment of the possible implications of this case goes beyond this contribution. See *inter alia* the comments of Behrens, "Das Internationale Gesellschaftsrecht nach dem Centros-Urteil des EuGH" (1999) IPRax 323–331; Bungert, "Konsequenzen der Centros-Entscheidung des EuGH für die Sitzanknüpfung des deutschen internationalen Gesellschaftsrechts" (1999) DB 1841–1844; Cascante, "Niederlassungsfreiheit contra Sitztheorie – Goodbye 'Daily Mail'?" (1999) RIW 450–451; De Kluiver, "De wet formeel buitenlandse vennootschappen op de tocht?" (1999) WPNR 527–528; De Wulf, "Brievenbusvennootschappen, vrij vestigingsrecht en werkelijke zetelleer" (1999) V&F 3–19; *Id.*, "Centros: vrijheid van vestiging zonder race to the bottom" (1999) *Ondernemingsrecht* 318–324; Freitag, "Der Wettbewerb der Rechtsordnungen im Internationalen Gesellschaftsrecht" (1999) EuZW 267–270; Geyrhalter, "Niederlassungsfreiheit contra Sitztheorie – Good Bye 'Daily Mail' ?" (1999) EWS 201–203; Höflinger, "Die Centros-Entscheidung des EuGH – auf dem Weg zu einer Überlagerungstheorie für Europa" (1999) DB 1206–1208; Kieninger, "Niederlassungsfreiheit als Rechtswahlfreiheit" (1999) ZGR 724–749; Kindler, "Niederlassungsfreiheit für Scheinauslandgesellschaften?" (1999) NJW 1993–2000; Meilicke (1999) DB 627–628; Menjucq, (1999) D., 553–557; Parleani, (1999) Rev Soc 391–398; Roth 37 *Common Market Law Review* 000–000; Sandrock, "Centros: ein Etappensieg für die Überlagerungstheorie" (1999) BB 1337–1345; Sedemund and Hausmann, "Niederlassungsfreiheit contra Sitztheorie – Abschied von Daily Mail?" (1999) BB 809–811; Sonnenberger and Großerichter, "Konfliktlinien zwischen internationalem Gesellschaftsrecht und Niederlassungsfreiheit" (1999) RIW 721–732; Werlauff, "Using a Foreign Company for Domestic Activities" (1999) *European Business Law Review* 306–313; Wymeersch, "Centros: A Landmark Decision in European Company Law", in T. Baums, K.J. Hopt and N. Horn (eds.), *Corporations, Capital Markets and Business in the Law. Liber Amicorum Richard M. Buxbaum* (Kluwer Law International, 2000), 629.

[107] Judgment of 5 November 2002 in Case C-208/00 (nyr).

[108] Similarly, the comments of the European employers' Association, UNICE: "UNICE seeks clarification on tax measures for migrating firms", European Report, 14 January 1998, No. 2282, business brief, 1.

If one opts for a system of competition between jurisdictions in the area of company law, another important distinction between American and (continental) European company law should be borne in mind as well. Apart from its state (as opposed to federal) character, American company law is also paradigmatically characterized by the fact that it primarily regulates matters concerning shareholders, and that it is above all enabling law.[109] American company law does not have a tradition of internalizing the public policy balancing act, such as between protection of investors, creditors and employees.[110] For example, protection of investors takes place mainly outside company law, under federal securities regulations,[111] and protection of creditors takes place primarily through federal bankruptcy legislation and the Uniform Commercial Code.[112] The "enabling" character of American company legislation underlines the view that company law is there in order to create an efficient framework so as to achieve economic and utilitarian (profit-maximizing) objectives: that is why the maximum possible room has to be left open to the freedom of the parties concerned.[113]

On the other hand, European legislatures, in particular continental European legislatures,[114] have tended in the course of time to enact more and more mandatory provisions, and perhaps felt themselves encouraged in that respect, to some extent, by European harmonization (Section 2.3). Although over the last few years in a number

---

[109] A number of years ago, Bebchuk tried to start a discussion on the limits of freedom of contract in this area: "The Debate on Contractual Freedom in Corporate Law" (1989) 89 *Columbia Law Review* 1395–1415; "Limiting Contractual Freedom in Corporate Law: The Desirable Constraints on Charter Amendments" (1989) 102 *Harvard Law Review* 1820–1860; see however the critical analysis by Romano, "Answering the Wrong Question: The Tenuous Case of Mandatory Corporate Laws" (1989) 89 *Colorado Law Review* 1599–1617. That does not mean at all that there are no proponents in the US apart from Bebchuk for mandatory corporate laws: see e.g. Brudney, "Corporate Governance, Agency Costs, and the Rhetoric of Contract" (1985) 85 *Colorado Law Review* 1403–1444; Eisenberg, *The Structure of the Corporation* (Boston, Little, Brown, 1976), 1–6 and 316–320; and, more "middle of the road", Coffee, "The Mandatory/Enabling Balance in Corporate Law: An Essay on the Judicial Role" (1989) 89 *Colorado Law Review* 1618–1691.

[110] See Buxbaum and Hopt, *Legal Harmonization and the Business Enterprise*, 128. This has its foundation in the conviction that broad social concerns should be regulated via external legislation, and not by means of "internal" company rules: see Buxbaum, "Juridification and Legitimation in Enterprise Law", in Daintith and Teubner (eds), *Juridification of Social Spheres* (Berlin/New York, De Gruyter, 1987), 241; Meier-Schatz, "American Legal Harmonization from a European Perspective" *European Business Law* 61, 63.

[111] As is well known, the two most important federal laws in this context are the Securities Act of 1933 (15 USC para. 77a–77aa) and the Securities Exchange Act of 1934 (15 USC para. 78a–78jj).

[112] See also Landau, "The Federal and State Roles in Regulating United States Business Corporations", in *Harmonisatie van vennootschaps- en effectenrecht. Ervaringen en vooruitzichten in Europa en de Verenigde Staten* (Deventer, Kluwer, 1988), 55, 59.

[113] See Winter, *op. cit.*, (1977) 6 *Journal of Legal Studies* 251; Buxbaum and Hopt, *Legal Harmonization and the Business Enterprise*, p. 119. See also Meier-Schatz, "Europäische Harmonisierung des Gesellschafts- und Kapitalmarktrechts" (1989) *Wirtschaft und Recht*, 84, 98; *Id.*, *op. cit.*, *European Business Law*, 63.

[114] On the somewhat particular position of English company law, caught between its "common law" roots, and the mainly civil-law inspired harmonization of company law, see Davies, *Gower's Principles of Modern Company Law* (6th edn, London, Sweet & Maxwell, 1997), p. 62.

of Member States the theme of increased contractual freedom has received more attention,[115] it is odd that in some other Member States, it is hardly discussed at all.[116] If one argues for a European "market for corporate charters" in order to obtain competition between jurisdictions, then one must also be aware that this process will imply an erosion of mandatory requirements and that, in order to realize policy aims such as protection of investors, creditors and employees, perhaps it will be necessary to harmonize more, and more intensively, at EU level, or even achieve uniformity by means of Regulations,[117] than has been the case up until now. For the rest, harmonization will be needed in any case in order to deal with certain externalities which can be expected also – and perhaps more – in a competition model (Section 3.3.2).

3.3. What role for the EU in the area of company law?

3.3.1. Facilitating the right of establishment

It is submitted that the prime objective for harmonization in the area of company law – for accounting and securities law, see Section 4.2 – should be to create the necessary conditions for companies to be able fully to exercise the freedom of establishment which they are granted by the EC Treaty. The *legal* arguments for this view are conclusive: if one reads the legal basis contained in Article 44(3) sub g EC in its context, and in the light of the EC Treaty objectives, it cannot be separated from the Treaty Chapter of which it is part or from the task assigned to the Commission and Council by the first sentence of Article 44(1), that is, to realize freedom of establishment, *inter alia* by means of harmonization. The Treaty objectives confirm this

---

[115] See, e.g. in Germany Lutter and Wiedemann (eds.), *Gestaltungsfreiheit im Gesellschaftsrecht* (Berlin/New York, De Gruyter, 1998). For France, see the debate about the need for more flexibility and contractual freedom in the law of public limited liability companies, which ultimately led to the SAS: Bisarra, "L'inadaptation du droit français des sociétés aux besoins des entreprises et les aléas des solutions" (1990) Rev Soc 553–566; Couret, "Les apports de la théorie micro-économique moderne à l'analyse du droit des sociétés" (1984) Rev Soc 243–258; Guyon, *Traité des contrats. Les sociétés. Aménagements statutaires et conventions entre associés* ((2nd edn) Paris, LGDJ 1995); le Fevre, "Le droit des sociétés redeviendra-t-il contractuel? Perspectives d'une société par actions simplifiée" (1992) *Rev Jurispr Comm* 89–105; Saintourens, "La flexibilité du droit des sociétés" (1987) Rev Trim Dr Comm 457–494. See, for the Netherlands, Timmerman, "Waarom hebben wij dwingend vennootschapsrecht?", in *Ondernemingsrechtelijke contracten* (Kluwer, Deventer, 1991), 1–10; *Id.*, "Is versoepeling van het Nederlandse n.v./b.v.-recht wenselijk?" (1992) TVVS 163–168; De Kluiver, "Het vennootschapsrecht dient te worden versoepeld … en verscherpt" (1994) TVVS 174–179.

[116] For example in Belgium. See nevertheless, with attention for contractualization or greater flexibility of company law, Simonart, "La contractualisation des sociétés, ou les aménagements contractuels des mécanismes sociétaires" (1995) RPS 75–130; Tilquin and Simonart, *Traité des sociétés*, I, 128–130. See also Corbisier and Maquet, "Une illustration de l'autonomie relative des dispositions statutaires et extrastatutaires et ce au détriment des premières", note by judgment of Spanish supreme court of 10 February 1992, (1995) RPS 45–56; Corbisier and Nicaise, "SAS: un exemple à suivre?" (1994) 33 *DAOR* 43–80.

[117] In which case the question arises as to the appropriate legal basis, in the EC Treaty, given that Article 44 (ex 54), para. 3, sub g, EC only creates the possibility for the use of directives.

interpretation: under Article 3(1)(h) EC, the approximation of national legislation is only required of the Community "to the extent required for the functioning of the common market". In other words, the EC Treaty itself imposes a functional view of harmonization: it is only intended for the abolition, or at least reduction, of disparities which cause barriers to free movement.[118]

Also in *political* terms, this position offers the best defence against Community decision-making being blocked by appeals to competence and legal basis problems and/or the subsidiarity principle. Developing the internal market and removing obstacles to the greatest possible freedom of movement for companies are objectives which, in the terms of Article 5, second para., EC, "cannot be sufficiently achieved by the Member States and can therefore, by reason of the scale or effects of the proposed action, be better achieved by the Community". The long-standing *status quo* – or even regression – in the legal conditions for cross-border seat transfers in the Member States' legal orders[119] is the best proof of this. Apart from a very few exceptions,[120] national company law rules are formulated in a domestic perspective, particularly as far as corporate concentrations[121] and mobility[122] are concerned.

Incidentally, it may be noted that harmonization is not the only possible way of dealing with company law obstacles to free movement. In some well-chosen cases, the Commission could consider starting infringement proceedings against Member States for breach of Articles 43 (ex 52) in conjunction with 48 (ex 58) EC – certainly

---

[118] *Cf.* the view of E. Stein, already developed in 1964: "The function of approximation is to reduce or eliminate disparities in national laws, regulations or administrative practices where they constitute *obstacles to economic intercourse* which cannot be removed through other legal devices in the armoury of the Community ...": "Assimilation of National Laws as a Function of European Integration" (1964) 58 Am. J. Int. L. 1, 29 (our emphasis). See in the same sense Rodière, "L'harmonisation des législations européennes dans le cadre de la CEE" (1965) RTDE 336, 346.

[119] See on this Wouters, *Het Europese vestigingsrecht voor ondernemingen*, paras 618–688.

[120] See Kreuzer, "Grenzüberschreitende Restrukturierung von Gesellschaften im Gemeinsamen Markt" (1994) EuZW 73, 74, n. 9, who refers to Article 3(2)–(6) of the Portuguese Companies Act of 2 September 1986.

[121] An illustration concerning Belgium is the Law of 29 June 1993 which transposes the Third and Sixth Directives into Belgian law. In the explanatory memorandum, the Government clung to the traditional view that the General Meeting cannot change the nationality of a company (Article 70 Belgian Companies Act), which means that a cross-border merger by which a Belgian company is swallowed up is legally impossible. The Government does consider it possible for a Belgian company to take over a foreign company, if the domestic law of the latter does not present any problems (*Doc. parl.*, Chamber of Representatives, 1989–90, No 1214/1, 3; the same reasoning is applied to divisions). The same reasoning is followed in Germany. One might share Tilquin's reservations, though, that if all Member States reason like this, intra-Community mergers remain virtually impossible: *Traité des fusions et scissions* (Brussels, Kluwer, 1993), p. 526, para. 741; see in this sense also Beitzke, "Les conflits de lois en matière de fusion de sociétés (droit communautaire et droit international privé)" (1967) Rev Crit Dr Int Privé 1, 5.

[122] For instance, the Belgian Companies Act only allows for the possibility of a domestic (statutory) transfer of seat: see Articles 81(3) and 138(3) Companies Act. In Belgium's defence, one might point out that, at least as far as seat transfers into Belgium are concerned, as a result of the *Lamot* case law of the Cour de cassation (12 November 1965, *Pas.*, 1966, I, 336, R.W., 1965–66, 91) Belgian law is characterized by more openness. However, the ambiguities and uncertainties attending this case law (see Wouters, *Het Europese vestigingsrecht voor ondernemingen*, paras 622–631) mean that a set of legal rules on cross-border seat transfers is particularly desirable.

given the more extensive effect which the Court of Justice accords to the right of establishment these days. In this context, the proceedings against Belgium brought by the Commission, for breach of Community law by the nationality requirements contained in the Law on non-profit-making associations, and the Law on international associations, should be greeted with enthusiasm.[123] Non-discriminatory obstacles which are not manifestly objectively justified and/or are disproportionate may infringe Article 43 (ex 52) EC.[124]

In addition, obviously, the creation of European legal persons and types of company, such as the EEIG, SE, EA, ECS and the EMS (see Section 2.1) or a European "private company",[125] has a positive effect on mobility – although much depends on the quality of the statutes developed for these legal forms, and on the extent to which these statutes refer back to national law.[126] As mentioned above, the SE statute does not give one high hopes in this respect (Section 3.1.4).

If this vision is adopted, then the most important priority for the Commission consists of identifying the real obstacles to cross-border mobility and mergers for companies, resulting from divergent national rules on business organizations, and eliminating them.[127] In this perspective, it would seem evident that – with a view to simplifying the exercise of the right of *primary* establishment – priority should be given to work on the Tenth Directive, on cross-border mergers, and the Fourteenth Directive, on cross-border seat transfers.[128] In addition, a thorough examination of the obstacles to *secondary* establishment of foreign companies is needed, and in particular – despite the Eleventh Directive – for branches; such obstacles still exist

---

[123] See Case C-172/98, *Commission* v. *Belgium*, judgment of 29 June 1999, nyr.

[124] See, e.g. for analysis of the Dutch proposed legislation on defensive tactics in relation to Article 43 (ex 52) EC, Wouters, "Het wetsvoorstel beschermingsconstructies in Europees perspectief", in *Het wetsvoorstel beschermingsconstructies*, papers of the Vereeniging "Handelsrecht" (Deventer, Tjeenk Willink, 1998), pp. 65–135. Quite obviously, discriminatory national company law rules would be generally prohibited under the EC Treaty's provisions outlawing discrimination on the basis of nationality: see Case C-122/96 *Saldanha and MTS Securities Corporation* v. *Hiross Holding* [1997] ECR I-5325, para. 23.

[125] See the initiative of the Paris Chamber of Commerce: Boucourechliev (ed.), *Propositions pour une société fermée européenne* (Luxemburg, Office of Official Publications EC, 1997). On this, Drury, "The Prospects for a European Close Company" (1998) *European Business Law Review* 24–29; Hommelhoff, "Die 'Société fermée européenne': eine supranationale Gesellschaftsform für kleine und mittlere Unternehmen im europäischen Binnenmarkt" (1997) WM 2101–2109. See also for the recent proposals by UNICE and EuroChambres for a European "close company" and the reaction of Commissioner Monti on this: Bulletin Quotidien Europe, 9 April 1999, 14. See on this theme, from a mainly comparative law perspective, De Kluiver and Van Gerven (eds) *The European Private Company?* (Antwerpen, Maklu, 1995).

[126] On the conflict of laws questions which arise in connection with e.g. the EEIG and the SE, see, e.g. Hauschka, "Entwicklungslinien und Integrationsfragen der gesellschaftsrechtlichen Akttypen des Europäischen Gemeinschaftsrechts" (1990) AG 85–103; Koppenhol-Laforce, "Het EESV en de internationaalprivaatrechtelijke complicaties", in *Aspecten van het EESV. Grensoverschrijdend en grensverleggend samenwerken* (Deventer, Kluwer, 1990), 79–108.

[127] In its advisory resolution of May 1966 concerning the draft for a first Directive, OJ 1966, 1519, point 3, the European Parliament already urged that an overview of obstacles for exercising the right of establishment which flow from national company law be drawn up. To our knowledge, such an overview has never been produced.

[128] This is also the conclusion reached by Schön, *op. cit.*, (1996) ZHR 244–246.

today as a result of divergent rules of national commercial and company law (and – although this is a different field of action – tax law[129]), which interfere with the freedom of choice as to legal form of a secondary establishment – i.e. subsidiary, branch or agency – guaranteed by Article 43 (ex 52) EC.[130]

Simplifying the exercise of the right of establishment can also provide a basis for the question to what extent EU action is needed concerning law on corporate groups. Rather than looking for a "European model", as in the draft Ninth Directive,[131] and for which there is hardly any real interest in practice,[132] one could examine whether and to what extent divergent rules concerning the relation between a company and its subsidiaries established in different Member States hinder the freedom of establishment. The problem of non-recognition of cross-border management agreements could be mentioned here, for instance.[133] At the same time, in this perspective, one could examine whether and how the problems of transnational vertical and horizontal formation of groups can be eased by harmonization initiatives.[134] The recent proposals by the Forum Europaeum Konzernrecht[135] offer interesting matter for

---

[129] The fiscally disadvantageous position of branches or permanent establishments has already led to a number of judgments by the Court of Justice: see, as well as the *avoir fiscal* case mentioned in the following footnote, Case C-330/91, *Commerzbank*, [1993] ECR I-4017, with annotation by Wouters in (1994) TRV 27, "Directe belastingen in de rechtspraak van het Europees Hof van Justitie: thema en variaties"; Case C-250/95, *Futura Participations*, [1997] ECR I-2471, with note by Wouters in (1997) TRV 302, "Verliesverrekening van vaste inrichtingen en het Europese vestigingsrecht". See also, most recently, Case C-311/97, *Royal Bank of Scotland*, judgment of 29 April 1999, nyr.

[130] This freedom of choice was recognized by the Court of Justice in the *avoir fiscal* case: Case 270/83, *Commission* v. *France*, [1986] ECR 273, para. 22. See on this Wouters, *Het Europese vestigingsrecht voor ondernemingen*, paras 210–212; Lauwaars and Timmermans, *Europees recht in kort bestek* (5th edn, Deventer, Tjeenk Willink, 1999), pp. 220–221.

[131] See, e.g. Bartman and Dorresteijn, *Van het concern* (2nd edn, Arnhem, Gouda Quint, 1994), pp. 273–276.

[132] This was the general feeling at the symposium held in early June 1993, on the occasion of the publication of the stimulating collection: Wymeersch (Ed.) *Groups of Companies in the EEC* (Berlin New York, De Gruyter, 1993): "Pas de demande pour un droit des groupes", L'Echo, 4 June 1993; "Laat Europese Gemeenschap het groepsrecht voor ondernemingen een stille dood sterven?", *Financieel-Ekonomische Tijd*, 17 June 1993.

[133] See Wouters, *Het Europese vestigingsrecht voor ondernemingen*, para. 610.

[134] See already at the time the proposals of Lutter, "Empfehlen sich für die Zusammenfassung europäischer Unternehmen neben oder statt der europäischen Handelsgesellschaft und der internationalen Fusion weitere Möglichkeiten der Gestaltung auf dem Gebiete des Gesellschaftsrechts?", *Verhandlungen des Achtundvierzigsten Deutschen Juristentages*, I (Munich, Beck, 1970), H5-H153, with an appendix containing a draft treaty; *Id.*, "Für einen Europäischen Vertragskonzern", (1971) *Zeitschrift für Schweizerisches Recht*, 267–291. The elaboration of European rules for transnational horizontal groups is also a theme which is dear to Wymeersch: *op. cit.*, in *40 Jahre Römische Verträge*, 202. As to the question of the usefulness of the SE as instrument for cross-border horizontal formation of groups, see Byttebier, "Binationale, horizontale groepsvorming: een zinvol alternatief voor de Europese Vennootschap?" (1994) TRV 119–127.

[135] Forum Europaeum Konzernrecht, "Konzernrecht für Europa" (1998) ZGR 672–772; for a French version, see Forum Europaeum sur le droit des groupes de sociétés, "Un droit des groupes de sociétés pour l'Europe" (1999) Rev Soc 43–80, 285–337; an extract in English has been published in (1999) *Common Market Law Review* 7–11. See Hopt, "Europäisches Konzernrecht?" (1999) EuZW 577; and the guest editorial of Lutter, "First steps for a European law on corporate groups" (1999) *Common Market Law Review* 1–5.

discussion on this, although their framework is much more ambitious than merely facilitating cross-border formation of groups.[136]

Another issue which certainly remains current in the view set out here is the need to follow carefully the problem of anti-takeover rules and other defensive measures. In actual fact, the exercise of the right of establishment by means of a public takeover bid is often curtailed by such rules and practices, much more than by divergent national regulations on the procedure of takeover bids (which is mainly what the Thirteenth Directive tries to bring closer together). The efforts by the EU thus far in this field, and the results achieved, are much too modest.[137] Limited, but well-directed, harmonization initiatives, which would restrain or where appropriate forbid the most draconian anti-takeover rules and therefore create a minimum of openness for listed companies (and for companies with wide share ownership), are still needed. The analysis and proposals of the High Level Group of Company Law Experts, in particular on introducing a so-called "break-through right" allowing the bidder to break through anti-takeover mechanisms and structures, are very interesting in this respect.

3.3.2. Tackling externalities

Alongside the facilitation of the right of establishment, the EU has the task – on the basis of Article 44(3)(g) – of dealing, by means of harmonization of legislation, with externalities which national company law rules create for the internal market and the EMU. Such externalities occur not just because of the exclusively internal focus of national legislation, mentioned above (Section 3.3.1) but could also result from competition between jurisdictions (Section 3.2.3).

The American experience indicates that externalities occur mostly in relation to protection of third parties, particularly creditors, and protection of minority shareholders.[138] Perhaps influenced in that direction by the German tradition, harmonization was

---

[136] See the comments by Timmerman, "Harmonisatie van het vennootschaps- en effectenrecht via het concernrecht" (1999) *Ondernemingsrecht* 102–104.

[137] That is the measures announced in the so-called "Bangemann memorandum" of 14 May 1990: Commission, *Communication relating to hindrances of public takeover or exchange bids*, published in Agence Europe, 17 May 1990, doc. 1619. See also Agence Europe, 9 May 1990, 6. This document resulted in two legislative initiatives: (i) an amendment to the Second Directive to control acquisition of a parent company's shares by its own subsidiaries, which led to Directive 92/101/EEC, and (ii) proposed amendments to the amended proposal for a Fifth Directive, which, together with the latter, remained blocked: see OJ 1991, C 7/4 and OJ 1991, C 321/9. For a discussion see Wouters, *op.cit.*, (1993) 30 *Common Market Law Review* 292–294. In a system of competition between state legislatures, such as in the US, the incentives for states to enact rules that excessively protect incumbent managers are not less great than in the EU nowadays: see, lastly, with reference to most of the earlier literature, L.A. Bebchuk and A. Ferrell, "Federalism and Takeover Law: The Race to Protect Managers from Takeovers", paper presented at the Colloquium organized by Tilburg University, *Convergence and Diversity in Corporate Governance Regimes and Capital Markets*, Eindhoven, 4–5 November 1999.

[138] See Bebchuk, "Federalism and the Corporation: The Desirable Limits on State Competition in Corporate Law", (1992) 105 *Harvard Law Review* 1435, 1485. The suggestions by Bebchuk for more federal "involvement" in company law were strongly criticized by Kostel, "A Public Choice Perspective on the Debate over Federal vs. State Corporate Law" (1993) 79 *Virginia Law Review* 2129–2154, who

originally particularly aimed at protection of *creditors*; the achievements of the First Directive in this area were mentioned above (Section, 3.1.1); the rules on capital contained in the Second Directive, and numerous provisions in the Third and Sixth Directives on mergers and divisions are also aimed at protection of creditors. A number of examples may demonstrate that this task of the European legislature, even on matters covered by the First Directive, is by no means completed. For instance, the scope of the "*prokura*" rule contained in Article 9 depends to a considerable extent on the national definition of what is an "organ" of the company. The scope of the rules on nullity in Articles 11–12, which the Court of Justice interprets very restrictively,[139] is not uncontroversial, especially since the French Cour de Cassation has ruled that these rules do not detract from the general ground for nullity *fraus omnia corrumpit*.[140] Also the rules on disclosure in the First Directive, at the time felt by many Member States to be innovative, are urgently in need of updating after a period of 30 years. It is high time that the possibilities to improve access to the basic data for limited liability companies via electronic systems were examined.[141] One may welcome the recent proposals of the simpler legislation for the internal market (SLIM) working group in this regard (Section 4.1). In this context, the Court's ruling in *Daihatsu* that the relevant information should be available not just to creditors, but to all third parties, is also to be welcomed.[142]

---

showed, using the example of the coming into being of the Williams Act (i.e. the American federal legislation on the procedure for and disclosure obligations in the framework of takeover bids), what forces come into play in the enactment of federal legislation. Also in the EU context such a perspective on harmonization of company law would be extremely interesting. The only author, to our knowledge, who has carried out such a thorough investigation for a company law directive (the First) is E. Stein in his standard work, cited *supra* n. 6.

139 See Case 136/87, *Ubbink*, [1988] ECR 4665, with note by Geens, (1988) TRV 1988, 440, "Het Hof van Justitie over de Eerste Richtlijn: het constituerend effect van openbaarmaking bij niet-opgerichte vennootschappen"; Case C-106/89, *Marleasing*, [1990] ECR I-4135, with note by J. and F. Bouckaert, (1991) TRV 36, "Het Marleasing arrest van het Europees Hof van Justitie en de nietigheidsgronden van art. 13ter Venn.W."

140 Cass. fr., 28 Jan. 1992, *Bull. Joly*, 1992, 419, with note by le Cannu; (1992) J.C.P., éd. E., II, 378, with note by Tisserand; (1993) D., 23, with note by Pages. Underlying this case is the idea that "les directives européennes et la jurisprudence de la CJCE ne sauraient écarter un principe général de droit aussi vénérable que *fraus omnia corrumpit*": Cozian and Viandier, *Droit des sociétés* (8th edn Paris, Litec, 1995), para. 229, p. 80.

141 See on this the interesting contribution by Noack, "The application of the modern method of communication in company law", in *Acts of the Conference on Company Law and the Single Market*, 97–109; *Id.*, "Modern Communications Methods and Company Law" (1998) Eur Bus L Rev, 100–106; see also, taking the new Dutch legislation on the Commercial register (*Handelsregisterwetgeving*) as point of departure, Meijers, "Een Europees handelsregister" (1998) TVVS 103–107.

142 The question whether employees are "third parties" in the sense of Article 44(3)(g) EC has always been controversial. See, e.g. in favor of this, Pipkorn, "Zur Entwicklung des europäischen Gesellschafts- und Unternehmensrechts" (1972) ZHR, 499, 513–514; arguing against this, Randelzhofer, "Art. 54", in Grabitz and Hilf (eds), *Kommentar zur Europäischen Union* (Munich, Beck), p. 8, para. 35; for a pragmatic approach see Eyles, *Das Niederlassungsrecht der Kapitalgesellschaften in der Europäischen Gemeinschaft* (Baden-Baden, Nomos, 1990), pp. 137–138.

In general, the EU initiatives for a more comprehensive system of disclosure of information by – especially but not exclusively publicly listed – companies, and the integration of national commercial registers, deserves strong support; they would tend to lower substantially the transaction costs associated with gathering information on trading partners.[143] The US experience indicates that the incentives for States to organize optimal disclosure of information for companies are insufficient.[144] Within the EU context, the German opposition to implementation and enforcement of the disclosure requirements in the First and Fourth Directives offers a good illustration of this.[145]

In the field of protection of *minority shareholders*, the achievements of the EU are much more modest: apart from a few specific provisions in the Second, Third and Sixth Directives,[146] there are primarily texts *de lege ferenda*, such as the mandatory bid included in the proposed Thirteenth Directive.[147] In the perspective of a European capital market in the process of integration – whereby private individuals or legal persons increasingly invest in companies from other Member States – this is by no means a mere theoretical question: the position of minority shareholders is particularly diverse throughout the Member States,[148] and a national legislature has little or no incentive to regulate the status of (foreign) minority shareholders sufficiently.[149]

---

[143] They also contribute to the European "market for corporate control" in the sense that they facilitate the search for information on potential target companies.

[144] Disclosure rules at the purely state level can end up being either under-regulatory or over-regulatory: see Easterbrook and Fischel, "Mandatory Disclosure and the Protection of Investors" (1984) 70 *Virginia Law Review* 669, 697; Meier-Schatz, *op. cit.*, *European Business Law*, 82.

[145] See on this Case C-97/96, *Daihatsu*, [1997] ECR I-6843 and Case C-191/95, *Commission* v. *Germany*, [1998] ECR I-5449. On the problems with implementation of the relevant provisions of the First and Fourth Directives, see the answer by Lord Cockfield, on behalf of the Commission, of 27 February 1986 to Written Question No. 2333/85 by F. Herman of 10 January 1986 (OJ 1986, C 126/36) and of 5 February 1988 to Written Questions No. 1478/87 by U. Braun-Moser of 19 October 1987 (OJ 1988, C 140/19).

[146] See, e.g. Article 20(1)(d) (exception to prohibition on the acquisition by a company of its own shares for the protection of minority shareholders) and Article 29 second Directives (pre-emptive right for existing shareholders when capital is increased); Article 28 Third Directive (right of minority shareholders to have their shares acquired in cases of merger with company holding 90% of shares); Article 5(2) Sixth Directive (right of minority shareholders to have their shares acquired in cases of disproportionate allocation of shares in the framework of a division).

[147] Article 3 Amended proposal for a Thirteenth Directive, with the title "protection of minority shareholders"; see also Article 10 ("mandatory bid"). See in addition, e.g. Article 16 amended proposal Fifth Directive (liability proceedings brought by minority shareholders); Article 8(2), revised proposal Tenth Directive, according to which a Member State can take measures for companies subject to its law which take part in a merger, in order to guarantee a suitable protection for minority shareholders who are against the merger.

[148] See, e.g. Ernst & Young, *The Simplification of the Operating Regulations for Public Limited Companies in the European Union*, pp. 49–50, para. 179; Miller, "Minority shareholder oppression in the private company in the European Community: a comparative analysis of the German, United Kingdom, and French close corporation problem" (1997) 30 *Cornell International Law Journal* 381–427. See at the time also Munyon, "Shareholders' Rights in the Common Market: A Comparative Study" (1976) 9 *Cornell International Law Journal* 191–238.

[149] *Cf.* at the time already Van Gerven, "Le droit d'établissement dans la Communauté économique européenne et la législation sur les sociétés dans les Etats-membres" (1965) RPS 53.

One can think here, for instance, of an initiative to grant shareholders with a minority holding, as of a certain percentage (5–10%), certain rights (e.g. to call for a special and independent investigation) and to harmonize their position with respect to buy-outs or the right to have their shares acquired.[150]

In combating these or other externalities, which do not directly concern the freedom of establishment, the Commission will have to carry out a subtle balancing act between the pros and cons of Community action, and also show respect for the principle of subsidiarity.

In taking into account potential advantages and disadvantages, as well as concern for optimal use of the limited personnel resources of the Commission, one must look above all at the question to what extent Community action really benefits the quality of national legislation. Thereby, account must be taken in particular of (i) the slowness (co-decision procedure) and the political nature of the Community decision-making process (diluted norms, opt-outs, transitional measures in order to reached a qualified majority), (ii) the fragmented character of harmonization measures (restricted to a particular subject, and to certain company forms), as a result of which the coherence of company law systems can come under pressure (but see Section, 2.3), and (iii) the danger of petrification of legal rules, given the cumbersome procedures which apply in order to change Community norms, and the corresponding *Sperrwirkung* effect which Directives which have been adopted exert on further development of national law.[151]

Possibly, the impact of the Amsterdam Protocol on subsidiarity will be felt primarily in the *form and intensity* of the EU action concerned. The Protocol stressed that the form of Community action should be "as simple as possible", that the Community "shall only legislate to the extent necessary" and that "other things being equal, directives shall be preferred to regulations and framework directives to detailed measures".[152] The Community measures shall – consistent with their objectives and with the EC Treaty – "leave as much scope for national decisions as possible", should (while respecting Community law) "respect well established national arrangements and the organization and working of Member States' legal systems", and should (subject to the need for proper enforcement) "provide Member States with alternative ways to achieve the objectives of the measures."[153]

The above should instill a sense of caution in the Commission, Council and Parliament: they will have to ask whether a binding legal instrument is necessary, or

---

[150] There turned out to be a great deal of support for this, according to the survey carried out by the Commission in 1997: see Blanquet, *op. cit.*, in *Aspects of the Conference on Company Law and the Single Market*, 18. Compare, in a group context, the proposals of the Forum Europaeum Konzernrecht concerning special investigation (*Sonderprüfung*) and buy-out of minority shareholders viz. their right to leave the company (*Auskauf – Austritt*).

[151] See on this *inter alia* Behrens, "Voraussetzungen und Grenzen der Rechtsfortbildung durch Rechtsvereinheitlichung" (1986) 19 *Rabels Zeitschrift* 26–33; Buxbaum and Hopt, *Legal Harmonization and the Business Enterprise*, 241–243; Kötz, "Rechtsvereinheitlichung – Nutzen, Kosten, Methoden, Ziele" (1986) 1 *Rabels Zeitschrift* 10–13; Timmermans, *op. cit.*, (1984) *Rabels Zeitschrift* 28–30.

[152] Point (6), Protocol on subsidiarity.

[153] Point (7), Protocol on subsidiarity.

whether in the current state of affairs a recommendation or communication concerning the subject in question is sufficient.[154] If it is judged necessary to legislate then the most obvious thing is a framework directive, with options presented to the Member States. The Commission seems to have been inspired by these guidelines in the revision of its proposal for a Thirteenth Directive (Section 2.2), but in such a way that the question seems justified whether it is not now more of an apparent than a real harmonization.[155] A similar criticism can be made of the Twelfth Directive on single-member private companies, the added value of which seems very limited.[156]

For the rest, the Commission would, in our view, do well not to wish to do all the drafting itself. One idea which has not received enough attention so far concerns the possibility that the EU might support initiatives for formulating non-binding model rules or codes of conduct on certain areas within company law, such as, for example, corporate governance, by (well-chosen and balanced) committees of experts, somewhat comparable to the activities of the American Law Institute and the American Bar Association in the US.[157] The activities of these expert committees could be followed up and coordinated by a Permanent Forum for Company Law, whose establishment the Commission has announced already a while ago and for which the High Level Group of Company Law maybe acts as a kind of precursor. After extensive discussions and consultations with all the groups concerned on the draft versions, the model rules and codes of conduct could be finalized under the aegis of the Commission. The result would obviously not be Community action,[158] but non-binding norms the authority, acceptance and implementation of which would entirely depend on their intrinsic quality. As (at least partial) alternative for the cumbersome, politicized and inflexible Community decision-making, this line of thought seems at least worth considering.

---

[154] Note that the Protocol on subsidiarity does not take over the passage from the Edinburgh guideline in which the preference is expressed for non-binding measures, such as recommendations and even voluntary codes of conduct.

[155] See also the criticism by Hopt, *op. cit.*, (1997) ZHR 379–393.

[156] *Cf.* the stinging criticism, based on Article 2(2) Twelfth Directive, by Lutter, "Mißglückte Rechtsangleichung: das Chaos der Ein-Personen-Gesellschaft in Europa", in Pfeiffer, Kummer and Scheuch (eds), *Festschrift für Hans Erich Brandner zum 70. Geburtstag* (Cologne, Schmidt, 1996), pp. 81–95. See also the interesting comparative analysis of H.E. Boschma, *De eenpersoons-bv* (Deventer, Kluwer, 1997).

[157] The American Law Institute (ALI) has, as is well known, formulated authoritative "Restatements" in the field of *inter alia* contract law, tort and conflict of laws. In the field of company law, its activities led to the publication of the extensive *Principles of Corporate Governance* in 1992. The American Bar Association (ABA) authored the (Revised) Model Business Corporation Act, which various American states have adopted and which is also – alongside the Delaware General Corporation Law – the model legislation on the basis of which company law is taught in many American law schools. See, in favor of the establishment of a "European Law Institute", Ebke, "Unternehmensrechtsangleichung in der Europäischen Union: Brauchen wir ein European Law Institute?", in Hübner and Ebke (eds), *Festschrift für Bernard Großfeld zum 65. Geburtstag* (Heidelberg, Recht und Wirtschaft, 1999), 189–221.

[158] Should the Commission wish to legislate, then it has to follow the procedures set out in the EC Treaty, and respect the competences of the Council and Parliament: the Commission learnt that lesson in connection with its former Communication on pension funds, in Case C-57/95, *France* v. *Commission*, [1997] ECR I-1627.

4. Challenges Facing Company, Accounting and Securities Law

4.1. The management of the acquis

Sensible management of the *acquis* in the field of company and accounting law is in itself already a formidable challenge for the future. After all, the *acquis* itself is not intrinsically safe or calm. In this area, the Commission bears a considerable responsibility, not just towards the present Member States of the EU and EEA, but even more towards the candidate Member States in Central and Eastern Europe. If the EU imposes its *acquis* on these countries as a condition for accession, this must concern sound norms of company and accounting law, and not outdated rules which will be more of a hindrance than a help to these countries in their transition to modern market economies. One should avoid at all costs that European company law and accounting rules would become what Manning, speaking of American corporate laws, at the time has termed "towering skyscrapers of rusted girders, internally welded together and containing nothing but wind".[159]

In the first place, particularly in areas such as accounting law, which are subject to intense internationalization, there will have to be constant monitoring of the compatibility of European norms with international standards. The Commission carried out this exercise for the first time in its Interpretative Communication of 7 January 1998 on certain Articles of the Fourth and Seventh Directives, which came after the report of a working group on the conformity of these Directives with international accounting standards (see also Section 4.2).[160] Meanwhile, it publishes on its website an increasing number of documents in which the Contact Committee (established under the European accounting Directives) examines the conformity of IAS Norms and IASC Interpretations on the one hand and the European accounting Directives on the other hand.[161]

But there is much more to be said. The urge for simplification and deregulation of Community law has led the Commission to subject the First and Second Directives to examination by a SLIM working group. Its proposals were submitted in October 1999.[162] As to the First Directive, they aim at introducing – after a transitional period

---

[159] Manning, "The Shareholder's Appraisal Remedy: An Essay for Frank Coker" (1962) *Yale Law Journal* 223, 245, n. 37.

[160] See Contact Committee on the Accounting Directives, *An examination of the conformity between the international accounting standards and the European accounting directives* (Brussels/Luxembourg, Office of Official Publications EC, 1996).

[161] See for these documents the recently modified sub-website on accounting of DG Internal Market: http://europa.eu.int/comm/dg15/en/company/account/ias/index.htm.

[162] See http://system04.rug.ac.be/fli. See, relating to these proposals, C. de Vos, "Het SLIM IV project van de Europese Commissie: harmonisatie door deregulering van het Europees vennootschapsrecht", (2000) TBH 608-613; Wymeersch, "European Company Law: the 'simpler legislation for the internal market' (SLIM) initiative of the EU Commission", working paper 2000–09 on the aforementioned website. On 3 June 2002, the Commission proposed amendments to the First Directive: see COM (2002) 279 final.

of five years – a system of electronic registration of companies and the filing of company documents in more than one Community language in order to improve access and dessimination of this information (currently, the disclosure system is based on paper copies which are usually only available in one Community language) (*cf.* Section 3.3.2). In addition, it was suggested to extend disclosure of the powers of representation of a limited liability company to company representatives with general powers of representation. On the Second Directive, the working group recommended various changes which essentially aim at simplifying procedures while protecting shareholders and creditors; among the proposed changes are suggestions aiming at a (partial) deregulation of financial assistance provided by a company to third parties in order to acquire its shares (Article 23),[163] and of the rules on preemptive rights of existing shareholders when capital is increased, so as to make these less obstructive for the company's financing.[164] The SLIM proposals are now also under consideration of the High Level Group of Company Law Experts.

All of this is just a start. The Commission will have to examine, actively and systematically, to what extent the texts in force are useful and effective, whether they reveal faults or omissions which call for supplementary action,[165] or are too far-reaching and/or call for simplification. Here, too, there is an important role for a Permanent Forum on Company Law. Via such a Forum, the Commission can be constantly made aware of shortcomings or practical problems to which the European rules lead. This need will grow if Community legal forms, such as the SE, EA, ECS and the EMS, really come into operation in future. In this context, work could already begin today on a re-evaluation of the EEIG Regulation, whereby in particular questions could be raised about the need to maintain all the restrictions it contains, especially in its Article 3 (Section 2.1).

For the rest, in our view the EU should not confine itself in this process to the adjustment of a few provisions in Directives and Regulations. Reflection is needed concerning fundamental legislative policy choices made at the time, such as for instance the use of a detailed (and highly inflexible) system of *ex ante* rules on capital formation

---

[163] For criticism of Article 23 Second Directive, although not supported by the same arguments, see Timmerman, *op. cit.*, (1996) AA 314; Wymeersch, *op. cit.*, in *40 Jahre Römische Verträge*, 195–196; *Id.*, "Article 23 of the second company law directive: the prohibition on financial assistance to acquire shares of the company", in Basedow, Hopt and Kötz (eds), *Festschrift für Ulrich Drobnig* (Siebeck, Mohr, 1998), 725–747. For recent developments in the direction of English law, see Adamides, "Financial assistance by a company for the purchase of its own shares: the case of management buyouts" (1998, January–February) *European Financial Services Law* 45–48.

[164] See especially Kübler, Mendelson and Mundheim, "Die Kosten des Bezugsrechts. Eine rechtsökonomische Analyse des amerikanischen Erfahrungsmaterials" (1999) AG 461–475; Kübler, "Aktienrechtsreform und Unternehmensverfassung" (1994) AG 141, 145–147; Wymeersch, "Das Bezugsrecht der alten Aktionären in der Europäischen Gemeinschaft: eine rechtsvergleichende Untersuchung" (1998) AG 382–393.

[165] *Cf.* Directive 92/101/EEC which amends the Second Directive in the area of subscription for and acquisition of a limited company's own shares by a subsidiary and Directive 90/605/EEC which extended the scope of application of the Fourth and Seventh Directives to include partnerships and limited partnerships (and similar legal forms in the various Member States) where all members having unlimited liability are themselves companies of the type already covered by the Directive, i.e. limited liability companies.

and maintenance in the Second Directive in the light of their practical operation, and the financing needs of companies.[166]

Another issue which is not unimportant is the possible undermining of the company law Directives in national legislation, case law or practice. The introduction of the SAS in France should be recalled, where a new company form was introduced partly to avoid the capital protection rules of the Second Directive (Section 3.2.1). Also, the manner in which national courts sometimes give their own, rather particular interpretation of Community Directives can be a cause for concern: the *IBH* case of the Bundesgerichtshof[167] and the *Verenigde Bootlieden* case of the (Netherlands) Hoge Raad[168] illustrate this. In general, it is astonishing that something of such practical importance as the capital protection rules of the Second Directive has led to virtually no preliminary references to the ECJ, leaving aside the continuing story of the Greek cases,[169] and two specific German cases (*Meilicke*[170] en *Siemens*).

---

[166] See recently the lively debate as to the desirability or not of this system at the Symposium "Unternehmensfinanzierung und gesetzliches Garantiekapital in Europa", with national reports in (1998) AG 345–375 and more in particular the diametrically opposed views of Lutter and Schuster, in their identically titled reports "Gesetzliches Garantiekapital als Problem europäischer und deutscher Rechtspolitik" (1998) AG 375–377 resp. 379–381. See also the evaluation of the EU system of capital protection compared with an *ex post* system of liability for evident undercapitalization, as applies in the US, by De Kluiver, *op. cit.*, in *Current Issues of Cross-Border Establishment of Companies in the European Union*, 312–314; Wilmet, "La sanction de la sous-capitalisation des sociétés anonymes: comparaison avec le droit des Etats-Unis" (1992) Rev Dr Int Comp 270–282; for the US itself, see Manning and Hanks, *Legal Capital* (3rd edn, Foundation Press, 1990), pp. 192–197. Belgium has in this respect already aroused comparative law interest with its obligation on founders to draw up a financial plan (Articles 29ter and 120ter Companies Act) and the liability rules for evident undercapitalization in cases of bankruptcy within three years of incorporation, contained in Articles 35, 6° and 123, 7° Companies Act: see De Kluiver, "Europe and the Private Company, An Introduction", in *The European Private Company?*, 21, 26.

[167] *IBH/Lemmerz BGHZ*, 110, 47 (1990) NJW 982, in which the Bundesgerichstshof on its own initiative ruled that the Second Directive does not exclude stricter national rules, to the extent that its provisions do not provide for a "Höchstmaßregelung". See the strong criticism of the BGH's failure to put a preliminary question to the Court of Justice, by, e.g. Frey, "Das IBH-Urteil" (1990) ZIP 288, 292–294; Joost, "Verdeckte Sacheinlagen" (1990) ZIP 549, 565; Steindorff, "Vorlagepflicht nach Article 177 Abs. 3 EWGV und europäisches Gesellschaftsrecht" (1992) ZHR 1–16. Since then, the BGH has improved its ways, as is evidenced by its preliminary question in the *Tomberger* and *Siemens* cases.

[168] Hoge Raad, 31 December 1993, (1994) NJ 436, with note by Maeijer. See Vletter-Van Dort, "Gelijke behandeling van aandeelhouders naar Nederlands recht", in De Kluiver and Wouters (eds), *Beginselen van vennootschapsrecht in binationaal perspectief* (Schoten, Intersentia, 1998), pp. 178–179. The case concerned the interpretation of Article 2:206a of the Netherlands Civil Code, which regulates the right of pre-emption of existing shareholders for new share issues, and is virtually identical to the relevant provisions relating to public limited liability companies (Article 2:96a Civil Code), which is based on the Second Directive. A request for a preliminary ruling would have been particularly desirable here; the fact that the case involved the provision relating to the B.V. (private limited company) and thus strictly speaking not a provision implementing the Second Directive, would not have posed problems for the Court of Justice: see Case C-28/95, *Leur-Bloem*, [1997] ECR I-4161.

[169] See Joined Cases C-19 & 20/90, *Karella and Karellas*, [1991] ECR I-2691; Case C-381/90, *Syndesmos Melon*, [1992] ECR I-2111; Joined Cases C-134 & 135/91, *Kerafina*, [1992] ECR I-5699; Case C-441/93, *Pafitis*, [1996] ECR I-1347; Case C-367/96, *Kefalas*, [1998] ECR I-2843; Case C-373/97, *Diamantis* [2000] ECR I-1705.

[170] Case C-83/91, *Meilicke*, [1992] ECR I-4871.

National courts should make more frequent use of the preliminary rulings procedure, in order to get clarity over what are sometimes rather unclear provisions. The case law of the Court in this context, up until today rather limited, but of increasing importance, is important for at least three reasons: (i) by its authority it contributes to a europeanization of national company and accounting rules[171] and private law doctrines, such as abuse of law;[172] (ii) it highlights from time to time the limitations of provisions of Directives, and can thereby give a signal that these may have to be improved (e.g. the non-coverage by Article 9 First Directive of problems concerning representation in case of conflicting interests in *Coöperatieve Rabobank*,[173] or the irrelevance of the directives on company accounts for fiscal objectives in *Futura Participations*); and (iii) it gives clarity as to the scope of the legal bases contained in the EC Treaty, in particular Article 44(3)(g) EC (*cf.* the hint, in the *Daily Mail* case, that a Community legislative initiative on transfer of seat would be appropriate).

4.2. The impact of EMU: towards a European SEC?

The impact of the Economic and Monetary Union on company, accounting and securities law has not been examined much so far, apart from technical details such as the redenomination of capital[174] and certain accounting adjustments.[175] An examination is needed of the impact the euro will have on the practical challenges and developments in this field, and in particular the question whether and to what extent new EU action is required. In our view, this impact will be enormous, both in the short term, and the middle and long terms.

In the *short term*, the introduction of the euro will be felt above all in the area of a greater transparency and comparability of provision of financial information. The lack of uniformity or even convergence of the national accounting standards of

---

[171] For instance, there is a lot to be done in Germany concerning the impact of *Tomberger*: see e.g. Herzig and Biener, *Europäisierung des Bilanzrechts: Konsequenzen der Tomberger-Entscheidung des EuGH für die handelsrechtliche Rechnungslegung und die steuerliche Gewinnermittlung* (Cologne, Schmidt, 1997).

[172] The Court of Justice has devoted some significant considerations to this in the case law, mentioned above, such as *Pafitis*, *Siemens*, *Kefalas*, *Centros* and most recently *Diamantis* (Case C-373/97, [2000] ECR I-1705).

[173] Case C-104/96, *Coöperatieve Rabobank* (in the Netherlands better known as "Mediasafe"), [1997] ECR I-7211, (1998) TRV, 41, with note by Geens, "Draagwijdte van artikel 9, 1° Eerste Richtlijn i.v.m. facultatieve bevoegdheden van de raad van bestuur".

[174] The Commission's view is that the Second Directive should not be altered to take account of the transition to the euro. In its view, this Directive creates the possibility for simplified procedures for capital increases and decreases with a view to "rounding" in cases of redenomination of capital and that the Second Directive already allows shares with no nominal value: Commission, *The impact of the changeover to the euro on Community policies, institutions and legislation*, Europaper No. 9, November 1997, 51–52. The possibility of shares with no nominal value has recently been introduced in German and French legislation, with a view to the introduction of the euro.

[175] See Commission, *Accounting for the introduction of the euro*, Europaper No. 2, July 1997; *Id.*, *Preparing Financial Information Systems for the euro*, Europaper No. 11, Dec. 1997.

the Eurozone[176] will then be painfully apparent: as is well-known, the Fourth and Seventh Directives leave Member States a great many options (62 in the former, 50 in the latter) and the national practice and interpretation of accounting rules, concepts and principles is still very divergent.[177] If it is desired to do justice to the principle of a "fair view" – which has been found by the ECJ to be essential[178] – then such diversity can no longer be maintained in a single market with a single currency. The question immediately arises as to what the EU should do. Nobody seems to be asking for a fundamental review of the accounting directives: the Member States not, because of the close link between accounting law and fiscal rules,[179] and remarkably enough the European Commission neither.[180] If there is no impetus for harmonization at European level, then convergence will have to come from another source. The Commission's daring initiative to propose a Regulation of the European Parliament and of the Council on the application of international accounting standards[181] shows that it has fundamentally chosen in favor of IAS rather than GAAP standards[182] (i.e. the American standards).

In the *medium and long term*, the euro and the EMU are expected to exert strong integrating influences on the European capital market.[183] The powerful tendency towards cross-border cooperation and even mergers between exchanges[184] means that pressure will increasingly work towards the convergence of listing conditions, the rules on periodic and occasional information and prospectuses, the organization

---

176 That is the eleven EU Member States which now participate in the third phase of EMU: Austria, Belgium, Finland, France, Germany, Ireland, Italy, Luxembourg, Netherlands, Portugal, Spain.

177 The study by the Fédération des Experts Comptables Européens, *Conceptual Accounting Frameworks in Europe*, Brussel, FEE, 1997, gives a good picture of this diversity. See, e.g. on the divergent application of the principles of "a fair view", Justice Arden, "A True and Fair View: Do the Member States of the EU Approach the Company Accounting Directives in Different Ways?" (1995) *Butterworths Journal of International Banking and Financial Law* 295.

178 Case C-234/94, *Tomberger*, [1996] ECR I-3133, correction order of 10 July 1997 (OJ 1997, C 318/3), (1996) TRV, 401, with note by Van Crombrugge, "De realisatie van dividenden in het Belgisch boekhoudrecht". See also on the impact of the principle of a true and fair view, Case C-275/97, *DE + ES Bauunternehmung GmbH* v. *Finanzamt Bergheim*, [1999] ECR I-5331.

179 See Schruff, "Accounting Standards in Practice", in Buxbaum, Hertig, Hirsch, and Hopt (eds), *European Economic and Business Law. Legal and Economic Analyses on Integration and Harmonization* (Berlin/New York, De Gruyter, 1996), pp. 163, 166.

180 See Van Hulle, "Respons", in *Knelpunten van dertig jaar vennootschapsrecht*, 359–362.

181 Meanwhile adopted: See Regulation (EC) No 1606/2002 of 19 July 2002, OJ 2002, L 243/1.

182 That is, the "Generally Accepted Accounting Principles" as established by the Financial Accounting Standards Board (FASB). Up until today, if a foreign, e.g. European, company wishes to be listed on an American stock exchange, the SEC requires that it carries out its financial reporting in accordance with the GAAP. On 29 February 1999, the SEC proposed adjusting its disclosure rules with regard to foreign private issuers so as to accord with the international disclosure rules which were endorsed by the International Organization of Securities Commissions (IOSCO) in September 1998.

183 See the report by a group of consultants chaired by Giovannini, *The impact of the introduction of the euro on capital markets*, Europaper No. 3, July 1997; see also Lannoo and Gros, *Capital Markets and EMU* (Brussels, CEPS, 1998).

184 See e.g. the plan by eight West-European exchanges to set up a common exchange for European top shares: "Pan-European exchange moves closer", *Financial Times*, 5 May 1999.

of market supervision and, last but not least, corporate governance. This must all lead to a thorough reconsideration of the present *acquis* of European directives in the field of securities law.[185] But inevitably the question will also arise as to the feasibility of a system of purely national stock exchange authorities – however closely they cooperate, also in the framework of the Investment Services Directive,[186] and however much support the idea of mutual recognition has gained. Already now, the crucial question presents itself, as to whether the time has come to take steps towards setting up a European "Securities and Exchange Commission", i.e. a European body which can supervise the securities market throughout the whole EU, and which disposes of the necessary regulatory and supervisory competences.[187] The future will tell whether the pragmatic line of the Lamfalussy proposals, which focus on optimalizing the use of comitology procedures in order to achieve more responsive law-making but which do not alter anything in terms of the actual supervision of securities markets, can be kept and whether the EU will not have to take a qualitative leap towards a more elaborated European supervisory system in the medium or long term.

5. Concluding Remarks

In this chapter, we have tried to take stock of the achievements of European action in the field of company law over the last 35 years, and at the same time we have tackled the question what role falls to the EU in the field of company, accounting and securities law in future. The golden years of European company law – in the sense of a strongly centralized harmonization of national company law rules – are long gone. Unlike the 1960s and 1970s, the impetus for new company law no longer comes from Brussels, but from the practical needs in the Member States, and – particularly as far as corporate governance is concerned – from the globalization of financial markets. Although a certain "competition for quality" between jurisdictions would seem to us to have a healthy effect on company law, we believe that there is still a role for EU harmonization in order to create the necessary conditions for

---

[185] See the rightly critical assessment of this *acquis*, especially the Listings Directive 79/279/EEC, by Ferrarini, "The European Regulation of Stock Exchanges: New Perspectives" (1999) *Common Market Law Review* 569–598. For a general picture taken in 1993, see Wouters, "EC Harmonization of National Rules concerning Securities Offerings, Stock Exchange Listing and Investment Services: An Overview" (1993) *European Business Law Review* 194–225.

[186] Council Directive 93/22/EEC of 10 May 1993 concerning the investment services in the securities field (OJ 1993, L 141/27).

[187] This question raises numerous considerations which go beyond the present contribution: see *inter alia* Hoppmann, "Europäische Börsenaufsicht" (1999) EWS 204–212; Karmel, "The Case for a European Securities Commission" (1999) 38 *Columbia Journal of Transnational Law* 9–43; Lannoo, *Does Europe Need an SEC?* (European Capital Markets Institute, November 1999); Lee, "Supervising EU Capital Markets: Do We Need a European SEC?", in *European Economic and Business Law*, 187–208; Thieffry, "Towards a European Securities Commission" (1999) *International Financial Law Review*, October, 14–18.

companies to be able to exercise their right of establishment smoothly, especially via the approximation of rules concerning branches, cross-border mergers and transfers of seat. At the same time, it is up to the EU – bearing in mind the principles of subsidiarity and proportionality – to combat externalities in the field of protection of shareholders and creditors. The further development of EU legal forms, such as the EEIG and SE, could be useful insofar as such legal forms offer real advantages compared with national company forms; only time will tell.

The important challenges for the future comprise the management of the existing *acquis* in these fields and the implications for European company, accounting and securities laws which result from EMU, the globalization of economies and financial markets, and the growing role of international standard-setting fora. For company accounts, the question arises how the EU can best and most urgently meet the challenge of internationalization: the answer is probably a well-coordinated participation in the various international fora which play a role in setting international accountancy standards. For securities law, the problem we are confronted with is whether it is time to consider the establishment of a European SEC, with strong regulatory and supervisory powers, for the rapidly integrating European capital markets.

In this whole context, the importance of taking a look in other parts of the world at solutions for – what are in fact common – problems, and the need for thorough comparative law studies cannot be sufficiently emphasized. This "third way", alongside harmonization from above, and a healthy degree of competition between jurisdictions, can in the coming years provide an important contribution to the formation of a European company and business culture with a place of its own in the world economy.[188]

---

[188] This is also the conclusion of Ebke, "Unternehmensrecht und Binnenmarkt – E pluribus unum?" (1998) *Rabels Zeitschrift* 195, 242; in the same sense, from the perspective of British company law, Justice Harden, "The Changing Face of Company Law" (1995) *Butterworths Journal of International Banking and Financial Law* 210, 213.

Chapter 4

Intellectual Property

*Annette Kur**

1. Introduction

Intellectual Property (IP) lawyers usually think of their subject as being rather far advanced in terms of legal integration. Even if that may be overly sanguine in view of the remaining tasks to be tackled before true harmonization is achieved, it is certainly right to say that in many aspects, both with respect to substantial and procedural matters, IP law in its different disciplines provides a test field for issues presenting typical challenges for European law, as legal harmonisation and/or unification are progressing. This concerns *inter alia* the methods for harmonisation, conflicts between primary and secondary Community law, the role of the ECJ, the establishment of administrative bodies and, in the future, of a Community judicial system.

In the following, an attempt will be made to give, first, a general overview of the present state of affairs in the various fields of European IP law**. Second, some issues of a more general, horizontal character shall be discussed with a view to emphasize those features which are linked, in one way or other, to themes addressed in other contributions in this volume, thus trying to add to the emerging image of a common European legal structure.

2. The Need for Harmonisation

Intellectual property is not only far advanced with respect to European harmonisation. It is an area which is and has always been on the forefront of internationalisation as well. The following reasons account for this: New thoughts – creations and inventions – tend to travel. Borders do not hold them. And wherever they go, they can easily be misappropriated by those who want to reap where they have not sown. To confine use and protection of new inventions, original creations or distinctive

---

* Max-Planck-Institute for Foreign and International Patent, Copyright and Unfair Competition Law, Munich. Lecturer at Munich University, at the University of Stockholm, and at the Swedish School of Economics.

** The following text reflects the situation in early summer 2002. Subsequent developments are indicated, to the extent possible, in footnotes 21a, 24, 25, 47, 48a and 76.

M. van Empel (ed.), "From Paris to Nice": Fifty Years of Legal Integration in Europe, 75–99.

signs to national territories therefore appears as a somewhat unrealistic concept. Nevertheless, this is exactly what the legal nature of such rights implies – they are in fact "territorial", meaning that in principle, protection ends one step behind the national borderlines. This situation quite obviously creates a demand for transnational protection, based on a system which is sophisticated enough to achieve a sufficient degree of mutual protection, while at the same time paying due respect to the sovereign powers of the foreign state(s) where protection is claimed.

Already at the end of the nineteenth century, two comprehensive international agreements have been concluded in the field of industrial property (patents, trademarks, designs and unfair competition) and copyright respectively – the Paris Convention[1] and the Berne Convention.[2] Shortly speaking, they both rely on the principle of national treatment – States must not deny to nationals of other Member States rights which they grant to their own nationals – and on the stipulation of certain essential minimum rights. Although this is no harmonisation in the strict meaning of the word, the system nevertheless has engendered over the years a certain amount of *de facto* approximation of legal standards in the fields concerned. When the European Economic Community (EEC) came into existence a bit less than 50 years ago, the minimum standards anchored in international IP law therefore already provided for a somewhat elevated threshold from which further harmonisation efforts could depart.

Of course, the fact that Community Member States did engage in such efforts was not a decision made simply out of a *l 'art pour l'art* kind of desire to harmonise, but it was driven by the wish to improve the proper functioning of the Common Market. And again, the territoriality principle played a role in the matter. The fact that IP rights are confined to national territories implies the possibility for a rightowner to oppose the circulation of goods to which the right pertains, unless they have been released on the market in the relevant territory by himself or with his consent. This is the general rule applying – subject to certain reservations with respect to trademark law[3] – in all former and present member countries. Quite obviously, when this rule is invoked in order to block the unauthorised importation of goods from one Member State to another, this entails a severe impediment for the free circulation of goods within the Common market.

---

[1] Paris Convention for the Protection of Industrial Property of 20 March 1883; revised at Brussels on 14 December 1900, at Washington on 2 June 1911, at The Hague on 6 November 1925, at London on 2 June 1934, at Lisbon on 31 October 1958 and at Stockholm on 14 July 1967; amended on 28 September 1979. Text available on the website of the World Intellectual Property Organisation (WIPO), at http://www.wipo.int/treaties/ip/paris/index.html.

[2] Berne Convention for the Protection of Literary and Artistic Works of 9 September 1886, completed at Paris on 4 May 1896, revised at Berlin on 13 November 1908, completed at Berne on 20 March 1914, revised at Rome on 2 June 1928, at Brussels on 26 June 1948, at Stockholm on 14 July 1967, and at Paris on 24 July 1971 (Paris Act); amended on 28 September 1979. Text available on the WIPO website, at http://www.wipo.int/treaties/ip/berne/index.html.

[3] Some countries have adopted a doctrine of global instead of only national exhaustion. This concerns in particular trademark law, where several EU Member States originally applied a rule of global exhaustion. After the implementation of the Trademark Directive (see below), it is no longer possible for Member States to maintain this principle, see ECJ decision C-355/96 Silhouette International/Hartlauer Handelsgesellschaft, 1998 ECR I-4799.

Intellectual property rights have indeed made their first prominent appearance on the European scene in the context of what is usually referred to as the parallel import cases.[4] Trademark or other IP right holders tried to enjoin independent traders from buying goods, at a low price, in one Member State in order to market them in another state where the price level maintained by the proprietor of the right and the dealers authorised by him was much higher. The ECJ has reacted to these practices by pointing out that the possibilities granted under national law to impede the free movement of goods in this manner had to be regarded as "measures having equivalent effect" in the meaning of Article 28, and that they could not be justified under Article 30 as being necessary in order to protect the specific subject matter of the respective property rights.[5] This line of jurisprudence has become known as establishing the doctrine of Community-wide exhaustion of IP rights.

This does however not mean that the ECJ has given precedence to the free movement of goods over the principle of territoriality. The Court only disregards the legal effects of the latter principle if and inasfar as the rightowner tries to impede the free movement of goods across internal borders, after having once exercised his or her fundamental entitlement to determine if, where and by whom the relevant goods shall be released on the Common Market. In all other aspects, the right remains intact. In particular, if the right to a trademark, patent or copyright belongs to different persons in different Member States, there is no doubt in principle that each proprietor is fully entitled to oppose the distribution of protected items in the country where he or she is in the position to claim a better right.

This result is uncontested.[6] It is a necessary consequence of the fact that when the EEC Treaty was concluded, national property rights were granted full immunity from

---

[4] See in particular ECJ decisions C-56/64 & 58/64, Etablissements Consten Sarl and Grundig VerkaufsGmbH/Commission, 1968 ECR 299; C-24/67 Parke Davis/Centrafarm, 1968 ECR 55; C-40/70 Sirena/Eda, 1971 ECR 69; C-78/70, Deutsche Grammophon Ges./Metro, 1971 ECR 487; C-15/74 Centrafarm B.V./Sterling Drug, 1974 ECR 1147; C-16/74 Centrafarm/Winthrop, 1974 ECR 1183; C-51/75 EMI Record/CBS, 1976 ECR 1183.

[5] In the first decisions mentioned in the previous footnote (up to "Deutsche Grammophon"), the ECJ decisions on parallel imports have mostly relied on the provisions concerning competition law, i.e. ex-Articles 85 and 86. Since then, however, the focus was shifted towards the provisions on free movement of goods, as is set out in the text above.

[6] This remark must be qualified with respect to trademark rights, which in the beginning have been treated slightly differently from the other IP rights. Thus, the ECJ pointed out in the Hag I case (C-192/73, ECR 731) that trademark rights could not be invoked *vis-à-vis* the marketing of a product stemming from a different right holder, if the two marks, although having separate owners at present, were of the same origin. The case concerned the trademark "Hag" for coffee, which had been transferred, subsequent to an expropriation in Belgium after the war, to the Belgian firm Van Zuylen Frères, whereas it still belonged to its original owners in Germany. In consequence of the ECJ's ruling, Van Zuylen Frères could not oppose the importation of German "Hag" coffee to Belgium. Fifteen years later, in the second Hag decision concerning the opposite situation, the Court ruled however differently and reversed its first ruling: It was now acknowledged that irrespective of "common origin", the specific subject matter of the trademark right would be encroached upon if the legitimate owner in Germany would have to tolerate importation of products bearing the same mark, but stemming from the Belgian firm (C-10/89, ECR I-3711). In another, subsequent ruling, the Court further declared that the same would apply even in case when the transfer of the mark to a different owner did not occur in consequence of an expropriation, but was effected by a voluntary act carried out by the owner himself (C-9/93, ECR I-2789 – Ideal Standard).

interference by the treaty provisions, including the provisions on the free movement of goods.[7] Still, the fact that national IP rights, apart from the parallel import cases mentioned above, can and often will result in a barrier against the shipping of goods from one Member Country to another, appears as undesirable in the long run. It was not least this aspect which has given rise, at a very early stage already, to the vision that the territorial confinements of IP rights should ultimately be overcome by the creation of unitary rights, which could be acquired through one single act taken out *vis-à-vis* one single authority, and having legal effect throughout the whole Community.

To create unitary rights has however not been feasible in all the fields of IP law, and even where this was envisaged as a primary goal, the pattern of legal integration has included a variety of other, complementary measures as well. An account of these shall be given in the following section.[8]

3. Developments in the Individual Fields

3.1 Trademark law

Trademark law was the first area where the visions concerning the creation of a Community right have been pursued in a consequent and ultimately successful manner. It was however not a quick and easy road to success. From the first studies and memoranda, which date back to the late fifties,[9] it has taken until 1994, i.e. more than 30 years of at times quite intense efforts, before the CTMR – the Community Trademark Regulation – was finally enacted.[10] Things simply cannot be rushed in Europe, and to develop something novel like the Community Trademark system is a step forward which should not be underestimated in its legal, political and psychological dimensions. *Inter alia*, it has involved the establishment of a completely new Community authority, the Office for Harmonisation of the Internal Market (OHIM) in Alicante/Spain,[11] which commenced its practical work in 1996, i.e. 2 years after the enactment of the CTMR.

---

[7] See Article 195 (ex-Article 222) of the EC Treaty.

[8] The following survey is not claimed to be complete. *Inter alia*, it does not include remarks on the pending proposal for utility model protection (Amended proposal for a European Parliament and Council Directive approximating the legal arrangements for the protection of inventions by utility model, COM/99/0309 final – COD 97/0356), or on plant variety protection pursuant to Council Regulation (EC) No 2100/94 of 27 July on Community plant variety rights.

[9] S. Hans *von der Groeben*, GRUR Int. 1959, 629 *et seq.*, stating the necessity to create a European (= Community) trademark, patent, and design. Von der Groeben was a member of the Commission at the time.

[10] Council Regulation (EC) No 40/94 of 20 December 1993 on the Community trade mark, OJ L 011/1, 14.01.1994.

[11] Detailed information about the office, its legal foundation and its practical work is available under www.oami.eu.int.

As regards national trademark law, different options have been considered in the process of development of the European trademark system. One of them was the model represented by the Benelux countries, where the national trademark systems had been abolished in favour of the unitary Benelux system created in 1975. Although the straightforward character of this solution may seem quite appealing, the opinion prevailed in Europe that it would not function equally well for a considerably larger group of countries, each of them carrying a much higher potential for eventually conflicting trademarks. It was therefore decided that instead of the Benelux model, a scheme of coexistence between a system operating at Community level and the pre-existing national systems should be followed. In order to remove obstacles against free trade which might result from existing disparities in the national laws, it was further decided to harmonize national trademark law to the extent this was considered necessary with a view to the proper functioning of the Internal Market. In their contents, the substantive rules set out in the harmonisation directive are congruent with the core provisions in the CTMR. Among others, this technique has the advantage that it prevents national legislatures from engaging in "unfair competition" with the Community system, by granting more favourable conditions for the acquisition and scope of rights than those anchored in the former set of rules. The Trademark Harmonisation Directive was enacted in 1990,[12] and the implementation process was completed in all EU countries in 1996.

The fact that the development of European trademark law occurs, at the same time, on two levels interacting with each other, results in a rather complex structure. Various actors involved in the play at different levels – the national authorities and courts in the Member States, the OHIM and its appeal boards, and the two courts in Luxembourg[13] – have to be observed as they influence each other and the process as a whole. And in order to complicate matters further, it must be realised that those actors in themselves do not always speak with one voice, but that they consist of a plurality of individuals with as many independent minds, which may foster their own ideas of what exactly should be the meaning and content of the European trademark law provisions.

This becomes particularly obvious at the OHIM in Alicante,[14] with the office and its Appeal Boards forming a congregation of individuals from all EU countries. The diversity of legal backgrounds – a clash of legal cultures in a nutshell – is sometimes reflected in diverging decisions of different OHIM Appeal Boards. And according to

---

[12] First Council Directive 89/104/EEC of 21 December 1988 to approximate the laws of the Member States relating to trade marks, OJ L 159/60, 10.06.1989.

[13] The Court of First Instance (CFI), which was established in 1998, is competent *inter alia* to decide appeals against decisions of the OHIM appeal boards, and its decisions are subject to revision for legal grounds by the ECJ. It seems apparent already now that the workload resulting from trademark appeals will be too much for the CFI, and that new, specialised chambers will have to be created on a level below the CFI in order to solve the problem. See also Section 4.4.

[14] It does however also apply, *mutatis mutandis*, in respect of national law, where opinions may be often divided between different bodies, for instance the Patent Office and the courts respectively, and even within one single authority.

oral testimony, this becomes even more apparent in the at times quite animated debates held between Board Members during the deliberations. Quite often, these debates concern procedural issues, not least because a number of details in the implementing regulations to the CTMR have been left open, with the task being imposed on OHIM and its Appeal Boards to develop, on the basis of procedural principles generally accepted in the Member States, their own, genuine rules of procedure. While this may pose difficult questions, it is certainly also a most valuable exercise, as it involves a good amount of comparative legal work with immediate practical relevance.

Also with respect to issues of substantive trademark law, it has turned out that there are still a number of open questions relating to the central provisions in the CTMR and in the Harmonisation Directive. The ECJ, and in particular the Advocate General, have already shown signs of slight irritation with this phenomenon, which is reflected in a relatively high number of questions submitted for preliminary decisions.[15] Indeed, the obvious need of national courts to seek clarification on a number of fundamental trademark law issues might be indicative of the fact that in spite of the efforts vested in the project during the long years of negotiation, it has not been possible to overcome the fundamental differences in the national attitudes towards the underlying objectives of trademark protection.[16] In other words, it cannot be excluded that the wording of the Regulation and Directive serves, to some extent, only as camouflage below which the original diversities linger on. If this were true, it would make the road towards true harmonisation even longer and more hazardous than it appeared at the outset.

3.2. Industrial designs

The two-tier coexistence model represented by trademark law has recently been implemented also in the area of industrial design legislation. The Design Directive dates from October 1998[17] and should have been implemented by October 2001,[18] whereas the Community Design Regulation[19] was enacted in December last year and has entered into force on 6 March 2002. As a novel feature, the Community Design

---

15 See the remark by Advocate General *Jacobs* in his Opinion of 26 November 1998, in the "Chevy" case, C-375/97 (1999 ECR 5421, at 5423), para. 1: "In the present case the Court is asked once again to venture into the largely uncharted territory of Community trade-mark law".

16 This concerns in particular the fundamental question whether trademarks enjoy full protection as a "normal" property right against any use which has not been authorized by the owner, or whether protection should be restricted in principle, i.e. unless extended protection is expressly granted, to the capacity of the mark to furnish a correct indication of the commercial origin of the merchandise to which it is applied.

17 Directive 98/71/EC of the European Parliament and of the Council of 13 October 1998 on the legal protection of designs, OJ L 289/28, 28.10.1998.

18 Only Denmark, France and Italy have met that limit. Until summer 2002, implementation has been effected also in the United Kingdom, Greece, and Portugal.

19 Council Regulation (EC) No 6/2002 of 12 December 2001 on Community designs, OJ L 03/1, 05.01.2002.

Regulation includes a design right which comes into existence without the formal act of registration, the Unregistered Community Design (UCD). The right is only valid for three years, and it only protects against copying, i.e. in contrast to the objective protection granted to registered design rights, it includes a subjective requirement.

While the UCD may be of interest for certain branches, like the fashion industry, where product styles are subject to constant change, it is expected that in the large majority of cases, protection also in the future will be sought and granted in the traditional way, i.e. by registration.[20] The Registered Community Design (RCD) will be administered by OHIM, i.e. the same authority in Alicante which has already gained experience in the field of Community marks. Preparations for the establishment of the necessary infrastructure have already been undertaken, and it is expected that the first applications will be handled by the office in early 2007.[21a]

Compared with European legislation in the trademark field, the time span between the first publication of preliminary proposals for a Community Design Regulation and a Harmonisation Directive in 1991[21] and the enactment of both instruments in 1998 and 2002 respectively has been relatively short. Indeed, in spite of some misgivings concerning the UDR and some quarrels concerning the notion of novelty,[22] most of the provisions involved have been uncontroversial. The only issue which has given rise to fierce debates concerned design protection for spare parts – or, more precisely: whether an exemption should be introduced for the manufacturing and selling of such parts for repair purposes ("repair clause"). In spite of several efforts by the Commission to propose compromise solutions,[23] the positions of the interested parties have remained unchanged throughout the whole process. Car manufacturers hold that a repair clause would amount to an intolerable encroachment on their vested rights, while the spare parts lobby argues that the grant and exercise of exclusive rights for spare parts would create a genuine product monopoly, and would therefore be irreconcilable with the true and legitimate function of industrial design protection.

When it became apparent that no chance existed for the time being to end the deadlock, it was decided that the directive should enter into force without a provision on spare parts. Instead, a so-called "freeze plus" solution was agreed upon, meaning that the present legal conditions must remain in force, unless Member

---

[20] Apart from the fact that protection of the RCD is independent of subjective requirement (see the text, above), it also has the advantage that its term of protection is much longer than for the UCD: Initial protection is granted for 5 years, and the term may be prolonged four times up to a period of 25 years.

[21] First published as an annex to the Green Paper on the legal protection of industrial designs, III/F/5131/91.

[21a] Applications have been received by the OHIM since 1st January 2003 and are handled since 1st April 2003.

[22] This concerned the question whether novelty should be assessed on an absolute, i.e. worldwide level, or whether the view and the knowledge of the interested circles who are active within the Community should be decisive. In the course of deliberations, both options have been tested by the Commission; the final versions of directive and CDR follow the latter approach.

[23] The Commission proposed first to allow for reproduction of spare parts for repair purposes after the expiry of three years after registration. The second proposal sought to establish a repair clause against payment of a "fair remuneration".

States decide to change their laws with a view to grant more liberal conditions for the marketing of spare parts. Consequently, even after the implementation of the directive in the Member States, different legal conditions will prevail in this economically not unimportant sector. In the Community Design Regulation, protection for spare parts has been excluded to the extent they are used for repair purposes. Otherwise, the freedom granted in the directive to national legislatures to adapt different solutions might have been undermined.

The Commission has been endowed with the task to elaborate, within three years after the date set for the implementation of the directive, a proposal on which a commonly acceptable solution for spare parts protection might be founded. For the time being however, it seems quite unlikely that such a solution is within actual reach.

3.3. Patent law

Patent law is certainly one of the key areas in IP law. It is also the area among all fields of IP where European structures have been dominating for the longest time. The European Patent Office (EPO) with its main branches in Munich and The Hague is well known to everyone regularly following the news agenda, its practices being under close scrutiny not least when it comes to the patenting of genes or computer-related inventions.

Nevertheless, when compared to trademarks and industrial designs, it has to be conceded that the patent system is less advanced in terms of Community law. In fact, it has not been possible as yet to implement the long-standing plans to establish a genuine Community patent system.[24] The most important of the many reasons accounting for this failure is languages,[25] which frequently, and particularly in this context, is but another word for "costs".

The existing trilingual system administered by the EPO for the time being is not based on an act of Community legislation, but it is founded on an international

---

[24] The original intention had been to establish the Community patent system on the basis of an international agreement, the Luxembourg or Community Patent Convention (CPC), which was concluded in 1975, but never entered into force. The proposal presently pending foresees the enactment of a Regulation on the matter, see Proposal for a Council Regulation on the Community Patent, Doc. 500 PC 0412. In early March 2003, a political agreement was reached in the Council that the proposal should be implemented. This includes a compromise solution on the language issue (see the following footnote).

[25] To be more precise, one has to distinguish in this respect between the issue of official languages used by the Office and the costs for translation of the patent. Both aspects were problematic with respect to the Community patent system. In the compromise solution found in the Council (see the previous footnote), it was decided that an application for a Community patent can be filed in any of the three official languages used in the EPO, and that a translation of the claims into every Community language must be filed when the patent is granted (unless this requirement is waived by a Member State with respect to its own official language). In the European patent system to which reference is made in the following text, the official languages used in the EPO have been confined to three (English, French and German), which is a big advantage compared to an All-European language system, and even compared to the five-language system (English, French, German, Spanish, Italian), which is applied by OHIM. However, translation costs for European patents entering into the national phase do pose a problem even within the basically trilingual EPC system.

convention, the European Patent Convention (EPC), which was concluded as early as 1973.[26] Its founding members were the Member States of the EEC at that time, but they also included a number of non-members. In that respect, the situation has remained unchanged, but of course the number of states adhering to the EPC is much higher nowadays.

The EPO accepts applications for European patents which are subjected to a centralized examination procedure. After the grant, the patents enter into the "national phase" which may comprise all or only a limited number of Member States, depending on the decision made by the rightowner. Thereafter, the patents continue to lead their own independent lives on the national level. This phenomenon is generally referred to as "bundle patents".

Unlike trademark and design law, the substantive provisions in the national patent law systems have not been subject to one comprehensive harmonisation directive. However, this does not mean that harmonisation is lacking on the level of national law. A blend of several factors accounts for this: Harmonisation of some central notions of patent law has been achieved by another international convention preceding the EPC, the so-called Strasbourg Convention.[27] Furthermore, the EPC as well as the proposed text of the Community Patent Convention have created a strong incentive for Member States to adapt their national laws to the envisaged European standards, even without being legally obliged to do so. This effect has been characterised by one of the fathers of the European Patent system, Kurt *Haertel*, as "cold harmonisation".

Finally, in some sensitive and economically important areas, it was found necessary to introduce specific, complementary EU legislation. *Inter alia*, two regulations have been enacted concerning the grant of a so-called supplementary protection certificate for inventions in the pharmaceutical[28] and the agro-chemical[29] sector. These legislative acts were founded on the consideration that, as the procedures for market admission of these substances are extremely time-consuming, a good part of the normal duration of patent protection would have passed before the rightowner would actually be in a position to reap the commercial benefit of his or her innovative activities.

Much public attention was raised by a rather recent directive in the highly controversial and sensitive field of biotechnological inventions.[30] It is widely known that this directive has been subject to a claim for annulment, filed by the Netherlands,

---

[26] Convention on the Grant of European Patents (EPC) signed in Munich 1973. Text available at the EPO website, at http://www.european-patent-office.org/legal/epc/index.html.

[27] Strasbourg Convention on the Unification of Certain Points of Substantive Law on Patents for Inventions, of 27 November 1963.

[28] Council Regulation (EEC) 1768/92 of 18 June 1992 concerning the creation of a supplementary protection certificate for medicinal products, OJ L 182/1, 02.07.1992.

[29] Regulation (EC) No 1610/96 of the European Parliament and of the Council of 23 July 1996 concerning the creation of a supplementary protection certificate for plant protection products, OJ L 198/30, 08.08.1996.

[30] Directive 98/44/EC of the European Parliament and of the Council of 6 July 1998 on the legal protection of biotechnological inventions, OJ L 213/13, 30.07.1998.

with support by Italy and Norway, and founded *inter alia* on insufficient ground for legislation, violation of the subsidiarity rule, and breach of order of public principles. The ECJ did not consider these arguments valid and rejected the claim.[31] It might be said that complainants have made it easy for the Court to find in favour of the directive, as they founded their case on political rather than legal arguments. In contrast, the point might be stressed that the decision demonstrates how prevalence is given in ECJ jurisprudence to economic in comparison to "moral" reasoning.[32]

The last item to be mentioned in this context concerns the pending proposal for a directive on protection of computer-implemented inventions,[33] or, to use the more popular term, for software patents. The present text of the EPC expressly excludes patent protection for software "as such".[34] While it has been held on one hand that this clause clashes with the obligation laid down in Article 27 TRIPS agreement[35] to grant protection for inventions "in all fields of technology", it has been criticised by others that the clause has been rendered void, or that its contents have at least been blurred, by the recent practice of the EPO and the German Federal Supreme Court, where patent protection was granted to inventions essentially consisting of a computer program.[36] Efforts to overcome the difficulties in the framework of a Diplomatic Conference for the revision of the EPC in autumn 2000, e.g. by removing the exclusion clauses and replacing it by the wording of Article 27 of the TRIPS agreement, have remained unsuccessful; the opposition from interesting circles arguing that this would have a freezing effect on the development of open source software programs proved to be too strong. The task to find a solution was therefore passed on to the Commission, which has come forward in spring 2002 with a proposal obviously trying to soothe the concerns of both sides involved. According to Article 4 of the proposal, computer implemented inventions shall be patentable, provided that they make a "technical contribution". It is however not very likely that this attempt to regulate an intricate problem will lead to an easy success.

---

[31] Decision C-377/98, 2001 ECR I-7079 – Netherlands/European Parliament and the Council of the European Union.

[32] See the contribution by Lorna *Woods*, in this volume.

[33] Proposal for a Directive of the European Parliament and Council on the patentability of computer implemented inventions, COM (2002) 92 final, 20.02.2002.

[34] See Article 53 EPC. In its relevant parts, the provision reads as follows: (1) European patents shall be granted for any inventions which are susceptible of industrial application, which are new and which involve an inventive step. (2) The following in particular shall not be regarded as inventions within the meaning of paragraph 1: ... (c) schemes, rules and methods for performing mental acts, playing games or doing business, *and programs for computers*; ... (3) The provisions of para. 2 shall exclude patentability of the subject-matter or activities referred to in that provision only to the extent to which a European patent application or European patent *relates to such subject-matter or activities as such*. (Emphasis added.)

[35] Agreement on Trade Related Aspects of Intellectual Property Rights, concluded as an annex to the WTO agreement. The text is available on the WTO website, at http://www.wto.org/english/docs_e/legal_e/final_e.htm.

[36] See, e.g. decisions of the Technical Board of Appeal, T 1173/97 of 08.071999 – IBM and T 0931/95 – Improved Pension Benefits System; see also decision by the German Supreme Court, GRUR Int. 200, 890 – Sprachanalyseeinrichtung.

3.4. Copyright

Compared to the fields considered in the previous paragraphs, harmonisation in copyright law has taken a very cautious and pragmatic step-by-step approach. The copyright directives, seven of which exist at present, have mostly dealt with specific, limited issues, typically where technical or economic developments have created an obvious and urgent need for uniform regulation in the Member States. The first of these directives concerned the protection of computer programs under copyright law[37] – certainly not a very central issue, in particular not from a continental *droit d'auteur* perspective, but nevertheless quite actual and without doubt of considerable practical relevance. The subsequent four directives have dealt with rental and lending rights,[38] satellite broadcasting and cable transmission,[39] duration of copyright,[40] and protection for databases.[41]

In view of the piecemeal approach taken in the directives just mentioned, it is difficult to say whether and to which extent they have the capability of revealing the contours of an emerging European copyright. For instance, it is sometimes emphasised that several of these directives have introduced subjective novelty as the mandatory threshold for protection. This is taken as an indication that this comparatively modest requirement will generally set the standard for protection in future European copyright law. Although this opinion does not lack plausibility, the issue is still far from being definitely settled for the time being.

Number six in the range of European copyright directives is more comprehensive in its contents than its predecessors. It deals with the "harmonisation of certain aspects of copyright and related rights in the information society" – "Infosoc Directive" is its short title.[42] Motivated by the need to provide a common European basis for the implementation of the obligations set out in the WIPO Internet Treaties of 1996, WCT[43] and WPPT,[44] by the Member States, the Infosoc Directive for the first time contains a comprehensive regulation of the fundamental rights granted to

---

37 Council Directive 91/250/EEC of 14 May 1991 on the legal protection of computer programs, OJ 1991 L 122/42, 17.05.1991.

38 Council Directive 92/100/EEC of 19 November 1992 on rental right and lending right and on certain rights related to copyright in the field of intellectual property, OJ 1992 L 346/61, 27.11.1992.

39 Council Directive 93/83/EEC of 27 September 1993 on the coordination of certain rules concerning copyright and rights related to copyright applicable to satellite broadcasting and cable retransmission, OJ L 248/15, 6.10.1993.

40 Council Directive 93/98/EEC of 29 October 1993 harmonising the term of protection of copyright and certain related rights, OJ 1993 L 290/9, 24.11.1993.

41 Directive 96/9/EC of the European Parliament and of the Council of 11 March 1996 on the legal protection of databases, OJ L 077/20, 27.03.1996.

42 Directive 2001/29/EC of the European Parliament and of the Council of 22 May 2001 on the harmonisation of certain aspects of copyright and related rights in the information society, OJ L 167/10, 22.06.2001.

43 WIPO Copyright Treaty; text available at the WIPO website, at http://www.wipo.int/treaties/ip/wct/index.html.

44 WIPO Performances and Phonograms Treaty, text available at http://www.wipo.int/treaties/ip/wppt/index.html.

authors and owners of neighbouring rights as well as a conclusive, although non-binding, catalogue of limitations. The arena of traditional copyright protection rules is further expanded by the introduction of provisions concerning circumvention of technical protection measures and the collection of data for administrative purposes.

There are plenty of interesting aspects in the Infosoc Directive, and to some of them we shall come back in the course of this presentation. At this point, it shall merely be added that it is hard to tell whether the Infosoc Directive with its comparatively broad approach constitutes a milestone in the history of European copyright or whether in view of its rather loose wording with respect to the fundamental rights, and its grotesquely extensive, yet non-binding catalogue of limitation clauses, it is "Unimportant, and Possibly Invalid", as it has been expressed by the Dutch professor Bernt *Hugenholtz*.[45] The final evaluation will have to wait until the implementation process has been completed and its effects become visible in practice.

The seventh and most recent piece of Community legislation in the field of copyright, the resale right directive,[46] is again quite specific in its content. It is remarkable and somewhat atypical, because the driving force in this case was not so much the need to cope with new technical developments and/or economic phenomena, but rather motives of social fairness and support *vis-à-vis* a frequently underprivileged group of artists. In addition to that, of course, also the disparities in national art markets created by different legal standards as regards the resale of art works have played a decisive role.

4. Further Issues to Discuss

In spite of the long way we have come in the past years, there are a lot of issues left on the agenda. Harmonisation is not fully completed in any of the areas included in the previous survey.[47] Trying to enumerate the various issues which might form the object of future harmonisation measures would however be a futile effort. Instead, as was pointed out in the beginning, the following remarks attempt to contribute to the discussion of issues of a more general character in the emerging structures of the European legal system.

4.1. Harmonisation methods

4.1.1. The maximum step: creation of unitary rights

As has become apparent in the previous survey, different harmonisation techniques have been employed in the individual disciplines of IP law. A maximum amount of

[45] See the title of the article by B. *Hugenholtz*, [2000] EIPR 499 *et seq.*

[46] Directive 2001/84/EC of the European Parliament and of the Council of 27 September 2001 on the resale right for the benefit of the author of an original work of art, OJ L 272/32, 13.10.2001.

[47] This regards in particular such practically important areas as sanctions for infringement of IP rights, where only the most fundamental rules have been harmonised as yet. The topic was only recently tackled in the Commission's proposal for a Directive of the European Parliament and of the Council on measures and procedures to ensure the enforcement of intellectual property rights of 30.1.2003, COM (2003) 46 final.

legal integration is achieved by the creation of unitary rights in the fields of trademark and industrial design law. This effect would even have been enhanced if the existing national systems had been dissolved completely[48] instead of "only" being subject to harmonisation directives. Indeed, some observers believe that this effect will occur by itself, meaning that the national systems will die out naturally in the long run. This scenario does indeed appear plausible in the field of industrial designs, provided that the Community design system will turn out to be the cheap and efficient tool for protection of product appearance it was meant to be. Whether this would actually lead to a complete abolishment of national design protection systems in some or even many Member States remains however to be seen. It appears arguable that the design directive would oblige Member States to maintain their national systems even in case there should be no more practical demand for it. Nevertheless, the national lawmaker is certainly free to severely reduce the administrative capacities in the national patent offices handling the administration of national design protection, should it turn out that specialised personnel is no longer needed for the purpose.

In trademark law, it is less likely anyway that the demand for protection on the national stage will vanish in the foreseeable future. In particular for small and medium enterprises, it still makes good sense to apply for protection on a national basis only, thus avoiding the risks ensuing from a Community wide assessment of protection requirements – i.e. assessment of the distinctive/descriptive character of the mark in all the languages spoken, and the absence of prior rights, registered or not, in all the Member States.

Another question to be posed in the context would be whether the two-tier model represented by trademark and industrial design law should be the ultimate goal also for the other areas of IP law. Inasfar as patent law is concerned, it has been the prevailing view for a long time that the system remains to be incomplete and suboptimal as long as a unitary right on the Community level is still lacking, and it is indeed difficult to imagine how legal integration should be progressing in the EU without a Community patent system being established. On the other hand, the example of patent law shows that to establish a Community right is not an aim in itself which must be pursued by all means: As long as it must be feared that the system would be overburdened with costs, meaning that it would hardly be possible for anyone else than big industry to make use of it, it is better not to install it for the time being, and to wait until the wish to establish a truly workable system supersedes political ambition and national misgivings, which typically lie at the bottom of the language issues presently at stake.[48a]

---

[48] It is another question whether it would have been legally feasible to dissolve the national systems. If that would have amounted in its practical effects to an expropriation of national rights (e.g. because it would no longer be possible to enforce them against the same or similar marks originally protected in a different territory), this would probably have violated the safeguarding clause concerning property rights in the EC treaty, Article 195.

[48a] A workable compromise solution appears to have been found in the Council in early March 2003 (see supra, no 24, 25). It is estimated that on the basis of the envisaged language regime, the costs for a Community patent will be some 25000 EUR for 25 Member States, which is half of the costs due at present for obtaining a patent in 8 European States.

As regards copyright, the question whether a genuine Community system is needed as a complement for, or constitutes a viable alternative to, harmonisation of national laws may seem absurd at first glance. The big advantage of a unitary right lies in the fact that it is acquired by one single act covering the whole territory of the Common Market. In copyright, this advantage is of comparatively little value, as the right is independent anyway of administrative structures – instead of registration, it comes into existence simply by the act of creation. Still, in contrast to the present situation, a Community copyright would be subject to only one exactly determined set of legal rules, whereas national copyright laws, even after full implementation of the existing directives, may still remain quite diverse in their details.

On the other hand, this is exactly the reason why the idea of a unitary Community Copyright is not considered as particularly appealing by the IP community. Strictly speaking, it would result in a far higher degree of harmonisation than what Member States are willing to concede at present. Of course, like in trademark and design law, the option would remain that national laws in all their diversities continue to co-exist with the unitary right. However, the consequences this would entail could hardly be called satisfactory. In a given conflict, it would be left to the rightholder to choose between two equally valid sets of rules, without the potential infringer being in a position to know beforehand which of the two sets will be governing.[49] The lack of legal security, this would imply, clearly outweighs any possible advantages of a coexistence model in the field of copyright.

The considerations concerning copyright further show that whilst the introduction of unitary rights certainly is the biggest step forward one can take with respect to legal integration, it is also a hazardous one, insofar as it removes any freedom of decision for the national lawmaker in the fields covered by the Regulation. In accordance with their strong legal impact, the ECJ has declared that the introduction of new rights on the Community level is left to the Council, and the decision can only be taken unanimously.[50] While this institutional safeguard is legally well-founded and understandable for political reasons, it must be realised that it drastically reduces the chances for adoption of legal measures on the level of Community rights with respect to issues which are politically and/or economically contentious, as, e.g. the introduction of global instead of regional exhaustion in trademark law, or the insertion of a repair clause into design legislation.

---

[49] Of course, it may happen also in the fields of trademark and industrial design law that the proprietor is in a position to choose between two different sets of rules. However, as national laws have been subject to comprehensive harmonisation in these fields, in particular as regards the scope of protection and possible limitations, the risk that the application of one or the other set of rules might lead to different results is much smaller. Furthermore, as both trademark and design rights regularly come into existence by registration (with reservations applying to the unregistered Community Design and unregistered trademark rights which may exist on the national level), the aspect of legal security poses lesser problems than with respect to copyright, as the potential infringer knows from the beginning that he may be sued for infringement of a Community right as well as – alternatively – for infringement of a national right.

[50] In its opinion 1/94 of 14 November 1994, concerning the competence of the EC and its Member States respectively to conclude the WTO/TRIPS agreement.

4.1.2. Harmonisation in contentious fields – possible reactions

Repair clauses and exhaustion of trademark rights represent but two of the many examples in IP law where the general desire to further European legal integration is contrasted with the unwillingness of national legislatures – motivated by the wish to preserve national values and traditions, or, probably more often, by economic considerations and concrete pressure exerted by domestic industries – to accept common solutions which are considered incompatible with their own legal approach. In this respect, IP law is certainly not different from any other legal area. One possible reaction to this dilemma is to leave the contested question out of the general harmonisation framework, as was done with respect to the spare parts issue in the Design Directive. Another method, which disguises rather than reveals the lack of agreement existing between Member States, can be found, e.g. in the Infosoc Directive, in particular in Article 5(3), the provision containing a lengthy catalogue of possible exemptions to be introduced in national law, without any of those provisos being of an obligatory character.

Article 5 of the Infosoc Directive is indeed a typical result of certain problems encountered with respect to EU legislation in the field. As it had been the ambition, in accordance with continental copyright tradition, to make the list of limitations contained therein conclusive instead of providing for an open "fair use" clause, every Member State and interest group struggled to get their own particular concerns expressly addressed and regulated, lest it should be completely banned from further consideration once implementation has been completed. It is hardly exaggerating to say that it mattered little in this process how well-founded and substantial these concerns were – the important thing was whether the party articulating them had sufficient lobbying impact to make an impression on the Commission and/or the other legislative bodies involved. The large variety of optional limitation clauses this has entailed is however not the only disadvantage connected with Article 5. In the long run, even more problems are likely to ensue from the fact that the directive does not allow the insertion by case law of new limitations which are founded on similar considerations, yet are not expressly mentioned in the present catalogue. In view of this unfortunate effect, Bernt *Hugenholtz* has made the point that "of course, the whole idea of drawing up a finite set of limitations was ill-conceived in the first place. The last thing the information industry needs in these dynamic times is rigid rules that are cast in concrete for the years to come".[51]

4.1.3. The flexibility problem

Indeed, lack of flexibility – legal rules being cast in concrete for many years – is (refering to lack of flexibility) a problem jeopardising the efficiency of European legal integration to no lesser degree than would the absence of sufficiently advanced harmonisation measures. With time progressing and in a rapidly changing socio-economic framework, the problems will probably become increasingly ponderous in

---

[51] [2000] EIPR 499, 501.

the future. The issue is elaborated in more detail in other presentations in this volume.[52] It suffices here to add that the flexibility problems may be enhanced by the two-tier solution – regulation plus harmonisation directive – employed in trademark and industrial design law, as regulations creating unitary rights on the Community level do not only require unanimity for their enactment, but consequently also for changes to be introduced therein. As the proper functioning of the system generally presupposes that regulation and directive are congruent in their core provisions, it makes little sense to change the directive without being in a position to do the same with the regulation – eventhough as a matter of principle, changes in the directive might be effected more easily under the co-decision procedure.

The possible solutions to be considered and discussed with a view to the flexibility problem are manifold. As was said before, one possible reaction with respect to IP law might be a re-evaluation of the theory that good legislation must provide for conclusive catalogues of limitation clauses. Without neglecting the advantages of this traditional technique, it must be realised that the purpose of legal security which such clauses are intended to serve can hardly be attained any longer in a satisfactory manner when the speed of technical and economic development together with the increasingly dense texture of IP protection create a permanent demand for a flexible assessment of what might be regarded as "fair use", in particular in copyright, but also, e.g. in trademark law.

Apart from such sector-specific solutions, a more general approach would have to reconsider the legislative procedures in the EU with a view to possible streamlining, and, finally, the partial transfer of responsibility to other bodies than the regular legislative organs of the EU.[53] The Commission is working on these matters, having proposed, in response to a request by the Lisbon Council, a number of measures for simplifying, improving and speeding up the legislative process.[54] *Inter alia*, the proposals comprise an enhanced use of the instruments of co-regulation and self-regulation. Whilst the risks ensuing from the various forms of co-regulation, as from comitology, for the democratic principle of Parliamentary control should not be underestimated,[55] it should be unproblematic to embark upon the proposed route towards more flexibility at least inasfar as it basically means to emphasise and strengthen the employment of widely accepted self-regulatory mechanisms like rules of conduct to be established within certain branches, or the conclusion of voluntary agreements between organisations representing different groups of stakeholders.

---

[52] See in particular Jan *Wouters* on company law.

[53] One specific variation of this approach is the delegation of rule-making to specialised agencies. The topic is of actual relevance in the patent field, where an important aim of the Diplomatic Conference for revision of the EPC which was held in Munich in November 2000 has been to transpose several provisions presently anchored in the Convention text into the implementing regulations, with the consequence that changes in those provisions can be effected more easily, by majority decision of the Administrative Council, instead of having to convene a Diplomatic Conference for the purpose.

[54] Interim Report from the Commission to the Stockholm European Council – Improving and simplifying the regulatory environment, COM/2001/0130/final.

[55] See on this problem *Langenbucher*, ZEuP 2002, 213 *et seq.*, with further references.

In IP law, this strategy is used to some extent, for instance – again in the Infosoc Directive – with respect to the conditions of "just compensation" for mass use of protected material, and, even more important, with respect to the terms for balancing the use of technical protection measures and the right of the public to access content. Although in the end, these issues can and must be regulated by the Member States if no solutions can be implemented in the framework of voluntary agreements, it is clear from the spirit and wording of the provisions that these solutions are expected to be elaborated by the stakeholders themselves in the first place.[56] It is interesting to note in this context that the preamble to the Infosoc Directive expressly acknowledges the concept of extended collective licenses,[57] which has been developed in the Nordic States. Where the system applies,[58] the agreements concluded between users of protected content and organisations representing the interests of a majority of copyright holders in the field concerned become binding in principle also for non-members (subject however to an opt-out clause), meaning that they become valid *erga omnes* in practice. Until now, this model has however not found a broader acceptance also in other EU states.

Leaving it at least partly to the stakeholders and their representatives to devise commonly acceptable solutions for concrete issues otherwise calling for detailed legal regulation certainly makes it easier to adapt a given scheme to the ever-changing needs of the marketplace and those active in the field. On the other hand, it is clear that the possibilities for soft law solutions are not unlimited. A firm legal framework is needed as a basis, and the technique only works in presence of general understanding and readiness to cooperate, i.e. it is not a feasible solution for matters which are fundamentally contentious. Furthermore, arrangements of the type mentioned above always entail a certain risk with respect to competition rules and must therefore be monitored closely.

4.1.4. Cold harmonisation

Finally, one word must be said about "cold harmonisation" in IP law, i.e. harmonisation which takes place without Member States being legally obliged to change their law. As was pointed out above, this technique has been successful in the patent field, whereas experiences are lacking in the other IP disciplines.

An actual variation of the "cold harmonisation" technique is represented by the country of origin principle, which has been anchored in Article 3 of the e-commerce directive[59] with respect to commercial communication via digital networks. Although not obliging member countries to harmonise the legal rules applying in the

---

[56] See in particular Article 6 para. 4 and recital no. 51 of the Infosoc Directive.

[57] Infosoc Directive, recital no. 18.

[58] Extended collective licences typically apply to reprographic reproduction of material to be used for teaching, and for retransmission of radio and tv programs under certain conditions and for certain purposes.

[59] Directive 2000/31/EC of the European Parliament and of the Council of 8 June 2000 on certain legal aspects of information society services, in particular electronic commerce, in the Internal Market (Directive on electronic commerce) OJ L 178/1, 17.07.2000.

field, it is generally expected that, as the country of origin principle will privilege entrepreneurs from countries with rather liberal standards, factual and political pressure will be exerted on legislatures in countries where stricter rules apply to adapt their own rules to the more lenient standards from abroad – an effect which according to some will initiate a "race to the bottom".[60] The directive expressly exempts IP rights from application of the country of origin principle.[61] Nevertheless, it may affect some of the areas where IP protection is supplemented by rules against unfair competition, in particular concerning modes of advertising and marketing, and it may thus contribute, for better or worse, to a *de facto* harmonisation in those adjacent areas.

4.2. The role of the Court

4.2.1. Secondary Community law

It was pointed out in the beginning that before harmonisation was actually achieved in the individual areas of IP law, a comprehensive body of ECJ case law had already been developed, mostly dealing with the impact of Articles 28 and 30 on the possibility to invoke IP rights with the aim to inhibit "grey" imports. It is interesting to note that in some of these decisions, the ECJ has deliberately pushed the efforts of the European legislature by pointing out that the Court was unable to react against existing impediments for cross border trade, as long as the area remained unharmonised.[62] As harmonisation is progressing and Member States have come to ends with their domestic implementation procedures, the main focus of ECJ jurisprudence is gradually shifted from primary to secondary Community law and to the interpretation of provisions contained therein.

As was pointed out above, the number of cases where clarification was sought from the ECJ with respect to the interpretation of provisions contained in the directive was and still is unexpectedly high in trademark law. One might say that this is indicative of the poor quality of the drafting, but of course, it may as well be attributable to the inherent complexities of the subject matter. Whatever the reasons may be – it has created a novel situation for those active in trademark law, especially in a country like Germany, which has always boasted of a very complex and refined

---

[60] The topic has been treated frequently, and mostly with a critical undertone, in the German literature; see, e.g. *Lehmann*, ZUM 1999, 180, 181; *Hoeren*, MMR 1999, 192, 194; *Mankowski*, GRUR Int. 1999, 909, 914; *Fezer/Koos*, IPRax 2000, 349, 354. So far, these fears have not been sustained in practice. The only legal rules which have been abolished by the German legislature not least with a view to the country of origin principle and the favourable effects it would entail for entrepreneurs from abroad were the provisions of prohibition of rebates and free gifts – rules which, according to the vast majority opinion, have been obsolete anyway for a long time.

[61] See Annex to the e-commerce directive, first item.

[62] See for instance C-144/81, 1982 ECR 2853 – Keurkoop/Nancy Kean Gifts; C-57/87, 1988 ECR 6039 – CICRA and Maxicar/Renault; C-238/87, 1988 ECR 6211 – Volvo AB/Erik Veng. All decisions concerned industrial designs, where harmonisation was only embarked upon at a rather late stage, i.e. shortly before completion of the Internal Market.

legal doctrine in the field, supported by a large body of case law and bookshelves full of specialised literature. It is difficult and maybe even painful to realise that the thousands of pages which have been written in German, from a German legal perspective, on specific trademark law problems have no more – and sometimes definitely less – impact on the ECJ, and thereby on the actual state of trademark law, than a single, well-written decision by the British High Court. Indeed, the strength principally inherent in a thoroughly developed, systematic approach can turn out to be a disadvantage, because and insofar as it is understood merely by specialists and cannot be communicated in simple words and comprehensible terms to judges who are not experts in the field.

For the legal profession, and not least for specialised academic circles in the Member States, it results from these considerations that in present times, it is better to attempt reducing than further enhancing the complexity and refinement of national legal doctrines, and to try conveying one's own ideas in a manner which can easily be grasped by persons not having grown up in one's own system, instead of using language which is hardly apt for communication outside an exclusive circle of fellow disciples.

But in spite of the efforts which may be undertaken in this respect, it remains a fact that it will never be easy to explain to the non-specialist judges at the ECJ the full impact and background of intricate questions arising in specific legal fields. The risk is therefore quite inevitable that each decision, although fair and understandable in its outcome as such, may create inconsistencies for the system as a whole. Furthermore, experience has shown that most ECJ decisions in the trademark field, while giving the requested answer to the questions posed by the referring court, give rise to at least as many novel questions for the national judiciary to deal with.

In brief, although the beneficial effect of the common judicial instance provided by the ECJ remains beyond any doubt, it would be mistaken to expect too much of it. For national courts, this means that it would be wise not to make inflationary use of the instrument of reference to the ECJ for preliminary decisions.[63] On the other hand, the vital interest of the parties involved in a conflict as well as of the public at large to obtain at least basic clarification with respect to the meaning of clauses contained in secondary Community law which are understood differently in the Member countries should neither be ignored nor underestimated. It might be a task for the future to devise instruments taking care of one or both aspects just mentioned – e.g. by giving the Court discretion to reject cases of a *de minimis* character, and/or by creating a route of direct access by the parties to the ECJ in case of apparent failure by a national court to refer contentious issues to Luxembourg.

---

[63] This happened in the field of advertising and marketing measures, where the ECJ, in consequence of the broad interpretation given to measures having equivalent effect in the sense of Article 28 in the Dassonville (C-8/74, 1974 ECR 837) and Cassis de Dijon (C-120/78, 1979 ECR 6349) decisions, was flooded with cases where national entrepreneurs wanted to get rid of national marketing rules restricting their business practices. In the end, the ECJ had to announce that they would no longer regard mere selling arrangements as "measures having equivalent effect", as long as they were non-discriminatory; C-267/91 & 268/91, 1993 ECR I-6097 – Keck & Mithouard.

4.2.2. Primary Community law

Apart from the interpretation of clauses contained in secondary Community law, issues of primary Community law still account for an important part of ECJ case law, also in the field of IP law. This applies e.g. to those – exceptional – cases where the legal foundations of a directive are challenged by one or more Member States, as in the ultimately unsuccessful claim for annulment of the Biotech Directive.[64] Of course, it also applies if a Member State has failed to comply with its Treaty obligations, e.g. to implement a directive within the prescribed time, as well as with respect to the liability *vis-à-vis* individuals this failure to implement may eventually entail. It is less clear to which extent primary Community law may come into play with respect to matters of substantive law even after harmonisation in the field concerned has been completed in the Member States. For instance, if secondary Community law allows for, or even makes mandatory, the introduction of clauses into national law, which in their practical effects clash with the free movement of goods – does the Court have to accept this effect as being the consequence of the sovereign decision of EU legislature, or must precedence be given to the fundamental freedoms as laid down in the EC Treaty?

This is not merely a theoretical question. The ECJ had to face this dilemma in at least one decision dealing with the interpretation of the trademark directive. Without being very explicit about it, the Court chose to uphold the approach taken in its previous case law, irrespective of the fact that this was incompatible with the exact wording of the relevant clause in the directive.[65] Similar problems may emerge in the future, e.g. in connection with the implementation of the Infosoc Directive. As was said before, this directive contains a very lengthy and conclusive, but mostly optional catalogue of limitations. Member States are therefore free to pick and choose from this catalogue whatever clauses they deem appropriate with respect to their national law. Will all restrictions of cross-border trade which might result from this approach have to be accepted as unavoidable? The example from trademark law mentioned above shows that this is unlikely at least in a case when the ECJ has already declared in its previous case law that certain practices are irreconcilable with the provisions in the EC treaty – like, for instance, to invoke copyright protection in the shapes

---

[64] See above, n. 31. A successful claim for annulment of a directive was launched, e.g. with respect to the directive on tobacco advertising; see ECJ decision C-376/98, 2000 ECR, I-8419 – Germany/European Parliament and Council.

[65] In ECJ C-379/97, 1999 ECR I-6954 – Pharmacia & Upjohn SA/Paranova A/S. The case concerned the question whether a parallel importer is entitled to "rebrand" an imported product, if the trademark owner uses (slightly) different marks in different countries for the same pharmaceutical. According to the wording of the trademark directive, this possibility should have been excluded, as exhaustion only takes place according to Article 7 if the product has been released on the market "under *that* trademark" (emphasis added). However, in the decision forming a precedence for this case, C-3/78, 1978 ECR 1823 – Centrafarm BV/American Home Products Corporation, the Court had held that to prohibit rebranding in certain cases might amount to the artificial partitioning of markets which could not be justified under (ex-)Article 36, and the Court did not see any reason to deviate from this finding in the actual case.

and/or labels of useful articles in order to enjoin a person legitimately trading in those goods from showing their images in advertising campaigns.[66]

This remark needs to be completed by at least a short glance at the competition provisions in the EC Treaty, Articles 81 and 82. The relationship between the competition rules on one hand and the limited kind of monopoly which is granted by IP rights on the other is and always has been a sensitive issue. Generally speaking, the ECJ has been following a rather cautious approach with regard to the IP/competition law relationship: While the manner in which use is made of such rights is certainly not immune against interference by the competition rules, it is acknowledged in principle that the mere refusal by the owner to grant licences or to otherwise tolerate use made by others of rights lawfully acquired by him will only be held to constitute inadmissible conduct in rare cases and under specific circumstances, e.g. in a situation when the rightowner fails to satisfy an apparent and serious market demand.[67]

The dogmatic foundation of this line of jurisprudence is still somewhat insecure. The topic was much debated in the aftermath of the Magill decision by the ECJ,[68] when the failure to grant licences by copyright owners for the compilation of TV programme listings was considered to constitute an abuse of market power. Many authors have considered this to be an outflow of the "essential facilities" doctrine, an interpretation which was however rendered less convincing by subsequent case law.[69] It is indeed doubtful that any legal theory will furnish a satisfactory answer to the problems involved. What it boils down to is that the ECJ sometimes, and certainly in a case like Magill, makes use of the competition rules in order to correct

---

[66] This was the situation in ECJ decision C-337/96, 1997 ECR I-6013 – Christian Dior/Evora BV. The ECJ ruled that copyright – just as trademark law – in the bottles and labels of Dior perfumes could not be invoked in order to stop their representation in advertisement brochures by a drug store chain. The Court motivated its finding by referring to previous case law, where it had been held that the "exclusive right of exploitation conferred by copyright" cannot be relied upon by its owner to prevent or restrict the importation of products having been lawfully marketed in another Member State by the right owner himself or with his consent. The Court chose to ignore the fact that in those cases, the right invoked by the owner concerned the distribution of products – which according to the general doctrine is indeed exhausted with first marketing – whereas in the actual case, the reproduction right was at stake, which, according at least to a majority view, is not subject to the exhaustion principle at all. Nevertheless, the result in this case was certainly sound, and, as was pointed out in the text above, it seems unlikely that the Court would be willing to abstain from it if a country chooses not to implement Article 5(3)j, i.e. the optional limitation clause in the Infosoc Directive on the basis of which the representation of images of products offered for sale could be declared legitimate in the future.

[67] See C-57/87, 1988 ECR 6039 – CICRA and Maxicar/Renault; C-238/87, 1988 ECR 6211 – Volvo AB/Erik Veng; see also the Magill decision cited in the next footnote.

[68] C-241/92 & 242/92, 1992 ECR I-743 – Radio Telefis Eireann (RTE) and Independent Television Publications (ITP)/Commission ("Magill").

[69] C-7/97, 1998 ECR I-7791 – Bronner. More light on the issue will probably be shed by the final decision in the pending case of IMS Health, which concerns copyright protection in the "brick structure" of a database concerning sales and prescribing of pharmaceutical products. The Commission found that the refusal to grant licences would amount to misuse of a dominant position and had ordered as an interim measure that IMS Health had to grant licences on request and on a non-discriminatory basis. The order of the interim measure was however suspended by the CFI (T-184/01 R) and the ECJ (C-481/01 P(R)). The appeal of IMS Health against the Commission decision is still pending before the CFI.

unwise decisions made by the national lawmaker or judiciary – in this case, to correct the decision that full copyright protection should be granted for simple programme listings. As was pointed out above, the same effect may eventually result also from ECJ rulings made on the basis of Articles 28 and 30, to the extent they set aside, e.g. the decision of national legislatures to grant full and unlimited copyright protection with respect to the representation of products and labels in advertisements.

The fact that the ECJ sometimes assumes, in these and similar cases, the role of a supervisor of national legislation without openly declaring it, and without having been expressly asked to do so, shall not be lamented here. At least in the cases this author is aware of, the results found by the ECJ have been sound, and, in particular with respect to the sometimes quite far-reaching effects of IP law, it is reassuring to know that there is an instance willing and capable to control and delimitate possibly detrimental impacts, even in cases when they are a direct consequence of national and/or secondary Community legislation, which cannot be declared invalid as such. From a legal, systematic point of view however, the situation is not fully satisfactory, and the cases where the Court has to intervene in the manner described should be kept to a minimum. Rather than to rely on an *ex post* control to be carried out by the ECJ on an insecure legal basis, legislatures on the national as well as the Community level should try their best in order to recognise potential imbalances and gross impediments for the freedom of competition arising from the grant of IP rights already in advance, and should provide for a wiser legislation, i.e. for sufficient safeguards to be included in the legislative acts proper.

4.3. European and international law

It was pointed out in the beginning that harmonisation of IP law had already been somewhat advanced on the international level at the time when the Treaty of Rome was concluded. A successful revision of the two main international instruments applying in the field, the Paris Convention and the Berne Convention, was concluded in 1967 and 1971 respectively. After that time however, a period of stagnation set in. The political and economic clash between East and West, North and South prevented any progress with respect to efforts initiated by industrialised countries to adapt the rules of international law to changing economic and technical conditions. For approximately 20 years, harmonisation implying the introduction of enhanced legal standards for protection of IP rights was only possible on a regional level, the European Communities being the most important and successful region in that respect.

It is well known that the situation has changed. By introducing IP in the Uruguay round of GATT negotiations which resulted in the WTO agreement and its Annex dealing with TRIPS,[70] it has been possible to raise the international standard for minimum protection of IP rights to a fairly advanced – some might even say exaggerated – level. Some of the provisions set out in TRIPS even went beyond the level of IP protection existing at the time in Europe. In some respects, they have even resulted

---

[70] The address under which the text can be found on the WTO website is indicated above, n. 35.

in a demand for changes in EU legislation in order to comply with international requirements.[71]

That international harmonisation efforts have gained new impetus in recent years could also be witnessed in the area of copyright, where the WIPO Internet Treaties of 1996 have entailed the need for the European Union to introduce harmonised legislation on copyright and related rights in the information society.[72]

These examples demonstrate that legal harmonisation of a regional character is no longer the sole and probably not even the most important pacemaker nowadays with respect to the adaptation of IP laws to new technical and economic developments. As the world grows together in the age of globalisation, there is an increasingly pressing need to find solutions which are applicable on a worldwide level. This does however not mean that regional harmonisation today is only of second rate importance. To the contrary – if appropriate solutions have been formulated and were put to a practical test already on the regional level, it becomes much easier to successfully influence the global developments.

For the EU, it results that one should always be aware of the global challenges, even when regional harmonisation projects are discussed. Spending too much time by merely reflecting one's own needs, and indulging in lengthy internal quarrels about national desires and divergencies might prove to create a severe impediment against an adequate representation of European positions on the international stage. In IP law, it is particularly obvious that a leading role can only be secured if determined efforts are undertaken within the EU to achieve a general agreement, with as much efficiency and as little internal frictions as possible, about the future legal framework for a harmonised, coherent and balanced system of IP protection.

The preceding considerations would be incomplete without adding some critical thoughts. With only slight exaggeration, it might be said that global harmonisation in the field of IP is under the dominating influence of three global players, the USA, the EU and Japan, who themselves are mainly driven by domestic industries and powerful lobbying groups. Small countries and particularly countries from less industrialised regions appear to have little to no vote in the matter. If that picture should prevail in the future, it risks to entail adverse consequences for IP rights in the long run, as the justification usually given for the grant of such rights – that they further the well-being of individuals and nations by rewarding innovation and creativeness – will lose credibility. Already at present, growing opposition against the economic impact of IP rights is building up in less developed countries,[73] and it is supported by an increasing number of NGO groups in the industrialised part of the

---

[71] This debate concerns most of all Article 27 TRIPS, pursuant to which patents must be available for inventions in all fields of technology. It is held by some that Article 52 EPC, which excludes computer programs "as such" from the notion of patentable inventions, is incompatible with this requirement. The recent proposal for an EU directive on computer-implemented inventions (see *supra*) can be viewed as a result of these discussions.

[72] See *supra*, Section 3.4.

[73] For the impact this criticism had on the agenda concluded at the WTO Ministerial Conference at Doha/Qatar, see the information available at http://www.wto.org/english/tratop_e/dda_e/dda_e.htm.

world. It would be much better, also for those representing European interests in international negotiations, to listen and react to those critical voices now, instead of waiting until acceptance of the system as a whole may be endangered.

4.4. The judicial system

It is a truism that to harmonise the law in the books is but the first step in a long and at times rather stony path towards truly harmonised practice. Law lives through those who apply it. A key role is therefore performed by authorities, courts and judges administering the rules incorporating the new European solutions.

Apart from the decisions made by the appeal boards in the EPO and at OHIM, the bulk of jurisprudence is still concentrated on the national level. Notwithstanding the tremendous importance of the landmark decisions handed down by the ECJ, they will always be very few in their number when compared to the total of cases which are submitted almost daily to the courts in the Member States. In this situation, it is of paramount importance that information and opinions are exchanged as much as possible between judges from different countries.[74] Furthermore, the situation calls for serious and intense considerations regarding the establishment of a common European court structure operating below and/or on a different level than the ECJ and the Court of First Instance.[75]

In the patent field, a fully elaborated proposal to create a common appeal court for litigation concerning Community patents ("COPAC") was already launched in 1985. Recently, the topic of creating common judicial structures for patent litigation in Europe was put on the agenda with renewed impetus.[76] The so-called Working Party on Litigation which had been commissioned with the task to elaborate a European protocol on patent litigation (EPLP) by the Intergovernmental Conference of the Member States of the EPO in 1999 has come forward with a proposal for the creation of a European Patent Judiciary (EPJ).[77] According to the proposal,

---

[74] For this purpose, regular (annual) meetings between specialised judges are organised by the EPO and OHIM respectively.

[75] Apart from the initiatives launched in the patent field which are discussed below, it is foreseen to install, below the Court of First Instance (CFI), a specialised court reviewing trademark cases coming up from the OHIM in Alicante. The CFI would then act as a (final) appeal instance for the legal issues involved. Without such a system, it would become increasingly difficult for the CFI as well as the ECJ to cope with the numerous cases in which appeals are filed against the decisions of OHIM appeal boards.

[76] The remarks made in the following text concern the European Patent Litigation Protocol Agreement, which was the most advanced proposal in early 2002. Meanwhile, the negotiations concerning the EPLA have come to a standstill after an intervention by the Commission challenging the competence of Member States to negotiate the EPLA, and precedence was given to the Community Patent System, for which a unitary judicial system shall be established by the year 2010.

[77] See the report on the proposed European Patent Litigation Protocol (EPLP), in 31 IIC 560 (2000). The proposal has been subject to many debates and changes. At the time of writing this article (July 2002), the version of the draft – now called European Patent Law Agreement (EPLA) – published on 31 May 2002 (WPL/SUB/2/02) has been subject to renewed considerations in a meeting of the Sub-Group of the Working Party on Litigation, which did however not lead to material changes.

a European Patent Court shall be established, comprising a Court of First Instance and a Court of Appeal, with competence to decide on infringement and validity of European patents. In addition, the European Patent Court shall also be competent to opine, in a non-binding manner, on questions concerning national patent law which are referred to it by the national courts. In response to misgivings voiced in the interested circles against the desirability and feasibility of a fully centralised court procedure in European patent litigation,[78] the proposal foresees that the Court of First Instance, in addition to a central chamber which is located at the seat of the EPJ and the Court of Appeal, may comprise Regional Divisions located in various Contracting states.

The adherence to the EPLP, which will be concluded as an international agreement, shall be optional for the Member States, i.e. it is left to the decision of the national legislatures whether they join the system or maintain their own. This will probably make it easier from a political point of view to get started with the development of a common court system in the highly specialised field of IP – something which in the long run might become a model even in other fields of the law.

Finally, at least short mention must be made of the special importance which the (former) Brussels Convention – now transformed into the Brussels-I-Regulation[79] – has attained in IP, in particular in patent law. We owe it to judges from the Netherlands (the name of Jan *Brinkhof* is inseparably linked to these developments), that the potential for consolidation of jurisdiction and for the release of cross-border injunctions has been realised in its full extent. Not everyone in Europe has been satisfied with this approach,[80] and in some respects, the Dutch jurisprudence may have been a little bit too bold.[81] Nevertheless, the fact remains that the courage and openmindedness which have triggered these practices are indispensable qualities when it comes to the development of a truly harmonised European practice – not only, but also in the field of IP law.

---

[78] See, e.g. *Pagenberg*, 31 IIC 481 (2000).

[79] Regulation 44/2001 [2001] OJ L12/1, January 16, 2001; in force since 1 March 2002.

[80] In particular British Courts have been very critical towards the Dutch approach. This is expressed *inter alia* in the cases *Fort Dodge Animal Health* v. *Akzo Nobel*, CA 27th October 1997, 1998 FSR 222 and in *Boston Scientific Ltd.* v. *Cordis Corp.*, CA 27th September 1997. The ECJ did not have an opportunity to rule on this matter as yet.

[81] This concerns in particular Article 6.1 of the former Brussels Convention, the multiple defendants rule. The rather far-reaching application of the rule in the framework of *kort geding* proceedings was changed when the Gerechtshof in Den Haag held in its decision of 23 April 1998 – *Expandable Grafts* v. *Boston Scientific* – that defendants who are not resident in the Netherlands should be subject to jurisdiction of Dutch courts in infringement proceedings only if the group of companies concerned had its headquarters in the Netherlands (so-called "spider in the web" rule).

Chapter 5

Legal Education and International Exchange

*Maria Sticchi Damiani**

1. Introduction

In choosing my approach to this topic I have certainly been influenced by my own personal experience as an academic engaged in international exchanges. For over 20 years, since I started teaching in my university, I thought that working in higher education and contributing to educate the young people of my country for their future lives and professions was a privilege, and I could not think of any more rewarding role for me to play in life. When I got involved in international exchanges in higher education, however – and this was about 15 years ago – I realized that my view of education had been transformed and expanded in such a way that international exchanges had become a key factor in it and I could no longer be active in the field without placing this factor at the heart of the process. Now I am even more convinced that no institution in Europe, indeed in the world, can properly educate its future generations in any discipline – be it law or economics or chemistry – without including these two terms into its mission statement: international and exchanges.

I take the term international as defining the space in which exchanges take place – Europe and beyond, but it is through the term exchange that I would like to approach the process that seems to be so relevant for higher education today, in law as in any other field. It is this term that has a potential for shaking the foundations of traditional education in our universities and breaking the barriers that have sometimes been built around and between institutions. Let me present this theme under three different headings: exchange of information, exchange of students, exchange of teachers.

2. Exchange of Information

Before the implementation of the interuniversity cooperation programmes launched by the European Commission in 1987, few contacts existed among higher education institutions within Europe, and between European institutions and those in the rest

* Professor, University LUISS Guido Carli, Rome – Member of the Socrates/Erasmus Sub-Committee, Brussels.

M. van Empel (ed.), "From Paris to Nice": Fifty Years of Legal Integration in Europe, 101–107.

of the world. When they existed, they were mainly originated by and relying on common research interests of individual academics who generally kept these contacts within a small circle of colleagues or doctoral students. The information exchanged was mainly related to the research projects being carried out and to the relevant literature. It was not until the first networks of European universities were set up in various disciplines that the need for information on the educational programmes available at partner institutions was urgently felt and a systematic exchange of materials began to take place.

Moreover, regular network meetings provided opportunities for the development of interpersonal relations, and opened informal communication channels among the representatives of the participating institutions. Having attended these meetings myself in the late 1980s and early 1990s, I do remember how eager we were to learn not only about the legal systems in other countries – a topic colleagues conversant in comparative law were already familiar with – but mainly on how legal education was structured and how specific programmes were organized in other institutions. We also exchanged information on the teaching materials being used, and on the local approaches to teaching/learning activities. This is how we became fully aware of the diversity of legal education in Europe and tried to share this awareness with colleagues in our institutions. Academic reactions at home were mixed: in some cases diversity was perceived as irrelevant to a deeply rooted national/institutional identity and caused greater entrenchment in well established teaching routines; in other cases, an exploratory attitude prevailed and interest was shown in different educational traditions, approaches, materials, as possible sources of enrichment for local programmes. In both cases, however, some sort of choice had been made – as a result of a confrontation with diverse realities – which had somehow shaken the tendency of European law departments to be rather self-referential.

As the awareness of diversity gradually developed in the institutions engaged in European cooperation, appropriate strategies and instruments for making diversity understandable were also devised. Transparency became a key issue for institutions who wanted to play the international game. Accordingly, transparency is one of the basic principles of the European Credit Transfer System (ECTS), launched in 1989 and now broadly used, on the grounds that each European institution should take responsibility for describing its distinctive character to readers who do not share the same background information or the same cultural presuppositions. In order to make diversity comparable, moreover, common principles should be adopted and an agreed framework should be used for presenting different contents. This applies to the ECTS credits allocated to teaching units, which are based on the common principle of student workload and determined as a proportion of the agreed conventional figure of 60 credits per year. It also applies to the structure, content and organization of educational programmes, which are described in ECTS information packages through an agreed format and sequencing of items. And to the results of the educational process, which are presented in ECTS Transcripts of Records also by using a common ECTS grading scale.

It is to be noted here that the pursuit of transparency under ECTS has generally triggered a process of self-analysis and self-awareness that in most cases has brought about interesting developments at the institutional level as well. In any case, the value of the transparency exercise is now being more and more associated with the quality of an institution.

3. Exchange of Students

Student exchange has been one of the most popular activities since the beginning of interuniversity cooperation in Europe. Students themselves have immediately seen the benefits of doing a period of study abroad with full recognition of the courses taken at another institution; they have seen the advantages in terms of language learning, personal growth and academic enrichment. Institutions have tried to satisfy this demand by signing agreements with suitable partners in other European countries and taking up the organizational responsibility of sending and receiving students: while international relations offices were set up to solve administrative and logistic problems, interested academics were appointed to advise students on programmes of study and guarantee a fair recognition procedure.

Recognition has definitely been the most sensitive area in the process, the principle that has met widespread resistance among academics and has generally been interpreted in the most restrictive way. Not many law professors, at least at the beginning, encouraged their students to study abroad for a semester or a year, because they were genuinely convinced that courses offered by another European institution would not be of great value to them. This approach was based in most cases on a national view of legal studies – traditionally adopted in many branches of law – as well as on limited personal experience in international contexts, which led most teachers to think that a period of study abroad would be a "waste of time" for their students. However, lack of encouragement did not stop many students from applying for an Erasmus grant and getting into the process of developing a programme of study which could be accepted for recognition. At this stage recognition was interpreted in many different ways: from "do anything that interests you as an addition to your curriculum, but real exams have to be taken here because none of the courses available abroad are completely equivalent to those offered here" to "do just an international law course in your semester abroad and we will accept it as a replacement of your course here, even though the content is not exactly the same" to "let's organize a full programme of study for your semester/year abroad that can enrich your curriculum without interfering with your national requirements". Many students accepted the first two interpretations of recognition because they were highly motivated to have an experience in another country, in another university and in another language, and certainly benefited from it. But they paid a high price for it in terms of prolongation of their studies, because their academic experience abroad did not fit properly into their home curriculum.

The restrictive attitude to recognition was based on the assumption that any course unit or educational activity provided in the national/institutional curriculum was a necessary component of it, and could only be replaced by courses to be done abroad if their content was deemed fully equivalent. Most academics, even those directly engaged in student exchanges, did not perceive or accept one of the basic principles underlying the recognition process, that was the principle of flexibility. A flexible approach to academic recognition means accepting the diversity of national education systems and appreciating the opportunity offered to students to expand their curriculum: this can be done by adding courses not available at their home institution and by introducing an international component in their education that would make it more attractive to the labour market. Of course, the international component – be it a course of an international nature or a specialization in an area of the national law of another country – should not be introduced in the curriculum at the expense of specific national components that are essential for acquiring the national qualification and/or for legal practice in the home country, but rather as an acceptable – even appreciated – alternative to the basic courses of an international nature or to the specializations left to the choice of students in the home curriculum.

It should be clear, therefore, that a period of studies abroad is no threat for the home curriculum if the required (basic/core) courses are clearly identified and some flexibility is used in determining the percentage of the whole study programme that is open to an international contribution. It is up to academic advisers to decide for how long their students can study abroad on the basis of this preliminary evaluation; and it is up to them to make the final decision on what are the most appropriate courses to be taken. At the same time, however, they have the obligation to design for each outgoing student a programme of study abroad which is equivalent in terms of workload to the programme s/he would have done at home, even though the course content is not the same. For those institutions implementing the ECTS system this means that 30 credits should be transferred back after a semester of study abroad and 60 credits should be gained in a year.

Although the ultimate decision on the programme of study rests with the academic adviser, it is to be hoped that students' interests and aspirations will be taken into account before the decision is made so that it can be agreed upon with them. In fact, agreement on the programme of study to be recognized is the second principle recognition is based on: such agreement should be reached between the student and his/her home institution before the student goes abroad and be honoured when s/he returns having completed the work assigned. In fact, ECTS recommends that a Learning Agreement be signed both by the academic adviser and the student before departure as a formal guarantee that there is no academic risk involved in the experience. If this is not done and decisions concerning recognition are postponed until the students come back, they will live through their period of study abroad with a feeling of uncertainty that might undermine their performance and would certainly make their experience less pleasant. Some students may even think they cannot accept the risk and withdraw from the programme.

It is my impression that, also because of the spreading of ECTS, a less restrictive, more flexible approach to recognition is gaining momentum in law faculties. Greater awareness of the international implications of the legal profession are making national curricula more open to integration with courses offered in other countries. Good quality information has offered a clear picture of educational supply in other European institutions. Years of cooperation with well-known partners have consolidated exchange patterns. And the positive response of the labour market to students with an international background has strengthened institutional motivation to support student mobility. It seems we are moving in the right direction, towards the third – more flexible – interpretation of academic recognition, even though some areas of resistance still remain.

It should be pointed out that, apart from the advantages for individual students, international student exchanges have also had positive effects on the institutions involved in the activity: they have benefited from having a certain number of students with an experience of study abroad, who have often started Erasmus students associations or similar groups with an international orientation. Or from having a small community of international students which, although scattered in various study programmes, tends to stick together and to present itself as a positive example of communication and understanding among people coming from diverse cultures. We should not underestimate the high symbolic value of this presence in institutions, especially when the general context is not international in nature and a small percentage of students can actually have the opportunity to study abroad.

It should also be mentioned that at the institutional level student exchanges have contributed to the promotion of language learning. This concerns not only those students who have actually decided to apply for a period of study abroad and see the language as an essential tool for performing the task, but also those who are just taking language courses as part of their regular curriculum, because their motivation to learn is somehow sustained by real, closer examples of international communication and foreign language use. Even the courses in the national language provided to guest students make local students aware that other people are making the same effort they are making to pursue the common goal of communication and cultural integration.

4. Exchange of Teachers

It is generally agreed that the exchange of teachers is one of the key factors in the internationalization process of European institutions. A study on this theme has been recently carried out by the University of Deusto within a European network of law faculties. Responses to questionnaires and structured interviews, as well as opinions expressed in group discussions, have shown widespread awareness of the tremendous potential of teacher mobility in Europe. First, it has been recognized that the mobility of teachers can be beneficial to the teachers themselves, in that it favours their personal and professional development, improves their awareness of other academic systems and teaching styles, and encourages a more critical and innovative approach to the teaching of their own subject. Second, it seems clear that academics who have gained experience abroad can bring new insights into curriculum development and teaching/learning methods of their own institution, thus contributing to the enhancement of its quality and reputation. Third, it has been pointed out that visiting professors can be very beneficial to the students they teach, because they bring to them a different view of the subject, different teaching methods and a different language: for the non-mobile students – and they are the majority in any law department – visiting professors can be the only taste of an experience of study abroad, their only chance to practice the foreign languages they have learned.

The importance of teacher exchanges at this particular point in time was also generally recognized by the respondents in the law faculties. Due to the Bologna/Prague process most European higher education systems are presently undergoing internal change, while converging towards the main common objective of constructing a European Higher Education Area. Being one of the key players in this process, academics need to be involved both at the national and the international level in the developments that are taking place. They know they cannot leave the management of change totally in the hands of the ministries or of the central administrations of their own institutions. Out of the specific objectives that have been set for European Institutions just one – the creation of easily readable and comparable degrees – is of administrative nature, whereas all the others are of academic concern: we all know that adoption of a credit accumulation system has significant implications for curriculum design and the adoption of the two cycles can have a tremendous impact on all academic activities. The discussion of quality assurance in Europe is also touching on a very sensitive academic issue. How can national changes be discussed without awareness and first-hand experience of the international framework that is being designed? The academics who have experienced a different teaching environment have also lived through the process of communicating, reflecting, understanding and finally negotiating the fairest approach to their audience and to themselves. They accept diversity and see it as an opportunity for expansion and development. Those academics seem to be better prepared to discuss the convergence issues with their colleagues from other countries, coordinate their efforts with them and find acceptable solutions at the European and the national level.

Although the potential benefits of teacher exchanges are generally recognized, this activity has not taken off yet at European level. Not only is the number of teachers exchanged still quite low in absolute terms, but also the percentage of visits actually performed falls short of the original plans made by the institutions. This shows that, even though there is an initial interest in the project, problems arise at the implementation stage. The Deusto study identifies some major obstacles, especially to short-term exchanges of the duration of about a week. At the institutional level, there seems to be inadequate information on this scheme as well as inadequate financial/logistic support for the academics who express an interest in it. At departmental level, there are often difficulties in making the right contacts and matching the demand/supply aspects of the exchanges: it is often difficult to find the right course for a professor who wants to visit a specific institution or to get the right professor for a course that requests a teaching input from European partners. At the personal level, it seems that academics are rather reluctant to commit themselves to teaching abroad much in advance, as they know that their engagements at home might interfere with this plan. They are aware, moreover, that accepting the challenge of teaching abroad would not bring them any special recognition in terms of academic prestige or career prospects.

Measures should definitely be taken to promote teacher exchanges at the institutional, departmental and personal level. The study recommends greater commitment from institutions in terms of funding and recognition but also a reconsideration of the whole concept adopted so far. Accordingly, the activities to be undertaken by a visiting professor should be redefined in broader terms than just a number of lectures, including discussions on curricula, materials, teaching methods, etc; the people to be involved in the scheme should be carefully targeted – in terms of age group, language competence, etc. – and adequately supported at all stages of the process; contacts between departments should be made through appropriate academic channels like institutional or thematic networks. It is hoped that institutions will take these suggestions into consideration and will play a more active role in promoting teacher exchanges in the future.

5. Conclusions

Through the exchanges of information, students and teachers carried out within EU-supported programmes, common principles and procedures have been developed that can be used in all international exchanges of European institutions. The principles of transparency, flexibility and agreement are now generally accepted as the foundations of any academic cooperation involving European institutions. It is our responsibility to implement these principles properly in our own national and institutional contexts by devising appropriate procedures for the solution of internal problems. In this way we shall contribute to developing a common "exchange culture" that can become one of the distinctive features of the European Higher Education Area.

Chapter 6

Culture and the European Union

*Lorna Woods**

Introduction

Culture was seen in the early days of the Community as lying within the exclusive competence of the Member States. With the Treaty of European Union (TEU), however, an express cultural competence was introduced into the TEC, against a shifting view of the Community's role in such matters. As such, it can be viewed as one of the examples of the perceived move away from a principally economic conception of the Community which characterised the TEU and, to a certain extent, subsequent treaty amendments. It might be questioned what significance, if any, this change in emphasis might have. Does the TEU mark a sharp turning point in the evolution of the law in this area, consequent on the broadening of the Community and reflecting the introduction of European citizenship, or does it constitute a refinement of the existing policy in terms both of the level of Community involvement and in the view of culture adopted? The chapter will address these questions, although a concrete answer may be difficult to find not least because of the potential breadth of "culture" and because of the constraints of time and space.

In considering these issues, the discussion will contrast the institutions' approach to culture in two different contexts. The first is the creation of the common market, which is a core activity of the Community. The approach to culture here can be broadly characterised as a negative approach. Cultural concerns are taken into account indirectly or as an exception to the main policy objective. Such an approach can be contrasted with a more positive approach when the Community seeks to develop law and policy in this area. A number of questions arise here. One might argue that the ability to develop a positive cultural policy comes into existence only with express Community competence. Further, the introduction of such express competence might influence the scope of negative competence, reflecting the broader scheme of values the Community has recognised with successive treaty amendments. A second set of issues concerns the issue of whose culture are we concerned about: the cultures of the Member States or that of the Union itself? One hypothesis here is that in its negative approach to culture, the Community is merely seeking to manage Member State difference and its impact on the common market project whereas in

* Reader in Law, University of Essex, Solicitor.

M. van Empel (ed.), "From Paris to Nice": Fifty Years of Legal Integration in Europe, 109–129.

its positive competence it may develop a pan-European culture. This latter point, indeed, links back to the broader view of the Community (and Union) post-Maastricht – culture, identity and citizenship being concepts that influence or interrelate with one another.[1] It should be noted at this point that this paper makes no comment as to the nature of European culture nor about its use.[2]

Before we can consider these issues further, we need to identify what is meant by culture? If there were a precise answer to this question, any analysis of this area would be considerably simpler. There is, however, no common understanding of the notion, although two main categories of culture can be identified. One relates culture to great works, whether within the spheres of art, music, science or otherwise. This view of culture relates to "the domain of the intellect in its manifestations within society".[3] Some views of culture on this basis would include science and education. Although such works have a societal context, they seem to be principally about individual endeavours, possibly also reflecting values that are not local/national. Music by Bach has been included within the capsule sent into outer space to represent human values to whatever is out there. Whilst one might question whether Bach's music represents global values, it certainly has transcended the national. Is culture in this context the same as heritage? There may well be some overlap; both high culture and heritage items tend to be rare, but there is a crucial difference. Something which has importance for heritage purposes may obtain this status through longevity rather than its intrinsic quality and, in many instances, heritage is linked to a particular society. At the other end of the scale, culture can take on a more anthropological hue; it represents the idea of "how we do things". Although representations of daily life – in film, in books and in art – could be considered high culture, the anthropological view of culture goes beyond representations of society to encompass the values of society.[4] In this context, culture is a very broad notion linked to the group and to particular societies, with no necessary longevity or quality. Heritage items may be items from day-to-day culture that have survived perhaps creating a link between the two categories of culture identified.

So what approach might the EU take to culture? Even though cultural competence has now been made express within the TEC,[5] there is no Community definition of culture. There is no generally understood legal version of culture either: examples

---

[1] M. Ross, "Cultural Protection: A Matter of Union Citizenship or Human Rights?" in *The European Union and Human Rights* (Martinus Nijhoff, 1995).

[2] Some of the difficulties in this area are outlined in, e.g. C. Belot and A. Smith, "Europe and Identity: A challenge for the Social Sciences" in U. Hedetoft (ed.) *Political Symbols, Symbolic Politics* (Ashgate, 1998).

[3] Oppermann *Kulturverwaltungsrecht*, p. 8 cited by M. Niedobitek, *The Cultural Dimension in EC Law* (Kluwer Law International, 1997).

[4] Although we might equate culture in this context to intangible matters, some intangible might also be considered highbrow, e.g. ballet. Both aspects can be considered cultural: UNESCO recognises intangible cultural concerns (e.g. folk dances) as well as tangible products.

[5] Originally introduced by the TEU as Article 128, it was amended and renumbered as Article 151 EC by ToA.

can be found for a high culture/heritage based view[6] or for a more anthropological view, e.g. through the protection of minorities.[7] The scope and development of culture within the EC thus comes down to the institutions' views and particularly that of the ECJ, as final arbiter of Community law.

A Cultural Policy by Exception?

Culture, in its different guises, can intersect with the EC and its policies in a number of ways. It can do so through the free movement of cultural goods, services and persons involved in the cultural sector or through the operation of competition rules. As a corollary, cultural arguments can be put forward to justify derogation from the operation of the four freedoms or from competition or state aid rules. Finally, it can be seen within positive Community action, either as part of harmonising measures or as more general flanking policy issues. Given the many ways cultural issues could arise, this chapter cannot pretend to give a detailed analysis of all potentially relevant areas. Instead, it will concentrate on areas where the potential for cultural concerns is clear; e.g. books, the audiovisual industries and languages. Even within these limited fields it is not the intention to provide a complete discussion of the various areas' development but rather to emphasise particular elements of the law.

How then does culture arise in the context of the former economic Community? Quite simply, the ECJ has determined that cultural goods and services fall within the Treaty. The argument was put before the ECJ in *Italian Art Treasures* Case[8] that cultural items should not be viewed as goods for the purpose of the TEC. This argument the Court rejected, setting down a definition of goods which paid no attention to cultural considerations, instead focusing on commercial considerations.[9] This emphasis we can see repeated in other areas, e.g. television. In *Sacchi*,[10] questions regarding the operation of a monopoly broadcaster arose. The ECJ did not consider in any great depth the arguments put forward concerning television's generally accepted societal function before it turned to apply Community competition policy. A similarly "blind" approach can be seen in *Steinhauser* v. *City of Biaritz*, which concerned terms for the renting of artists' studios and which was dealt with under the freedom of establishment.[11] Within the field of competition rules, an opera

---

[6] Convention on the Protection of Underwater Cultural Heritage, 2 November 2001; *Unidroit Convention on Stolen or Illegally Exported Cultural Objects*, 24 June 1995; Convention Concerning of the World Cultural and Natural Heritage, 16 November 1972.

[7] Convention on Indigenous and Tribal People, 27 June 1989; see reasoning of the European Court of Human Rights in, e.g. *Cyprus* v. *Turkey*, ECHR, judgment 10 May 2001 and in *Chapman* v. *UK*, ECHR, judgment 18 January 2001.

[8] Case 7/68 *Commission* v. *Italy* [1968] ECR 428.

[9] "... products which can be valued in money and which are capable, as such, of forming the subject matter of commercial transactions". This approach was re-iterated in Case 18/71 *Eunomia di Porro* [1971] ECR 811 and Case 48/71 *Commission* v. *Italy* [1972] ECR 529.

[10] Case 155/78 *Sacchi* [1974] ECR 409.

[11] Case 197/84 *Steinhauser* v. *City of Biarritz* [1985] ECR 1819.

singer was found to constitute an "undertaking".[12] This approach would seem not to be the operation of a Community cultural policy but almost the negation of such a policy, as cultural goods, services and actors are seen through an economic lens and their cultural context ignored.

We might argue that such an approach is necessary to avoid the ECJ having to make difficult distinctions between what is properly considered cultural and what, not. This can be no easy matter given that we have not even identified one definition of culture. Further, given the value of some cultural goods and services, this desire to include those whose livelihoods are in this area is unsurprising, especially against the background of a less developed European Community. Nonetheless, the value of cultural artefacts or performances now falls to be judged by EC standards. The wide scope of application of EC law and the inclusion of cultural items makes the scope of any derogation very significant. It functions to balance not only the competing claims to competence but also competing policy objectives. This means that the ECJ is in the position to determine the hierarchy of the competing values within the Community legal order; the concern is that the value of such competing policy objectives will be judged by reference to an economic scale. Derogation is about the space left to Member States. The question is, how big is this space?

Given the importance of the derogation, it may seem surprising that there was little overt mention of "culture" in the original version of TEC. The possible exception to this statement can be found in Article 30 (ex-36), which deals with exceptions to the prohibition on quantitative restrictions on imports and exports and measures having equivalent effect.[13] There, we see a reference to "the protection of national treasures possessing artistic, historic or archaeological value". This provision seems to be aimed at ensuring that Member States can, in isolated cases, take action to prevent important works leaving that particular Member State. There have been no cases on this provision, probably because there is secondary legislation in the area.[14] A couple of points should, however, be noted. The provision is tightly focussed: it is not aimed at stimulating new works but preserving the status quo and, on this basis, it is re-emphasising the difference between the Member States. Each Member State is permitted to reserve works for that state alone, and the exception to free movement would seem to be based on individual Member States and their individual histories. One might ask, what about the regional or even the pan-European? Further, although there are textual differences between the various language versions, which might raise questions as to the precise importance of the artefacts to be protected,[15] this element of Article 30 concerns a highbrow or heritage based view of culture and one, unsurprisingly in the context, that is focussed on goods rather than intangible cultural items. Scientific achievement, save as it constitutes historic artefacts, would seem also to be excluded from this view of culture. Presumably it is for the Member

---

12 Commission Decision 78/516 *RAI/UNITEL*, Decision of 26 May 1978, OJ [1978] L 157/39.

13 Articles 28 and 29 EC, respectively.

14 Directive 93/7/EEC on the return of objects unlawfully removed OJ [1993] L 74/74.

15 The English and French versions refer to "national treasures" whereas the other language versions refer to "artistic heritage".

States to decide individually, at least in the first instance, what falls within the scope of this exception although the significance of the work and its significance to that state would have to be demonstrated.

The other express ground of derogation found within the original version of the Treaty of relevance here is the reference to "commercial and industrial property". This term the ECJ has interpreted as including copyright. Copyright has clear links with artistic works, however, whether the way the ECJ has sought to reconcile the exercise of such rights (usually by private actors) with the needs of the internal market can be considered to constitute cultural policy is far from clear. The emphasis within the EU is more on ensuring free movement and ensuring individuals are recompensed for work rather than directly for any particular cultural purpose. Certainly, the emphasis in the judgments relating to copyright is on their economic aspect rather than on their moral rights;[16] and other intellectual property rights – e.g. patents – have little to do with cultural concerns. Although the ECJ did refer to Article 151 in the more recent *Metronome Musik case*,[17] it almost immediately went on to discuss the impact of forms of piracy on authors' remuneration.[18] The priority here was economic: the production of cultural and artistic works did not appear to have a separate value. Any impact on culture might at best then be seen as being indirect.

Finally, in terms of the negative scope of culture, the position of "mandatory requirements" or issues of overriding public interest should be noted. As regards arguments that seek to rely directly on the nature of culture itself, the starting point for the case law in this area is probably *Leclerc* v. "*Au blé vert*" *et al.*[19] Although the French government had sought to raise the issue of culture in relation to national rules concerning newspapers and their distribution, the Court had not had to discuss cultural concerns expressly.[20] This case concerned the "loi lang" which imposed retail prices for books. The aim of the rule was to protect books, as cultural media, from the adverse effects of untrammelled competition and so encourage diversity and protect the cultural level of publication. This is a clear example of the negative form of cultural policy and it seems that, in its desire to prevent "dumbing down", is probably concerned with the more limited version of culture. Member States' desire to protect the cultural industries from this sort of pressure arises also in the audiovisual field and is discussed further below. In this case, the rule was challenged under both Article 28 (as it now is) and the competition provisions read in conjunction with Article 10 EC. In seeking to justify this rule, the French government relied on the *Cassis de Dijon* mandatory requirements.[21] The government was unsuccessful. The reasoning by which the Court reached its conclusion is somewhat opaque and it is

---

[16] Cases 55 & 57/80 *Musik Vertrieb membran GmbH and K-Tel International* v. *GEMA* [1981] ECR 147, [1981] 2 CMLR 44.

[17] Case C-200/96 *Metronome Musik GmbH* v. *Musik Point Hokamp GmbH* [1998] ECR I-1953, para. 23.

[18] *Ibid.*, para. 24.

[19] Case 229/83 [1985] ECR 1.

[20] Case 269/83 *Commission* v. *France* [1985] ECR I-837, at p. 838.

[21] Case 120/78 *Rewe* v. *Bundesmonopolverwaltung für Branntwein* [1979] ECR 649.

therefore not entirely clear why the French Government's arguments were not accepted. One possible interpretation was that the rule was perceived as having discriminatory effects thereby excluding reliance on mandatory requirements.[22] This view is supported by the later case, *Cognet*, concerning the amended French rules which did not tie imported books to the French price and were therefore indistinctly applicable.[23] The rules in this case were held to be compatible with Article 28. Alternatively, the ECJ has always viewed price fixing as problematic, and has generally not accepted arguments based on mandatory requirements in respect of such rules.[24] *Leclerc*, and even *Cognet*, left the position of cultural policy as a ground of justification unclear: the question was at best left open; it was certainly not welcomed.

Further, albeit limited, clarification of the position came with the ECJ's response to similar arguments in respect of other cultural goods, videos, in *Cinéthèque*.[25] The rules in issue concerned the prohibition of the sale of videos within a certain time of the relevant film's cinema release. The argument was that the rule was to protect the film industry and thereby culture. In this case, the ECJ accepted the argument, although the precise scope of its ruling was, again, unclear. Two possible interpretations arise: that the ECJ accepted culture in general (or cultural policy); or a more narrow view which limited its ruling to the facts of the case, i.e. the film specific interest identified in the case. Thus, although in principle the Court here seems to have accepted some form of culture as a mandatory requirement, *Cinéthèque* cannot be seen as evidence of unhesitating support for Member States' cultural policies, especially those policies that seek to protect an anthropological view of culture.

The audiovisual sector, this time the television industry, has also given rise to some cases in which the importance of culture was considered. Although the fact that the television sector, despite its undoubted influence in cultural, political and scientific fields,[26] would be subject to the rule rigour of Community rules had long been established,[27] the scope of any exception based on cultural considerations was not really elaborated until the "*Mediawet*" cases.[28] These cases consist of a preliminary reference and an action by the Commission but both actions concerned the same

---

[22] In fact the ECJ viewed the rule as being both discriminatory and indistinctly applicable; it is presumed that once a rule has discriminatory effects, the indistinctly applicable element cannot be severed – see Kuyper's note on this case (1985) *Common Market Law Review* 801.

[23] Case 355/85 *Cognet* [1986] ECR 3231.

[24] See e.g. Case 231/83 *Cullet* v. *Centre Leclerc* [1985] ECR 305, [1985] 2 CMLR 524.

[25] Cases 60 and 61/84 *Cinéthèque SA* v. *Fédération nationale des cinémas françaises* [1985] ECR 2605, [1986] 1 CMLR 365.

[26] These values have been accepted by the Community institutions; indeed the Commission has also seen the broadcast media as having a role to play in the formation of identity: The Digital Age: European Audio-visual Policy. A Report from the High Level Group on Audio-visual Policy. URL: *Http://europa.eu.int/comm/dg10/avpolicy/key_doc/hlg1_en.html*. See also the European Parliament Resolution on the Role of the Media: OJ [1985] C-288/113.

[27] Case 155/78 *Sacchi, supra* n. 10; see also Case 352/85 *Bond van Adverteerders* [1988] ECR 2085; Case 52/79 *Debauve* [1980] ECR 833.

[28] Case C-288/89 *Stichting Collective Antennevoorziening Gouda* v. *Commissariat voor de media* [1991] ECR I-4007; Case C-353/89 *Commission* v. *Netherlands* (Mediawet) [1991] ECR I-4069.

national rules. The Dutch rules at issue granted to one body alone the right to sell advertising time on television and limited the broadcast of advertising on private channels. The reasoning behind this rule was to allow the profits from advertising to be distributed amongst the Dutch media (including the press), so as to free the media from some of the constraints of commercial considerations and thus encourage the reflection of the views of the various cultural, philosophical and social sections of Dutch society. Although this might seem on the face of it to be a broad, anthropological view of culture, the ECJ's reasoning opens up a number of questions about the values that the Court accepted needed protection. Is the Court concerned with culture *per se* or with cultural diversity? Further, if we are talking about cultural diversity, is this code for a wide range of "quality" programmes, or are we just concerned with seeing different views represented? In short, could we argue that cultural diversity here is an attempt to open Member States' audiovisual markets up to non-national products, arguably serving internal market ends? Although this latter point might seem to import to the ECJ some Machiavellian motives, the reasoning in the *Mediawet* judgments is ambiguous. On the one hand, we can see a specific reference to the "cultural tasks" of the system – such as managing a sound library, keeping film archives and managing orchestras and choirs.[29] Further, the ECJ did seem to accept that the maintenance of programme quality itself could be an object of cultural policy. On the other hand, the ECJ referred specifically to Article 10 ECHR, almost turning the issue into a question of freedom of expression and of equality of access.[30] Moreover, it seems that the ECJ did not accept that culture is linked to a particular state: broadcasters cannot be under an obligation to have "all or some of their programmes produced by a Dutch undertaking".[31] The matter has not been clarified by subsequent rulings: in *Commission* v. *Belgium* – another television case – the ECJ seemed to accept that diversity and culture were separate issues, however, without clarifying what culture itself meant.[32]

Although the *Mediawet*[33] judgments accepted the principle of cultural diversity, in the final analysis the Dutch rules were felt to be too far reaching. The same sort of reasoning can be seen in the *Tourist Guide cases*:[34] the ECJ accepted that the

---

[29] Case C-353/89 *Commission* v. *Netherlands* (Mediawet), *supra* n. 28, at para. 29.

[30] On the issue of the link between freedom of expression and culture see arguments about the application of Article 81 in Case 243/83 *Binon* [1985] ECR 2015.

[31] Case C-353/89 *Commission* v. *Netherlands* (Mediawet), *supra* n. 28, at para. 31. Note, however, the European programme quotas are permissible under the Television without Frontiers Directive, Council Directive (89/552/EEC) of 3rd October 1989 on the coordination of certain provisions laid down by law, regulation or administrative action in Member States concerning the pursuit of Broadcasting Activities as amended in 1997 by Directive 97/36/EC of the European Parliament and of the Council of 30th June 1997, and, in many Member States, in practice this turns into a national requirement.

[32] Case C-11/95 *Commission* v. *Belgium* [1996] ECR I-4115.

[33] Case C-353/89 *Commission* v. *Netherlands* (Mediawet), *supra* n. 28.

[34] Case C-198/89 *Commission* v. *Greece* [1991] ECR I-727. Similar concerns arose in Case C-180/89 *Commission* v. *Italy* (Tour Guides) [1991] ECR I-709. The Court at para. 19 accepted the cultural exception as arising thus: "The interest in conservation of the national historical and artistic heritage is safeguarded by the tourist guide, who constitutes an intermediary between the visitor and the cultural asset. In the specific case of an organized tour by a group of foreign tourists, the protection of that

proper appreciation of a country's heritage as being a principle worthy of protection. Indeed, when discussing high culture, the ECJ seems to accept a broad notion of what might fall within its terms. For example, in this case the rule related not to the protection of historic monuments themselves, but to tour guides who would tell tourists about those monuments. The ECJ then continued to discount the national rules in practice. It argued that:

> ... the requirement in question contained in the Greek legislation goes beyond what is necessary to ensure the safeguarding of that interest inasmuch as it makes the activities of a tourist guide accompanying groups of tourists from another Member State subject to the possession of a licence ...
>
> It follows that in view of the scale of the restrictions it imposes, the legislation in issue is disproportionate in relation to the objective pursued...

One might suggest that what the Court gives with one hand, it is taking away with the other, using the proportionality test to limit the scope of any derogation from treaty freedoms.

Concerns about maintaining quality and diversity have also arisen regarding the operation of competition and state aid rules in relation to both books and the audiovisual sector. The cases can be divided into two categories: those where the competition rules apply in their normal context – that is concerning the actions of private parties; and those in which governmental action is involved (including the state aid rules). Looking at the first type of situation, a number of publishers and booksellers decided to enter agreements regulating the price of books so as to ensure the availability of a wide range of books. The Dutch books agreement[35] and the net book agreement relating to the United Kingdom and Ireland[36] are two examples of such agreements to which the Commission took exception. The Dutch agreement was entered into by Dutch and Flemish booksellers and publishers and it established a system of collective exclusive dealing and resale price maintenance. The Commission concluded the agreement fell within the prohibition on anti-competitive agreements in Article 81(1). As with many of the free movement cases the issue then turned on the scope of the exemption, here contained in Article 81(3) EC.

---

interest is important inasmuch as, regard being had to their different cultural origins and the limited duration of such visits, the tourists retain only such image and knowledge of the cultural asset as may be conveyed to them by the tourist guide." Museums and the qualifications required for those who work in them occurred again in the case of Case C-234/97 *Fernández de Bobadilla* [1999] ECR I-4773. The Advocate General commented that "[I]n determining the level of education and expertise appropriate, the Spanish authorities are entitled to be influenced by the richness of the artistic heritage of which the Prado is custodian." This argument is not, however, based on respect for Spanish culture itself. The ECJ in its judgment did not pick up the point.

[35] Commission Decision 82/123, Commission Decision of 25 November 1981, OJ [1982] L 54/36; Joined Cases 43 and 63/82 *VBVB and VBBB* v. *Commission* [1984] ECR 19.

[36] Commission Decision 89/44 *Publishers Association – Net Book Agreements*, Decision of 12 December 1988, IV 27.393 and IV 27.394 OJ [1989] L 22/12; Case C-360/92P *Publishers Association* v. *Commission of the European Communities* [1995] ECR I-23.

The justification put forward was based on the need to ensure diversity and, again, implicitly at protecting publishers and therefore authors from the pressure to "dumb down". This latter point seems linked rather to the protection and stimulation of high culture products rather than mass culture. The Commission accepted the arguments in principle; the problem lay in whether the restrictions were necessary. In rejecting the Dutch publishers' arguments, the Commission emphasised the fact that prices were increased overall to the benefit of a small group of readers. The Commission's decision was upheld on appeal.

In the Commission's reasoning we can find two main points of note relevant here. The first is the parallel approach between derogation from the four freedoms and the exemption from Article 81. In both instances, the institutions may be happy to accept a principle as being worthy of protection but the difficulty arises in showing that the particular restrictions are indispensable (or proportionate). In the *Net Book Agreement case*, the publishers on appeal to the ECJ argued that the Commission would state that a rule was not indispensable without really being put to proof about the availability of a (legal) similarly effective alternative. Further, in the Dutch case, the ECJ and the Commission implicitly made a judgment about the relative value of benefits to be passed on to consumers, seeing the increase in price as crucial. Cost would seem to be a more important consideration than variety and, arguably, quality.

Similar issues arose in relation to the UK net book agreement,[37] although this agreement was not so restrictive as the Dutch agreement. The Commission sought to rely on its approach in the *Dutch Books case*[38] and, again, ended up before the ECJ, via the CFI. Despite the advice of the Advocate General, the ECJ in this case allowed the appeal. This judgment should not be seen as evidence of a significant change in the institutions' approach to culture or cultural diversity. The ECJ's concern in this case related to the fact that the Commission had seemingly tried to turn its argument in the *Dutch Books case* into a general proposition about the effects of such agreements and whether such agreements are capable of exemption under Article 81(3). An assessment should have been made on the facts of the case. According to the ECJ, the Commission in particular failed to take into account the benefits of the agreement in the Irish market. Although the publishers won their case, they subsequently abandoned the net book agreement: the long-term effects of this have yet to be assessed.

Subsequent agreements regarding net book prices have been cleared by the Commission,[39] but this has more to do with a lack of effect on intra Community trade than a greater emphasis being given to non-price concerns under Article 81(3). The Council has since agreed a Resolution on book price fixing emphasising the dual character of books as the bearers of cultural values and as merchandise as well as the

---

[37] Case C-360/92P *Publishers Association* v. *Commission of the European Communities, ibid.*

[38] Joined Cases 43 and 63/82 *VBVB and VBBB* v. *Commission, supra* n. 35.

[39] Press Release IP/00/651.

Commission's obligation

> when applying competition rules and rules on the free movement of goods, to take account of the specific value of the book as a cultural object and the importance of books in promoting cultural diversity, and of the cross-border dimension of the book market.[40]

Given that the Council has made similar resolutions in the past, it remains to be seen what impact this Resolution will have on the Commission's approach.

State aid is another area in which cultural concerns have been raised. Aid to the film industry is regularly accepted by the Commission as falling within the scope of culture, and the Council has described the industry as constituting a cultural industry par excellence',[41] as is aid to the book industry.[42] Since TEU, a specific cultural exception has been permitted, although aid to both film and book industries had been granted prior to that treaty and found to fall within the then existing exceptions to the state aid rules. Article 87(3)(d) EC now provides that aid to promote culture and heritage conservation may be compatible with the common market. The terms of this provision have parallels with the approach in Article 30, focussing on high culture and heritage. One might, however, question what is held to constitute culture for the purposes of state aid. In the *BBC News 24* case,[43] the United Kingdom did not argue that the cultural exception was relevant in the context of the provision of a 24-hour news channel, a point which the Commission noted. In the Commission's view the exception could not in any event have been used, as BBC News 24 dealt with information rather than cultural needs.[44] This approach, however, is certainly open to criticism on the basis that it is not possible to make such a clear distinction between news, information and culture, and arguably this is a distinction the ECJ has not yet accepted.[45] Even accepting the distinction, where does the boundary between information and culture lie? The difficulty is compounded by the Commission's own lack of clarity in this area: in a decision relating to the Swedish aid to its film production and film related activities, the Commission took the view that "quality short and feature films, documentaries and school cinema" fell within the cultural exception.[46] Although films can be seen as cultural, are not documentaries informational?

---

[40] Council resolution of 12 February 2001 on the application of national fixed book-price systems, OJ [2001] C 073/5.

[41] Council resolution of 12 February 2001 national aid to the film and audiovisual industries *Official Journal* [2001] C 073/3, para. 10(a).

[42] Case T-155/98 *SIDE* v. *Commission*, judgment 28 February 2002.

[43] *State Aid No 88/98 – United Kingdom*, Commission Decision 14 December 1999.

[44] *Ibid.*, para. 36.

[45] In the Hahn Report, the European Parliament noted "European unification will only be achieved if Europeans want it. Europeans will only want it if there is such a thing as a European identity. A European identity will only develop if Europeans are adequately informed." Report on radio and television broadcasting in the European Community' EP Doc. 1-1013/81 of 23 February 1982, p. 8.

[46] European Commission (2000) *Bull EU* 1/2, pt 1.3.90.

Article 86(2) operates to protect providers of certain public services from the full operation of competition rules.[47] It seems accepted by both the Commission and the Court that public service broadcasters in fulfilling their public service broadcasting remit may fall within the scope of this provision, potentially justifying licence fees and other advantages that they may have been granted. Article 86(2) is not a cultural exception save in so far as public service broadcasting is perceived as fulfilling a cultural function; it can also be used in respect of other public interest services.[48] It also gets us no further in determining what might be meant by culture. The Commission when considering this point originally seemed minded to take a limited view of the type of broadcasting that might be provided within the terms of this provision; for example light entertainment was thought at one stage to be excluded. More recently, perhaps in the light of the Protocol on Public Service Broadcasting annexed to the ToA, the Commission has adopted a more "hands off" approach. In its recent guidelines[49] on the subject, the Commission has left it to the Member States each to define public service broadcasting within the context of their respective territories. This approach clearly allows more space for Member States to fund broadcasters as they see fit, and potentially allows a broader notion of cultural, and other, values to be protected. This approach in relation to state aid does not affect the application of the free movement rules, so Member States' audiovisual markets still cannot be cordoned off.

So far the exemptions we have considered have been mainly addressed towards heritage and higher cultural concerns. Are there any provisions which might specifically protect a lower view of culture? Returning to Article 30, public morality can also been seen as having a connection with anthropological culture, as the scope of this particular exception will reflect the values of each particular Member State, a point noted recently by Advocate General Jacobs in the *Biotechnological Inventions* case.[50] Unlike the rules relating to national treasures and industrial and commercial policy, this exception finds a reflection in the express treaty derogation relating to services, establishment and workers and a similar view can be discerned in the case law on services.[51] From early case law,[52] the ECJ has held that the question of the scope of public morality must be for the individual Member State. Although it will ensure that Member States are not seeking to impose different standards on imports than on domestic products (or services), the ECJ has not involved itself too much in

---

47 The relationship between Article 86(2) and the free movement rules is far from clear, as the Danish waste case illustrates: Case C-209/98 *Entreprenørforeningens Affald/Miljøsektion (FFAD)* v. *Københavens Kommune* [2000] ECR I-3743, [2001] 2 CMLR 938.

48 Referred to in Article 86(2) as services of general economic interest.

49 Commission Communication on the application of State aid rules to public service broadcasting OJ [2001] C 320/1.

50 Case C-377/98 *Netherlands* v. *European Parliament and the Council of the European Union* [2001] ECR I-7079, Opinion, para. 99.

51 Case C-275/92 *HM Customs and Excise* v. *Gerhart Schindler and Jorg Schindler* [1994] ECR I-1039.

52 Case 34/79 *R* v. *Henn and Darby* [1979] ECR 3795; Case 121/85 *Conegate Ltd* v. *Commissioners of Customs and Excise* [1986] ECR 1007.

the question of whether there is a legitimate question of public morality in the first place.[53] Clearly, here, we see the individuality of Member States being allowed room as an exception to Community policy, the difficulty being, as ever, the application of the proportionality/necessity test.

One other area linked to the anthropological end of the cultural scale recognised within the treaties is that of language. The importance of language to communities is implicitly recognised by the fact that the official languages of the Member States are all official languages of the Communities (and now the Union). Minority languages do not receive this level of recognition, although the Community has taken some action to protect them.[54] The importance of language in the context of culture (and identity) has also been recognised by the ECJ, most famously in the *Groener* case.[55] The case concerned Irish rules which required teachers to be able to speak Irish, although the language of instruction would be English. The ECJ in this case noted that Irish was, constitutionally, the first language in Ireland and then argued:

> although Irish is not spoken by the whole population, the policy followed for many years has been designed not only to maintain but also promote the use of Irish as a means of expressing national identity and culture.[56]

Although the rule was permissible, the ECJ commented on the proportionality of the measures to implement it. Although language requirements might be acceptable, it would not be proportionate to require the Irish language tests or teaching to take place in Ireland.

The ruling was criticised at the time, not least because it seems to go against the express wording of Article 3 Regulation 1612/68. This provision provided that restrictions could be imposed on non-native speakers where language was necessary for them to carry out their job; it clearly was not necessary for that purpose here. This point emphasises the value that the ECJ has placed on the cultural argument in *Groener*.[57] It would seem, however, that *Groener* was a one off case, dependant on particular history. In passing, it should be noted that the usual contrast made between *Groener* and the "language teachers" cases is not relevant here. In those cases the ability of the language speakers related to their own language, not that of the host Member State; the cultural question as regards derogation from free movement does not therefore arise.

---

[53] Arguably, an exception to this point is the ruling in Case C-1/96 *R* v. *Minister for Agriculture, Fisheries and Food, ex parte Compassion in World Farming Ltd* [1998] ECR I-1251, in which the ECJ ruled that the welfare of animals could not constitute public policy as it was dealt with under health grounds.

[54] The European Parliament has made numerous resolutions on this subject. In more concrete terms, we can find a number of "soft law" provisions regarding linguistic minorities, e.g. the establishment of the European Bureau of Lesser Used Languages; and the MERCATOR network.

[55] Case 378/87 *Groener* v. *Minister for Education* [1989] ECR 3987.

[56] *Ibid.*, para. 18.

[57] Case 378/87 *Groener* v. *Minister for Education, supra* n. 55.

Language and cultural identity have arisen more recently.[58] In *Bickel and Franz*,[59] the rules in question were Italian rules which gave the German language the same status as Italian in relations between citizens and the public administration and the court system in a province of Italy in which there is a strong German speaking minority. Bickel, an Austrian, who was on holiday in the area sought to rely on these rules when he was charged with drunk driving and possession of a knife. When the matter was referred to the ECJ, the Italian Government argued that the rules only applied to the citizens of the province in question as the aim of the rule was, in the terms of the statute itself, to "recognise the ethnic and cultural identity" of individuals belonging to the protected minority. Although the ECJ agreed that protecting a minority could constitute a legitimate aim,[60] the ECJ relied on its pre-Maastricht jurisprudence[61] to hold that a rule which operated, as this did, on the basis of residency constituted discrimination contrary to Article 12 EC.[62] Although the case may give rise to a number of questions concerning its precise scope and ramifications, this ruling is unsurprising. Leaving the Italian rule intact would have deprived an individual of an advantage which would not have adversely affected the minority the rule sought to protect. Given the focus in *Groener*[63] on the national importance of the Irish rule, *Bickel and Franz* is a significant development as it accepts culture and identity as worthy of protection in particular in connection with minorities. Nonetheless, although the ECJ accepted the principle, in practice it still found a problem with the national rules themselves. Again it could be argued that the ECJ takes a broad approach to the scope of the heads of derogation but counters that by taking a restrictive approach to the assessment of the proportionality of the measure.

The gap between principle and the assessment of the national rule's proportionality can also be seen in the jurisprudence relating to language requirements on product labels. Initially, this was seen not as a cultural issue but as a matter relating to consumer protection, and the ECJ has interpreted the relevant provisions of the labelling directive narrowly. Although not required by a black letter interpretation of the directive itself, the ECJ looked to the directive's purpose to conclude that a national rule requiring that labelling be exclusively in the language of the region in which the product was to be sold was contrary to the terms of the directive and of Article 28.[64] In a subsequent post-Maastricht case, *Peeters II*,[65] it further held that a Member State could not specify that the language most commonly spoken in an area be used in labelling, even if that Member State did not preclude the possibility

---

[58] The following cases were decided after the ToA had been agreed but before it came into force.

[59] Case C-274/96 *Bickel and Franz* [1998] ECR I-7637.

[60] *Ibid.*, para. 29.

[61] Case 137/84 *Mutsch* [1985] ECR 2681.

[62] For further difficulties arising from this area of Italy, see Case C-281/98 *Angonese* v. *Cassa di Rispamio di Bolzano SpA* [2000] ECR I-4139.

[63] Case 378/87 *Groener* v. *Minister for Education, supra* n. 55.

[64] Case C-369/89 *Piageme* v. *Peeters* [1991] ECR I-2971, the same approach has recently been taken in Case C-366/98 *Yannick Geffroy* v. *Casino France SNC* [2000] ECR I-6579.

[65] Case C-85/94 *Piageme* v. *Peeters* [1995] ECR I-2955.

of other languages additionally being used on the label. It was only in *Goerres*[66] where the Member State got it right: there the national rules that a specific language for use on labels may be identified where producers *alternatively* may use a language easily understood by purchasers. This line of case law does seem to prioritise the concerns of the ECJ not to burden producers with extra labelling costs at the expense of consumers being able easily to understand the information on the label. What is particularly interesting from the perspective of a cultural analysis is that in the second *Peeters* case, the Belgian government sought to argue that Member States were free to impose higher standards than those laid down in the directive in the light of the introduction of the specific consumer protection and cultural competence. This argument the ECJ rejected.

Culture and the anthropological version of culture intersect in areas other than language requirements. We could argue that measures that protect the traditional way of doing things, e.g. the brewing of beer or baking of bread, are also cultural. They have, however, tended to be discussed by the Court, somewhat unsympathetically,[67] in the context of consumer protection or public health. The ECJ has seemed to want to break down what it sees as consumer prejudices in all areas of trade.[68] A recent example is the case of *Gourmet Products International*.[69] That case concerned the Swedish rules limiting the advertising of alcohol. The ECJ recognised the link between the product on the one hand and tradition and culture on the other, but seemed more interested in removing barriers to trade by obliterating those links between individuals and the individual Member State. Are we seeing the beginning of a distinction in the level of freedom allowed to Member States to protect culture when we are considering (very) low culture rather than high culture?

A Community Cultural Policy?

The final element we need to consider is the possibility of Community taking action in the cultural sphere. As already noted, the EC Treaty did not originally contain express cultural competence, although it took action in the internal market in the area of cultural industries. The early General Programme and on the abolition on restrictions on freedom of establishment[70] and the freedom to provide services included the film industry as "recreation services" and a number of directives were enacted in

---

[66] Case C-385/96 *Goerres* [1998] ECR I-3341.

[67] See, e.g. S. Weatherill, "Recent case law concerning the Free Movement of Goods: Mapping the Frontiers of Market Deregulation" (1999) 36 *Common Market Law Review* 51 on the ECJ's approach to consumer protection measures.

[68] See, e.g. Case 207/83 *Commission* v. *United Kingdom* (Origin Marking) [1985] ECR 201, [1985] 2 CMLR 259; Case 407/85 *Drei Glocken GmbH* v. *USL Centro-Sud & Provincia Autonoma di Bolzano* [1988] ECR 4233 but note the comments of the Advocate General in this case.

[69] Case C-405/98 *Konsumentombudsmannen* v. *Gourmet International Products AB* [2001] ECR I-1795, [2001] 2 CMLR 672.

[70] No. 36/62 OJ [1962] p. 7, Sp Edn (Second Series) IX, p. 7.

this area.[71] The thrust of these endeavours was, however, part of the overarching aim of ensuring free movement. Similarly, despite the rhetoric, the Community's actions in the field of copyright were angled towards the need to remove barriers to trade arising from different approaches to copyright within the various Member States rather than directly to ensuring, e.g. cultural diversity.

Another example of Community legislation with mixed motives is the Television without Frontiers Directive.[72] It clearly had the aim of creating a single market in television programmes, but cross border broadcasting was also seen as an important means of "establishing an ever closer Union amongst the peoples of Europe",[73] though precisely how this might be achieved was never fully explained.[74] Whatever the values identified in the recitals, the directive aimed at minimum harmonisation and although Member States remained free to regulate their own broadcasters, a market access clause ensured that intra-EC broadcasts could not be stopped save on limited grounds.[75] Clearly these provisions serve free movement, but is this an attempt to ensure Europeans understand each other by virtue of watching each other's television programmes, or just an attempt to generate a secondary market for European television programming?[76] If so, it has sadly failed as most non-national programming seems to emanate originally from the United States.

Similar tensions can be found underlying the MEDIA programme. Again, the Commission's first action in this area pre-dated the introduction of formal cultural competence by TEU: the basis for the MEDIA proposal was in 1986 and, in 1990, turned into a full-scale project.[77] In approving the project, the assessing experts emphasised the cultural nature of the film industry, but also the economic.[78]

---

[71] See, e.g. Council Directive 65/264/EEC on specialist cinemas, import and screen quotas and dubbing of films OJ Sp Edn 1965–6, p. 62; Council Directive 68/369/EEC on the Freedom of self-employed persons to provide services in film distribution OJ Sp Edn 1986 (II), p. 520; and Council Directive 70/451 on the Freedom of self-employed persons to provide services in film production, OJ Sp Edn 1970 (II), p. 620.

[72] Council Directive 89/552/EEC, *supra* n. 31.

[73] See Recitals to the Directive, *supra* n. 31. See also Explanatory Memorandum to the Proposal for the Directive COM (86) 146 final.

[74] The cultural elements also gave rise to concerns that the Community did not have competence in this area: Wallace & Goldberg, "The EEC Directive on Television Broadcasting" (1989) 9 *Yearbook of European Law* 175.

[75] The overarching public policy concerns relate to the protection of children, and prohibition of racial or religious hatred (Article 22 and 22a), as defined by the Member States. There is no one pan-European understanding of these concepts and to the extent that any commonality exists, it seems to have been driven by the Article 10 ECHR case law and the Recommendations and Conventions of the Council of Europe.

[76] See also the quota provisions which seek to preserve European culture and European programme making industries. For difficulties with these provisions see Harrison and Woods [2001] *Entertainment Law Review* 5–14.

[77] Council Decision 90/685/EEC of 21 December 1990 concerning the implementation of an action programme to promote the development of the European audiovisual industry (MEDIA) (1991–1995) OJ [1990] L 380/37.

[78] Commission *Encouraging Europe's Media Industry – a Review of Media 92* (COM (90) 132 final).

Nonetheless, the MEDIA programme is one of the main pillars in the Community audiovisual policy to address the threat to cultural diversity in film and programme production.[79] The assessment of the programme's success tends to be based on economic factors, such as market share rather than qualitative or cultural grounds. In terms of European culture many of the films tend to be primarily from one Member State, or a co-production with the United States.

One might argue that the economic emphasis in these Community initiatives was dictated by the fact that the Community did not, at that stage, have cultural competence. This consideration, however, would appear not to have deterred the institutions in others instances, a fact which undermines such an argument. Even prior to Maastricht, there were specific references to culture and to European culture within the then EEC. The European Parliament might be seen as one of the early driving forces in this field. It passed an resolution in 1974 regarding the preservation of European cultural heritage[80] and in subsequent years adopted resolutions on various subjects, such as the creation of an European youth orchestra.[81] Council actions in this area could be characterised as cautious: as Niedobitek noted, originally the resolutions it made were made by the representative ministers acting as representatives of the Member States rather than in Council.[82] The resolutions concerned measures such as sculpture competitions and the establishment of the European City of Culture. Some of these actions, notably the resolution concerning the promotion of the translation of important works of European culture, contained no specific Treaty base. It was in 1988 that the Council itself passed two resolutions: one established a committee to work in the cultural field and its organisation;[83] the other identified the scope of its work which included the books and audiovisual sectors; training in the cultural industries and business sponsorship.[84] On the whole, these early culture specific actions can be seen as quite limited in impact, and certainly limited to highbrow and representational notions of culture; they are also based on individual Member States' culture and heritage.

The TEU, following numerous proposals to this broad effect, saw the introduction of cultural competence. This provision bears certain structural similarities with other flanking policies for which the EC gained express competence at the same time. Thus, Article 151(1) provides:

> The Community shall contribute to the flowering of the cultures of the Member States, while respecting their national and regional diversity and at the same time bringing the common cultural heritage to the fore.

---

79 R. Collins, "Unity in Diversity? The European single Market in Broadcasting and the Audio-visual, 1982–92" (1994) 32 *Journal of Common Market Studies* 89.

80 OJ [1974] C-62/5.

81 OJ [1976] C-79/8.

82 Niedobitek, *supra* n. 3.

83 OJ [1988] C-197/1.

84 OJ [1988] C-197/2.

This reflects the wording used in the list of activities of the Community set out in Article 3 EC. Article 151(2) details specific areas in which Community action is foreseen: the dissemination of culture and history of European peoples; the safeguarding of cultural heritage of European significance; non-commercial cultural exchanges; and artistic and literary creation. Article 151(4) requires the Community to

> take cultural aspects into account in its action under other provision of this Treaty, in particular in order to respect and to promote the diversity of its cultures.

Paragraph (5) provides the procedures the Community must follow in taking action under Article 151; it specifically excludes harmonising measures.

Perhaps now, in the light of the changes from Maastricht, we might seek to re-characterise the EC's policy or identify a turning point following which Member States' cultural concerns are given full weight and further, that the EC itself recognises a cultural policy that is not driven by economic concerns. The position of Article 151 is not that simple, however. The difficulties arise both from the terms in which the provision is drafted and the way in which it has been used. The first, most obvious point is that the notion of "culture" is not defined and the reference to the "flowering" of cultures is not the most easily understood legal obligation in the Treaty. Perhaps some guidance in this respect might be obtained from the terms of Article 151(2), which gives us some sort of idea of the provision's scope, although this is clearly a non-exhaustive list of activities. On this basis, the provision is taking a narrow view of culture and the institutions' activities in the cultural field reflect this: the actions the Commission has undertaken reflect what might be termed the unequivocal scope of the provision: heritage; artistic activities and books and reading. These tend to be based on the existing Member States' frameworks and emphasise diversity.[85] The advantage of the breadth of the Community action, however, has the potential to develop rather than viewing culture only a historic matter. We might not have a European culture now, but might we in the future?

There seems also to be an internal tension: the provision requires respect for both the commonalities between the Member States and for their differences, and it requires such respect to occur simultaneously. While no doubt such a balance is not impossible, it might be difficult to achieve in practice. One might argue that the steps the Commission have taken do, in fact, respect both aspects of culture. By ensuring that information about each Member States' heritage and culture is disseminated through other Member States, so facilitating mutual tolerance and thereby facilitating the creation or strengthening of a more cohesive Union. The effect of such policies is difficult to measure a fact which is compounded by the fact that the effectiveness of cultural understanding in such an endeavour is by no means proven. Such an approach, however, does have the advantage of balancing fears the individual Member States' identity will be submerged under a homogenous Euro-culture, a point re-emphasised by the changes to Article 151 made by the Treaty of Amsterdam.

---

[85] Even the Council Resolution on Architectural Quality in Urban and Rural Environment OJ [2001] C73/6 refers to the importance of "urban diversity".

Another difficulty concerns the relationship between this provision and other treaty objectives. There are two points to note: Article 151(4) requires that cultural policies be taken into account in other Community policies. Article 151(5) identifies the types of legislative action the Community may take, specifically excluding harmonisation. Community action is thus also limited in type: it cannot, e.g. impose standards: its role is to foster and to facilitate Community action. As with other policy areas, notably public health,[86] the limitation on harmonisation raises the question of the provision's impact on Article 95 (and equivalent service provisions) and whether the provision is an attempt to limit the Community's competence and preclude harmonising action in the field at all. For example, such an interpretation could throw into difficulties the revision of the Television without Frontiers Directive. This argument is unlikely for a number of reasons. The revisions of the Treaty have been subject to the *acquis communautaire*.[87] Further, although using the Article 151 EC as a base for harmonising measures is precluded, the provision is silent on the subject of internal market driven measures, or measures based on other treaty provisions, which happen to have an impact in the field of competence defined by Article 151.[88]

The difficulties of identifying an appropriate treaty base are exemplified in the linguistic diversity decision.[89] The decision focussed on linguistic diversity in the Information Society and was based on former Article 130. The European Parliament challenged the decision on the basis that it should additionally have been based on what is now Article 151; it had tried to emphasise through the drafting process the cultural aspect of the decision, and amend the draft decision accordingly. In the Commission's view, the decision was economic. It was aimed at encouraging the provision of multilingual services and that any social or cultural benefit was merely a spin off despite the inclusion in the decision of the objective of contributing to "the promotion of linguistic diversity of the Community". The ECJ reviewed its usual case law on treaty base before commenting that

> as regards the marginalisation of the languages that remain excluded from the Information Society, it is not a risk of a specifically cultural nature.

Although the ECJ accepted that there might be some loss of cultural heritage through such marginalisation, this was of little significance compared with

> the difference in treatment between economic operators in the Community who enjoy greater or lesser advantages depending on whether or not the language they use is widespread.[90]

---

[86] See the difficulties with the Tobacco Advertising cases: Case C-376/98 *Germany* v. *European Parliament and Council of the European Union* (Tobacco Advertising Directive) [2000] ECR I-8419.

[87] Article 2 TEU.

[88] See reasoning of ECJ in Case C-376/98 *Tobacco Advertising Directive* cases, *supra* n. 86.

[89] Case C-42/97 *European Parliament* v. *Council of the European Union* [1999] ECR I-869.

[90] *Ibid.*, para. 50.

There are a couple of points that could be made here. The first is that, post-Amsterdam, the ECJ still seems to be taking a primarily economic view of questions such as these. Of course, the matter was raised in the context of identifying the appropriate treaty base for the decision and the Court's reasoning must be understood against this backdrop. It is therefore not assessing whether cultural issues should be taken into account but, given the terms of the decision itself, what is the appropriate base for that action? Certainly it must be right that the mere mention of culture of itself cannot bring cultural policy into play. Further, as the ECJ pointed out, it is less necessary to use the Article 151 treaty base when Article 151(4) requires cultural issues to be taken into consideration in the context of other Community policies. This argument, however, raises the question of what sort of consideration would cultural policies get in such circumstances?

A number of the resolutions of the Council and the guidance issued by the Commission in a number of areas which impinge on cultural policy make reference to Article 151, e.g. the Council Resolution on national aid to the film and audiovisual industries;[91] Council Resolution on exchange of information and experience concerning conditions for professional artists in the context of EU enlargement;[92] Council Resolution on the Fixed Book Price System.[93] As might be expected from the way Article 151(4) will come into play, these examples all concerns the protection of Member State policies against the operation of internal market and competition concerns. Whether these resolutions constitute sufficient action on the part of the political institutions is debatable as some of the more recent case law discussed earlier in this chapter illustrates. The Council has this year agreed a further resolution, which emphasises the centrality of culture to European integration and requests the Commission to update its study on implementation of Article 151(4). This indicates that the Council may think that more work needs to be done.

What then of the judicial arm of the European institutions; how have the CFI and ECJ approached the obligation to take culture into account? As we have seen, the ECJ did not take much account of the cultural argument in the context of labelling requirements. The issue has also been raised in a number of cases concerning the broadcasting and book industries. Perhaps the earliest of these cases in *Commission* v. *Belgium*,[94] which concerned the Television without Frontiers Directive[95] and the interpretation of the jurisdiction clause. In that case, the Belgian government argued that in interpreting the Television without Frontiers Directive, and particularly the individual Member State's rights to take action to ensure that incoming transmissions complied with the terms of the directive even if that states did not have

---

[91] Council Resolution of 12 February 2001 national aid to the film and audiovisual industries OJ [2001] C073/3.

[92] Council Resolution of 23 July 2001 on exchange of information and experience concerning conditions for professional artists in the context of EU enlargement OJ [2001] C213/9.

[93] Council Resolution of 12 February 2001 on the application of national fixed book-price systems OJ [2001] C073/5.

[94] Case C-11/95 *Commission* v. *Belgium* [1996] ECR I-4115.

[95] Council Directive 89/552, *supra* n. 31.

responsibility for regulation of the broadcaster, the ECJ should take into account Article 151 (then Article 128). The ECJ accepted that the Community should take cultural aspects into account in its action under other provisions of the Treaty, but concluded that Article 151 could not justify the imposition of potential barriers to trade.[96] Whatever one makes of the reasoning, it seems clear that internal market concerns were prioritised here.

A similarly terse approach has been taken by the ECJ more recently in *Échirolles Distribution*,[97] a case concerning the fixing of prices for books, in which it was argued that the ECJ should revise its jurisprudence on free movement of goods in the light of the completion of the internal market. Despite the fact that some arguments concerning the cultural value of books were put before the ECJ, the Court contented itself with dealing with the question of the legal consequences of Articles 3 and 14, arguing that those provisions

> must be read in conjunction with the provisions of the Treaty designed to implement those objectives. Since Articles 28, 30 and 81 of the Treaty have not been amended, the Court's interpretation of them in *Leclerc*, in conjunction with Article 10 of the Treaty, cannot be called into question.[98]

Although this statement addresses some of the issues raised before the ECJ, it leaves the status of Article 151(4) unclear. Although the completion of the internal market was not seen as changing the law, this case cannot be seen as a resounding defence of other values in the Treaty.

Conclusions

At the beginning of this chapter, a number of hypotheses concerning the development of European Community's approach to culture were identified. From the overview presented, although some changes are identifiable in specific areas, it would seem that it is not possible to verify any of the hypotheses, which given the change in Treaty competence initially seems somewhat surprising. As regards the negative scope of culture, the institutions do not seem to have adopted any clear, let alone consistent, approach to issues to be considered as falling within a cultural exception, although there is a slight tendency towards preferring the emblematic and intellectual view of culture rather than an anthropological version. Despite this statement, it is also possible to detect a certain respect for the need to ensure diversity of culture, perhaps linked to concerns about freedom of expression and the respect for human rights. To a certain extent, some lack of coherence in this area is understandable. Culture is a concept that has relevance in many areas and it is often difficult to

---

96 Case C-11/95 *Commission* v. *Belgium, supra* n. 94, at para. 50.

97 Case C-9/99 *Échirolles Distribution SA* v. *Association du Dauphiné* [2000] ECR I-8207.

98 *Ibid.*, para. 24.

produce a synthesis of such cross-cutting themes. In any event, in many cases the ECJ was responding to arguments put forward by the Member States. Not only is it impossible to define categories of such arguments in advance, but the ECJ would also find its field of enquiry defined by the issues that Member States chose to bring forward under this heading. The ECJ was therefore responding to the different conceptions of culture within the Member States, a fact which is reflected in the fragmented jurisprudence. What is clear in this context is the stringent application of necessity and proportionality tests, so as to limit the practical scope of any such derogation. Culture may be recognised but it is still not high on the list of values recognised within the Community order, and Article 151(4) would seem to have had little influence on the jurisprudence in this area. The positive aspect of culture within the Community – or Union – currently shows very little change. Many of the types of action undertaken now under Article 151 have predecessors in action taken at the Community level. It would seem then that Article 151 is still a recognition of the status quo rather than the basis for development of a pan European culture and all that that might imply; the emphasis seems rather on the diversity of the cultural traditions. The final point to make is that the Community and Union have developed and that process will continue. An assessment of the same issues 10 and 20 years hence may show a completely different picture. For the time being, however, the European Community's view on culture seems no more than a reflection of the general issues facing the Union at the moment – the creation of unity in diversity.

Chapter 7

State Intervention in the Economy: From State Monopolies to Regulated Industries

*Erik Pijnacker Hordijk**

1. Introduction: From 1982 to 2002 via 1992

Not only in the 1950s but also in the early 1980s, when I studied Community law at University, utilities were still largely the domain of public monopolies.[1] The legality of these monopolies – or, for that matter, of other service monopolies – was never seriously questioned under Community law. In its 1974 Sacchi judgment,[2] the Court had stated that Member States were entitled "for considerations of public interest, of a non-economic nature" to create legal monopolies in the field of broadcasting. It was generally held to be beyond doubt that identical considerations would apply to, e.g. telephony and postal services. The mere thought that the legal monopoly of the national PTT could be held to restrict the freedom to provide services and the freedom of establishment simply did not arise, if only because there were no candidates seeking to exploit those freedoms. Moreover, those fundamental freedoms at the time were held to extend to discriminations on grounds of nationality only.[3] The granting of an exclusive right to a single body involved no such discrimination, since it affected without distinction all operators who might be interested in the activity concerned.[4] As to legal monopolies for the supply of goods, the only limits to their existence were those imposed by Article 37 EEC Treaty.

The role of Article 90 EEC Treaty was close to none. As the Court had stated in *GB-INNO* v. *ATAB*,[5] Article 90(1) EEC Treaty was only a particular application of certain general principles which bind the Member States. In other words: it did not

---

* Erik Pijnacker Hordijk is a partner with De Brauw Blackstone Westbroek, practising from The Hague.

[1] In this chapter, the term "monopolies" is – unless indicated otherwise – meant to refer to companies holding exclusive rights for the supply of certain goods or the provision of certain services that have been granted by public authorities of the Member States.

[2] Case 155/73, Sacchi, [1974] ECR 409.

[3] It is recalled that in *Säger* v. *Dennemeyer* (Case C-76/90, [1991] ECR I-4221), the Court for the first time interpreted the principle of freedom to provide services so as to extend to all restrictions including those that are indistinctly applicable to nationals and non-nationals.

[4] Cf. case C-124/97, Läärä, [1999] ECR I-6067, at rec. 28.

[5] Case 13/77, INNO/ATAB, [1977] ECR 2115, rec. 42.

M. van Empel (ed.), "From Paris to Nice": Fifty Years of Legal Integration in Europe, 131–149.

add anything to the scope of the other Treaty Articles it referred to. Moreover, in Port de Mertert,[6] the Court had denied direct effect to Article 90(2) EEC Treaty. The Treaty Article did not lay down an unconditional rule, as its application involved "an appraisal of the requirements, on the one hand, of the particular task entrusted to the undertaking concerned and, on the other hand, the protection of the interests of the Community."[7] This appraisal, the Court added, "depends on the objectives of general economic policy pursued by the States under the supervision of the Commission."[8] As the Commission had virtually never used its powers under Article 90(3) EEC Treaty,[9] Article 90(2) remained dormant.

Certainly, there existed some legal monopolies that had triggered case law or had otherwise attracted attention in the world of Community law; notably the French and Italian tobacco monopolies[10] and the German "Branntweinmonopol".[11] But not the (true) utilities. The lack of interest for the public utilities from a Community perspective was not as surprising as it may seem today: geographic markets were mostly national, and neither market forces nor technological developments pushed hard for the development of a true single market.

Anno 2002, the landscape has changed quite dramatically. Many monopolies have been abolished, often as a result of the application of – primary or secondary – Community law. Most utilities sectors are in a situation of constant change. In the telecommunications sector, all legal monopolies have been abolished. In the electricity and gas sectors, the Council of Ministers recently agreed to prohibit all remaining monopoly rights by 2007. There is political agreement on the fading out of the postal monopolies. The internal market for air transport services has been liberalised completely. Markets for a number of airport services have been liberalised, and a similar program will soon be adopted for seaports. On the other hand, rail and road transport – is so far as transport of passengers is concerned – remain political stumble-blocks. And last but not least: liberalising the supply of drinking water is still a non-issue on the level of the Community.

Where entire sectors have been liberalised EU-wide, this has without exception been the result of legislative actions initiated at a Community level. Some Member States may have moved faster or may have liberalised to a greater extent than others, but in all cases Community legislation has set a minimum standard. These Community-wide liberalisation programs should be distinguished from cases in which a particular legal monopoly was challenged before a national court – and

---

6 Case 10-71, Port de Mertert, [1971] ECR 723.

7 *Ibid.*, rec. 14.

8 *Ibid.*, rec. 15. In light hereof, the Court declined to review the possible negative impact of certain "privileges" granted to the Port de Mertert by the Luxembourg authorities for the competitive position of other undertakings. By the same token, the Court would have refused under Article 90(2) EEC Treaty, the possible negative impact of legal monopolies on the competitive position of third parties.

9 The only exception being Commission Directive 80/723/EEC of 25 June 1980 on the transparency of financial relations between Member States and public undertakings, OJ L 195, 29.7.1980.

10 For example, case 59/75, Manghera, [1976] ECR 91.

11 For example, case 45/75, Rewe, [1975] ECR 181.

via the route of Article 234 EC indirectly before the Court of Justice – on an *ad hoc* basis. The appraisal of the legal monopolies of institutions such as the German *Bundesanstalt für Arbeit*, French insemination centres (for cows), Dutch pension funds for various industrial sectors and for various liberal professions, and German medical aid organisations, falls outside the scope of any Community program. Nevertheless, these legal monopolies have contributed to creating a highly interesting body of case-law.

Obviously, the increased "interest" for monopolies – more particularly utilities monopolies – is not a result of the autonomous development of Community law. Factors that will have played a role are technological developments, the increasing maturity of the markets concerned, the general prosperity of society as a result of which the social dimension of utilities is less at the forefront than the competitiveness of the services rendered, the impact of the Commission's "1992 Program" and, finally, the stronger focus of the European governments on competition as a major instrument of economic policy generally. De-monopolisation often goes hand in hand with privatisation. Strictly speaking, however, for the appraisal of legal monopolies under Community law, the nature of the ownership of the monopoly should not make a difference.[12] For that reason, and also in order not further complicate the subject, I will leave privatisation aspects of de-monopolisation efforts aside in this chapter.

Against this background, I will, in this chapter, first address the status of primary Community law as regards the assessment of legal monopolies. Second, I will address issues relating to the choice of the legal basis of secondary Community law dealing with the abolition of exclusive rights. Third, I will briefly discuss some issues that arise in the post-monopoly era: abolishing monopolies is one thing, but what comes next?

2. The Assessment of Legal Monopolies Under Primary Community Law Anno 2002 Generally

2.1. The basic approach by the Court

When analysing the assessment of legal monopolies under *primary* Community law, one will have to focus on the case-law of the Court of Justice. When making the exercise, one should bear in mind that the relevant rules of primary Community law have horizontal direct effect, which means that they can be relied upon before national courts in disputes between private parties. This partly explains why most of the relevant case-law consists of preliminary rulings. The cases in which the Commission has challenged legal monopolies maintained by Member States through direct actions pursuant to Article 226 EC are extremely limited. Moreover, the outcome of those cases was not always favourable to the Commission. This suggests that in

---

12 *Cf.* Article 295 EC: "This Treaty shall in no way prejudice the rules in Membership States governing the system of property ownership."

practice the supervision of legal monopolies is primarily a matter for private parties. As will be shown below, this is only a partial truth. Even though the Court of Justice has developed a set of basic rules that render the legal position of monopolies highly vulnerable in principle, the outcome of most cases shows that in real terms the Court is rather hesitant to effectively declare monopolies contrary to the Treaty.

As to the basic approach of the Court, the following should be noted.

It is by now well established that legal monopolies for the provision of services – even though not discriminatory in nature – are to be qualified as restrictions of the freedom to provide services and the freedom of establishment.[13] In order to justify legal monopolies in the light of these fundamental freedoms, they need to be justified by overriding reasons relating to the public interest. Moreover, they need to meet the necessity test and the proportionality test. In practice, the review of exclusive rights seems to be rather lenient. The catalogue of overriding interests – which includes such interests as the protection of the recipients of the service concerned (or consumers generally) and the maintenance of order in society – is not limited.[14] Moreover, in the absence of harmonisation at the Community level, it is in principle up to the Member States to choose what they consider an adequate level of protection: "the mere fact that a Member State has opted for a system of protection which differs from that adopted by another Member State cannot affect the assessment of the need for, and proportionality of, the provisions enacted to that end. Those provisions must be assessed solely by reference to the objectives pursued by the national authorities of the Member State concerned and the level of protection which they are intended to provide."[15] The latter element in the assessment of legal monopolies is particularly important; it limits the scope for (national) courts searching for a common Communitarian denominator in the absence of guidance from the Community's legislator.

It is rather the Court's renewed interpretation of Article 90 EEC Treaty (now Article 86 EC) in combination with the competition rules that has become the main route to challenge the legality of legal monopolies as such.[16] The Court's creativity in this field has been quite extraordinary. It is recalled that Article 86(1) EC does not prohibit as such the granting (and maintaining) of exclusive rights by Member States. Article 86(1) EC merely specifies that the Member States have to comply with the rules of the Treaty. Article 86(2) EC addresses the special position of undertakings "entrusted with the operation of services of general economic interest": such undertakings shall be subject to the rules of the Treaty "in so far as the application of such rules does not obstruct the performance, in law or in fact, of the particular tasks

---

[13] See for an outspoken example case C-124/97, Läärä, [1999] ECR I-6067.

[14] The overriding interests are not necessarily to be of a non-economic nature; protecting the coherence of the tax system can hardly be called a non-economic interest (*cf.* case C-204/90, Bachmann, [1992] ECR 249).

[15] Case C-124/97, Läärä, [1999] ECR I-6067, rec. 36.

[16] According to its wording, Article 86(1) covers "special and exclusive rights". Unless the opposite follows from the context, references throughout this paper to "exclusive rights" and to "monopoly rights" should be meant to include references to "special rights". See for a definition of the notion of special rights case C-302/94, BT, [1996] ECR I-6417.

assigned to them." It goes without saying that, according to its wording, Article 86(2) EC does not address the creation of monopolies by the laws of the Member States either. How then may Article 86 be construed so as to limit the freedom of Member States to grant exclusive rights?

2.2. The Court's case law regarding Article 86 EC

In a series of preliminary rulings, all of which were rendered in 1991, the Court gave a new impetus to the interpretation of Article 86 EC. The first case was Höfner.[17] To understand the case, one should have a closer look at the facts. The case concerned a refusal to pay an invoice issued by one private party to another private party. It only indirectly concerned the exclusive right of employment procurement of the German Bundesanstalt für Arbeit (BfA), in so far as it extended to executive recruitment activities. Höfner and Elser had been hired by Macrotron as executive recruitment consultants. Their invoice was turned down by Macrotron who after having used their services made a point of the fact that the provision of those services was in violation of the legal monopoly of the BfA and, hence, illegal. Obviously, Höfner and Elser did not accept this rather opportunistic ground to refuse payment, and argued that the law granting the exclusive rights to the BfA was incompatible with the freedom of establishment and the freedom to provide services, as well as the competition rules. The national court referred the case to Luxembourg for a preliminary ruling. The Court of Justice first of all found that it could not rule on the fundamental freedoms issue since the facts of the case did not involve any cross-border element.[18] It then found a way out by reviewing the legality of the monopoly rights under Articles (now) 86 and 82 EC taken together. The Court recognised that the simple fact of creating a dominant position by granting an exclusive right within the meaning of Article 86(1) EC does not as such violate Article 82 EC. However, the Court pointed out that this may be different in a case where the statutory provision at stake creates a situation in which the holder of the right cannot avoid infringing Article 82 EC. The Court then went on to state that such an *inevitable* abuse may occur when the owner of the exclusive right "is manifestly not in a position to satisfy the demand prevailing on the market" for the services covered by the exclusive right. Thus, the invoice of Höfner and Elser was saved.

> I have always found the Court's reasoning in Höfner and Elser highly questionable. On the merits, the case was not a competition case, but had everything to do with the freedom to provide services. The BfA was found to systematically abuse a dominant position, without even having been heard. Categorising the failure to satisfy the demand that is prevailing in the market as an abuse, lends itself easily

---

[17] Case C-4/90, *Höfner and Elser* v. *Macrotron*, [1991] ECR I-1979.

[18] It is well-established case-law that the four freedoms cannot be relied upon before national courts in disputes the facts of which have no bearing on cross-border trade. In the present case, all parties involved (as well as the BfA) were German and there were no cross-border services at stake.

to abuse by litigants who for one reason or another are not satisfied with the level of service granted by a legal monopoly. The Court may have wanted to help out Höfner and Elser, but should have left it to the national court to find an adequate response to the pettifoggery of Macrotron.

In the subsequent ERT[19] and Merci Convenzionali[20] judgments, the Court took it even a step further stating that a violation of Articles 86 and 82 EC occurs where exclusive rights are *liable to create a situation* where the holder of the right is *led to* abuse its dominant position. The Merci Convenzionali case is particularly remarkable, since the Court deduced the abuse-proneness of the Genoese port company merely from its past performance.[21] The ERT judgment is the most convincing of the series. The Court held *combining* exclusive rights to transmit (national) broadcast program and exclusive rights to retransmit (foreign) broadcast programs within the hands of a single undertaking to be incompatible with Article 86(1) EC, "where those rights are liable to create a situation in which that undertaking is led to infringe Article (82) by virtue of a discriminatory broadcasting policy which favours its own programmes, unless the application of Article (82) obstructs the performance of the particular tasks entrusted to it."[22] In this case, it was not the granting of exclusive rights as such, but rather the conflict of interest created by the combination of the two exclusive rights, that was questioned.[23]

The last case in the series is *RTT* v. *GB-INNO*.[24] RTT, the (then) Belgian national telephony monopoly, had been granted by the Belgian government the power to lay down the standards for telephone equipment and to check that economic operators meet those standards. The Court recalled that behaviour of an undertaking that is dominant on a given market aiming at monopolising an ancillary activity on a different market, constitutes an abuse within the meaning of Article 82 EC. It was clear, however, that in the present case Article 82 EC could not come into play since the necessary initiative of RTT was failing. The Court, however, held that "where the extension of the dominant position (...) results from a State measure, such a measure constitutes an infringement of Article (86) in conjunction with Article (82) of the Treaty."[25] This is the only type of case where the Court has found Article 86 EC to apply to a State measure without having established a causal link with an underlying infringement of the competition rules by an undertaking.[26]

---

19 Case C-260/89, ERT, [1991] ECR I-2925.

20 Case C-179/90, Merci Convenzionali, [1991] ECR I-5889.

21 See the opinion of advocate-general Van Gerven for an account of the performance of the monopoly holder.

22 *Ibid.*, rec. 37.

23 The Court reached the same result applying the Treaty rules on the freedom to provide services.

24 Case C-18/88, *RTT* v. *GB-INNO*, [1991] ECR I-5941.

25 *Ibid.*, rec. 21.

26 *Cf.* the case law concerning the combined application of Article 10 EC and the competition rules. In *Leclerc* v. *Thouars* (case 229/83, [1985] ECR 1, rec. 15), the Court had held that (now) Articles 3(1) sub g and 10 EC might be applied to State measures which render "corporate behaviour of the type prohibited by Article (81(1)) superfluous", thus suggesting that State measures that have the same *effect* as

These four cases have in common that they all focus on the combined application of Articles 86(1) and 82 EC. Article 86(2) EC did not come into play, because there was nothing to be justified in the light of the criteria of that Article. The link between the first two paragraphs of Article 86 EC was made in 1993 in the Corbeau judgment.[27] The case concerned the "extension" of the monopoly of the Belgian postal services to certain courier services. It was beyond dispute that the Régie des Postes was an "Article 86(2) undertaking" in so far it concerned the traditional postal service. But how about the courier services? The Court started out by emphasising that Article 86(1) and (2) EC should be read together. As to the latter provision, the Court stated that it "permits the Member States to confer on undertakings to which they entrust the operation of services of general economic interest, exclusive rights which may hinder the application of the rules of the Treaty on competition in so far as restrictions on competition, or even the exclusion of all competition, by other economic operators are necessary to ensure the performance of the particular tasks assigned to the undertakings possessed of the exclusive right. (…) The question which falls to be considered is therefore the extent to which a restriction on competition or even the exclusion of all competition from other economic operators is necessary in order to allow the holder of the exclusive right to perform the task of general interest and in particular to have the benefit of economically acceptable conditions."[28] This wording suggests that the Court would henceforth only be willing to accept exclusive rights to the extent they were considered necessary to allow "Article 86(2) undertakings" to carry out their tasks under economically acceptable conditions. On the other hand, this wording also makes clear that the conditions for the application of Article 86(2) EC should not be construed to narrowly: competing courier services from third parties should only be allowed "in so far as such specific services (…) do not compromise the economic equilibrium of the service of general economic interest by the holder of the exclusive right".[29]

At this point in time, the state of the case-law was not particularly coherent. In later years, the Court has had the opportunity to refine its jurisprudence to some extent. In its 1994 La Crespelle judgment,[30] the Court reiterated the old starting point that the mere creation of a dominant position through the grant of an exclusive right does not as such violate Article 82 and 86(1) EC taken together, thus quieting the speculations over the meaning of the Corbeau judgment.

---

anti-competitive agreements of undertakings fall within the scope of the said Treaty Articles. This suggestion was, however, finally discarded, in case C-245/91, Ohra, [1993] ECR I-5872 and case C-2/91, Meng, [1993] ECR I-5791, in which the Court made it clear that Articles 3(1) sub g and 10 EC may only come into play when there is an underlying anti-competitive agreement. *Cf.* also the Dutch pension fund cases (case C-67/96, Albany, [1999] ECR I-5751 and others), in which the Court held that a State measures meant to reinforce the effects of a collective labour agreement falls outside the scope of Articles 3(1) sub g and 10 EC, for the mere reason that the said collective labour agreement falls outside the scope of Article 81 EC.

27 Case C-320/91, Corbeau, [1993] I-2533.

28 *Ibid.*, rec. 14 and 16.

29 *Ibid.*, rec. 19.

30 Case C-323/93, La Crespelle, [1994] ECR I-5077.

The so-called Article 37 judgments[31] of October 1997[32] are interesting, not only because they confirm that Article 86(2) forms an exception with regard to the competition rules *as well as* the Treaty rules on free movement,[33] including Article 37 EEC Treaty (now Article 31 EC) that addresses "monopolies of a commercial character". The Commission had challenged under (now) Article 226 EC exclusive import rights applied granted by a number of Member States to public utilities in the electricity and gas sectors. The Member States all argued – for different reasons – that the import monopolies were justified in the light of Article 86(2) EC. The Court did not go so far as to explicitly endorse the defences raised by the Member States,[34] but dismissed the applications of the Commission on the ground that it had insufficiently rebutted those defences. Nevertheless, it is clear from these judgments that the Court considered the defences raised by the Member States favourably. Thus, the judgment in case C-157/95, *Commission* v. *Netherlands*, shows that the Court was sympathetic to the argument that the import monopoly for electricity for public distribution was an indispensable element of the national market organisation for the electricity sector. The judgments are interesting, because they show that Article 86 EC may not be the ideal legal instrument to force through the liberalisation of entire sectors on a Community level. I will come back to that in the next chapter.

The judgments in the Article 37 cases should be contrasted with the earlier Almelo judgment,[35] in which the Court left it to the national judge to answer the question whether exclusive supply arrangements between public electricity distribution companies in The Netherlands – which formed an integrating part of the Dutch public electricity supply system – might be justified in the light of Article 86(2) EC.[36]

---

[31] Some of the vary rare cases that are not preliminary rulings but in which the Commission itself took the initiative to proceed.

[32] Case C-157/94, *Commission* v. *Netherlands*, [1997] ECR I-5699; case C-158/94, *Commission* v. *Italy*, [1997] ECR I-5789; case C-159/94, *Commission* v. *France*, [1997] ECR I-5815; case C-160/94, *Commission* v. *Spain*, [1997] ECR I-5851.

[33] In case 72/83, Campus Oil, [1984] ECR 2727, the Court still had held that Article 86(2) EC cannot exempt Member States from their obligations under Article 28 EC.

[34] The Court did not deny that the Member States have to demonstrate that the conditions for the application of Article 86(2) EC are met. However, referring to Corbeau it pointed out that those conditions "are fulfilled if maintenance of those rights is necessary to enable the holder of them to perform the tasks of general economic interest assigned to it under economically acceptable conditions" (case C-157/94, rec. 53). Moreover, the Court held that "that burden of proof cannot be so extensive as to require the Member State, when setting out in detail the reasons for which, in the event of elimination of the contested measures, the performance, under economically acceptable conditions, of the tasks of general economic interest which it has entrusted to an undertaking would, in its view, be jeopardised, to go even further and prove, positively, that no other conceivable measure, which by definition would be hypothetical, could enable those tasks to be performed under the same conditions" (*ibid.*, rec. 58).

[35] Case C-393/92, Almelo, [1994] ECR I-1477.

[36] The referring court concluded that the exclusive agreements were *not* justified, because the defendant electricity company had failed to demonstrate that the overall system could not have been organised in a different way involving less restrictions (Court of Appeal Arnhem, 22 October 1996, not reported). The approach followed by the Court of Appeal is manifestly incompatible with the approach followed by the Court of Justice in the Article 37 cases; *cf.* n. 34 *supra* on the burden of proof.

The 1998 Dusseldorp judgment once again reinforced the confusion about the scope of the Article 86(1)/82 combination. The Court reiterated the Höfner and Merci judgments in a slightly altered wording: "a Member State breaches the prohibitions (of Article 86 in conjunction with Article 82) if it adopts any law, regulation or administrative provision which *enables* an undertaking on which it has conferred exclusive rights to abuse its dominant position" (italics added).[37] The Court then went on to hold that a legal provision imposing an obligation to deliver oil filters to a given undertaking that held the exclusive right to incinerate dangerous waste "has the effect of favouring the national undertaking by enabling it to process waste intended for processing by a third undertaking. It therefore results in the restriction of outlets in a manner contrary to Article (86(1)) in conjunction with Article (82) of the Treaty."[38] The Court seems to overlook that the said restriction of outlets is inherent in the granting of exclusive rights as such, and has nothing to do with abusive behaviour by the undertaking enjoying the exclusive rights. Thus, once again the Court follows a line which leads to the conclusion that any exclusive right is almost *per se* incompatible with the Article 86(1)/82 combination. Indeed, the reasoning applied by the Court in Dusseldorp, suggests that the only relevant question is whether the exclusive right may be justified by a task of general economic interest within the meaning of Article 86(2) EC.

The same quasi-automatic infringement approach was followed in the subsequent Dutch Sectoral Pension Fund cases.[39] In this case, an employer wishing to opt out of the existing system of compulsory affiliation to the pension scheme for the economic sector in which he was active argued that the pension fund managing the scheme (and enjoying exclusive rights in that connection) provided benefits that were inadequate compared to what could be offered by (private) insurance companies. The Court assessed the position of the pension fund in the light of the Höfner criterion, i.e. whether it was manifestly incapable of satisfying the demand prevailing on the market. In this connection, the Court held: "(d)outbtless, some undertakings in the sector might wish to provide their workers with a pension scheme superior to the one offered by the Fund. However, the fact that such undertakings are unable to entrust the management of such pension scheme to a single insurer and the resulting restriction of competition derive directly from the exclusive right conferred on the sectoral pension fund. It is therefore necessary to consider whether (...) the exclusive right of the sectoral pension fund to manage the supplementary pensions in a given sector and the resultant restriction of competition may be justified under Article (86(2)) of the Treaty as a measure necessary for the performance of a particular social task of general interest with which the fund has been charged."[40] Thus, the mere fact that the applicant in the main action argued that others than the monopolist might offer superior services was a sufficient reason for the Court to pass on to

---

[37] Case C-203/96, Dusseldorp, [1998] ECR I-4075, rec. 61.

[38] *Ibid.*, rec. 63.

[39] Case C-67/96, Albany, [1999] ECR I-5751; joined cases C-115/97 – C-117/97, Brentjens, [1999] ECR I-6025; case C-219/97, Drijvende Bokken, [1999] ECR I-6121.

[40] Brentjens, rec. 97–98.

the Article 86(2) justification test. This, it is submitted, is precisely the perverse consequence that may be drawn from the Höfner approach: whenever a customer complains about the type of service provided by the holder of an exclusive right, the monopolist concerned may be held not to satisfy the demand prevailing on the market. The final outcome, however, was positive for the pension fund: the Court accepted the argument that the compulsory affiliation was necessary because the fund in view of various solidarity elements in the scheme could not be as competitive as a private insurance company.

The subsequent Pavlov case,[41] which concerned a similar compulsory pension scheme, albeit this time for a specific (liberal) profession, shows that the Court will not at all times feel forced to follow the Höfner route. In Pavlov, the Court stopped short of an Article 86(2) analysis, because the applicants in the main action had not raised any objections against the level of the services provided by the pension fund concerned.

Finally, in the Ambulanz Glöckner case,[42] the Court once again applied the extension approach of *RTT* v. *GB-INNO*, and moreover made it clear that Corbeau should be read as a straightforward extension case as well.[43] The case concerned ambulance transport. In the German *Land* of Nordrhein-Westfalen, emergency ambulance transport had been entrusted to four medical aid associations. In addition, the associations had been granted a quasi-monopoly to carry out the commercially more interesting normal passenger transport by ambulance. Confronted with another extension of a legal monopoly by a government act, the Court once again found it necessary to assess the extension in the light of Article 86(2) EC. Unlike in the Corbeau case, the Court did not leave the final analysis tot the national court, but decided the matter on the merits.[44]

2.3. *Concluding remarks*

Looking back at the case law on Article 86 EC of the last 10 years, it appears that the Court started off very ambitiously by applying Article 86(1) EC in conjunction with the competition rules in such a way that legal monopolies of whatever nature might be open to challenge. On the other hand, the Court seems to have relaxed its justification test under Article 86(2) EC. Even though there may still be cases where exclusive rights may pass the test of Article 86(1)/82 without needing to have recourse to a justification under Article 86(2) – Pavlov being a notable

---

[41] Joined cases C-180/98 – C-184/98, Pavlov, [2000] ECR I-6451.

[42] Case C-475/99, Ambulanz Glöckner, 25 October 2001, nyr.

[43] In other words, it was only the *extension* of the monopoly for the traditional postal service to courier services that the Court had meant to assess under Article 86(2) EC in its Corbeau judgment.

[44] This seems inconsistent with the division of tasks between the national courts and the Court of Justice under Article 234 EC. However, the Court may have learned from Corbeau that it may be very difficult for a national court to second-guess what exactly the economic analysis should be that the Court would wish it to make.

example – under the law as it stands in most cases a justification under Article 86(2) EC will be needed. This being said, the Court would be well advised to limit the scope of its Höfner-rule to cases of *manifest* impossibility to satisfy a demand that is *generally prevailing* in the market, and not the individual demand of a given market player.

In so far as the assessment under Article 86(2) EC is concerned, one may well see in the next years a convergence with the appraisal under the "overriding interests" exception in the sphere of the free movement of services. After all, the exception of Article 86(2) EC also applies in the area of the four freedoms, and the Court so far has never felt the need to have recourse to Article 86(2) EC in the sphere of services. Within the context of the freedom to provide services, it is as a matter of principle still considered permissible for a Member State to entrust the provision of specific services to a specific body, provided there is an adequate, coherent general interest justification. This justification will often imply that the body performing the said services can be considered an "Article 86(2) undertaking". Be this as it may, convergence is necessary to ensure a coherent application of the Treaty.

Finally, it should be noted that most if not all the cases in which the Court came to a negative assessment about a given legal monopoly concerned "fringe" cases: one should not overlook the fact that Höfner, *RTT* v. *GB-INNO* and Corbeau all concerned side-activities of an otherwise unchallenged monopoly. Indeed, one should continue putting the case-law of the Court in perspective.

3. Secondary Community Law and Monopolies: Legislation Meant at Liberalising Markets

3.1. Introduction

Since 1988, the Community legislator – i.e. the Council, the Council and the European Parliament, or the Commission – has adopted a variety of Directives aiming at liberalising specific markets. In this chapter, I will not deal with all of those Directives. To focus the debate, I will rather concentrate on a couple of issues that come up when looking in particular to the approach followed by the Community legislator with regard to the telecommunications and the energy sectors, as well as the non-action of the Community legislator in the field of drinking water.

3.2. Liberalisation versus harmonisation: the use of Articles 86(3) and 95 EC as a legal basis for legislation

The first sector to be liberalised on the Community level was the telecommunications sector, the first liberalisation directive dating from 1988: Commission Directive 88/301/EEC on competition in the markets in telecommunications terminal equipment.[45] The Directive was based on Article 86(3) EC Treaty. Its object was the

[45] OJ 1988, L 131/73.

abolition of the existing exclusive rights of the national telecom operators with regard to importing, marketing, maintenance, etc., of terminal equipment. In the preamble of the directive, the Commission states that maintaining these exclusive rights should be held incompatible not only with basic rules on free movement of goods and services, but also with the competition rules. The reasons given for intervening on the basis of Article 86(3) in conjunction with (now) Article 28 EC are very succinct:

> 3. Article (28 EC) prohibits quantitative restrictions on imports from other Member States and all measures of equivalent effect. The grant of special or exclusive rights to import and market goods to one organisation can, and often does, lead to restrictions on imports from other Member States.

The grounds to act on the basis of the competition rules are set out as follows:

> 13. The telecommunications bodies hold individually or jointly a monopoly on their national telecommunications network. The national networks are markets. Therefore, the bodies each individually or jointly hold a dominant position in a substantial part of the market in question within the meaning of Article (82). The effect of the special or exclusive rights granted to such bodies by the State to import and market terminal equipment is to:
>
> – restrict users to renting such equipment, when it would often be cheaper for them, at least in the long term, to purchase this equipment. This effectively makes contracts for the use of networks subject to acceptance by the user of additional services which have no connection with the subject of the contracts,
> – limit outlets and impede technical progress since the range of equipment offered by the telecommunications bodies is necessarily limited and will not be the best available to meet the requirements of a significant proportion of users.
>
> Such conduct is expressly prohibited by Article (82)(d) and (b), and is likely significantly to affect trade between Member States.
>
> At all events, such special or exclusive rights in regard to the terminal equipment market give rise to a situation which is contrary to the objective of Article (3(1) sub g) of the Treaty, which provides for the institution of a system ensuring that competition in the common market is not distorted, and requires a fortiori that competition must not be eliminated. Member States have an obligation under Article (10) of the Treaty to abstain from any measure which could jeopardize the attainment of the objectives of the Treaty, including Article (3(1) sub g).
>
> The exclusive rights to import and market terminal equipment must therefore be regarded as incompatible with Article (82) in conjunction with Article 3, and the grant or maintenance of such rights by a Member State is prohibited under Article (86(1)).

The Directive was challenged before the Court by France.[46] France argued, *inter alia*, that the Commission had encroached on the power conferred on the Council by Articles (now) 83 and (now) 95 EC. The Court dismissed this argument for the following reasons:

> 24 Article (95) is concerned with the adoption of measures for the approximation of the provisions laid down by law, regulation or administrative action in Member States which have as their object the establishment and functioning of the internal market. Article (83) is concerned with the adoption of any appropriate regulations or directives to give effect to the principles set out in Articles (81 and 82), that is to say the competition rules applicable to all undertakings. As for Article (86), it is concerned with measures adopted by the Member States in relation to undertakings with which they have specific links referred to in the provisions of that article. It is only with regard to such measures that Article (86) imposes on the Commission a duty of supervision which may, where necessary, be exercised through the adoption of directives and decisions addressed to the Member States.
>
> 25 It must therefore be held that the subject-matter of the power conferred on the Commission by Article (86(3)) is different from, and more specific than, that of the powers conferred on the Council by either Article (95) or Article (83).

France furthermore challenged the legality of the provision in the Directive obliging the Member States to withdraw the existing exclusive rights. The Court dismissed this plea in law as well, thereby focusing strongly on the incompatibility of those rights with Article 28 EC. The competition rules are mentioned only in passing:

> 41 In that regard it should be borne in mind, in the first place, that, as the Court has consistently held, Articles 2 and 3 of the Treaty set out to establish a market characterised by the free movement of goods where the terms of competition are not distorted (…). Article (28) *et seq.* must therefore be interpreted in the light of that principle, which means that the competition aspect of Article (3(1) sub (g)) of the Treaty has to be taken into account.

The difference in emphasis between the preamble of the Directive and the Court's ruling is striking: the Commission focussing on the competition rules and the Court on the rules on free movement. Equally striking is the difference with the approach followed by the Court in the cases discussed in Section 2, in which the Court itself put the competition rules on the forefront.

Meanwhile, the Commission continued to pursue the route of Article 86(3) EC for the telecommunications sector. In 1990, it had adopted a first directive on competition in the markets for telecommunications services (Directive 90/388/EEC[47]),

---

[46] Case C-202/88, *France* v. *Commission*, [1991] ECR I-1223.

[47] Commission Directive 90/388/EEC of 28 June 1988 on competition in the markets for telecommunications services, OJ 1988, L 192/10.

which was later on amended several times. The final and most fundamental amending directive was adopted in 1996: Directive 96/19/EC with regard to the implementation of full competition on telecommunications markets.[48] As the name indicates, this amendment was meant to abolish all remaining monopoly rights in the telecommunications sector.

In the telecommunications sector, the Community has followed a two-pronged approach: on the one hand liberalisation directives adopted by the Commission based on Article 86(3) EC, on the other hand (a whole series of) harmonisation directives adopted by the Council (later on the Council and the European Parliament jointly) based on Article 95 EC. The first harmonisation directive dates from 1990: Directive 90/387/EEC concerning open network provision.[49] The distinction between liberalisation and harmonisation is not always that clear. At first sight, one might argue that the liberalisation directives are driven by the aim to create a system of undistorted competition within the common market, whereas the harmonisation directives would primarily aim at breaking up the internal frontiers that hinder the completion of the internal market. In reality, these are two sides of the same coin, as was emphasised by the Court in its judgment in *France* v. *Commission* (rec. 41, quoted above). Moreover, the liberalisation directives do not only deal with the abolition of exclusive rights. Thus, for instance, Article 6 of the first liberalisation directive (Directive 88/295), stipulates that drawing up technical specifications for terminal equipment, monitoring their application and granting type-approval is to be entrusted to a body independent of undertakings active in the telecommunications sector. Why this obligation should be qualified as "liberalisation" rather than "harmonisation" remains unclear. In fact, there are quite a number of subject matters that are first addressed in liberalisation directives, and later on worked out further in detail in harmonisation directives. Allocation of numbers and interconnection between networks are just two examples.

Despite the support received from the Court, the (partial) Article 86(3) EC approach has remained unique for the telecommunications sector. In other sectors, the Commission based its liberalisation initiatives on Article 95 EC.[50] Notable examples are Directive 96/92/EC concerning the internal market in electricity[51] and Directive 98/30/EC concerning the internal market for gas.[52] Both directives contain elements which may be qualified as "liberalisation" and elements which should rather be brought under the heading of "harmonisation". The gradual opening up of the market is a typical liberalisation element. Thus, under Article 18 of Directive

---

[48] Commission Directive 96/19/EC of 13 March 1996 amending Directive 90/388/EEC with regard to the implementation of full competition in telecommunications markets, OJ 1996, L 74/13.

[49] Council Directive 90/387/EEC of 28 June 1990 on the establishment of the internal market for telecommunications services through the implementation of open network provision, OJ 1990, L 192/1.

[50] Or, for that matter, the relevant provisions of the Treaty concerning the transport sector.

[51] Directive 96/92/EC of the European Parliament and of the Council of 19 December 1996 concerning common rules for the internal market in electricity, OJ 1997, L 27/20.

[52] Directive 98/30/EC of the European Parliament and of the Council of 22 June 1998 concerning common rules for the internal market in natural gas, OJ 1998, L 204/1.

(as it stands at the time this paper is written), the Member States are required to open up the market equal to at least 20% by mid-2000, increasing to 28% by mid-2003 and 33% by mid-2018. This opening should be effected by granting access rights to the transmission system to sufficiently widely defined categories of "eligible customers". The group of eligible customers should at the outset include in any event gas-fired power generators and other end-users consuming more than 25 million m^3 per annum. This obligation obviously means that exclusive rights that incumbent gas companies may have had in supplying these categories of end users will have to be abolished.

3.3. The choice between Article 86(3) and 95 EC: why Article 86(3) should be considered an unsuitable basis for liberalisation legislation

The choice for an integrated approach, combining "liberalisation" and "harmonisation" elements in directives based on Article 95 EC, should be endorsed. Not only because the two elements – to the extent a clear distinction between them can at all be drawn – are closely interconnected in substance. But also because Article 86(3) EC should not be considered an adequate legal basis for Community wide liberalisation operations. I would like to highlight a number of reasons in this connection.

First, an argument of a "constitutional" nature: the Treaty does not formally require the involvement of the Council and the European Parliament in the decision making process under Article 86(3) EC. Clearly, Article 86(3) EC had not been designed by the authors of the Treaty to enable the *pouvoir exécutif* to act as a true legislator. Despite the Court's support of the Commission's initiatives regarding the telecommunications sector, it should be recognised that Community wide liberalisation legislation suffers from a democratic deficit when it may be (and is) adopted by the Commission using autonomous powers under Article 86(3) EC.

Second, the issues to be addressed in a liberalisation Directive are often far too complex and far reaching in nature to be qualified as a straightforward application of Article 86(1) and (2) EC. This again despite the support given by the Court to the Commission's approach in the telecommunications sector.

Third, it should be borne in mind that Article 86(3) EC is meant to specify the obligations that ensue from Article 86(1) and (2) EC. These Treaty provisions have direct effect, which implies that they can (and must) be applied by national courts. It may be argued that the Commission, acting as legislator under Article 86(3) EC, has wider powers than courts of the Member States when reviewing the same national measures on an *ad hoc* basis. However, there is no clear basis in the Court's case-law, nor, for that matter, in the concept of direct effect, to draw such a distinction. The interplay between the first liberalisation directive for the telecommunications sector (Directive 88/301/EEC) and the *RTT* v. *GB-INNO* case may help to illustrate the issue. In the latter case, the Court of Justice followed a reasoning based on Article 86(1) EC that in its outcome coincided very well with the rules set forth by the Commission in its liberalisation directive (the facts of the Court cases predated the entry into force of the directive). In the context of a legislative liberalisation operation, it may sound obvious that Member States are obliged to entrust the granting of type approval for certain equipment to a body that is totally independent of any operator on the market for that equipment.[53] It remains, however, difficult to see how such an obligation may be inferred *directly* from the application of primary Community law.

The question when and under which conditions a sector or market is to be liberalised is primarily a political question and not a (purely) legal question. In other words: neither the obligation as such nor the time-frame to be followed should be made (fully) dependent on the application of primary Community law.

This can be clarified by an example. In Directive 96/19/EC the Commission proclaimed that the time was ripe for the total liberalisation of the telecommunications sector. Member States were ordered to withdraw all special and exclusive rights for voice telephony and the establishment and provision of public telecommunications services before 1 January 1998. It is clear that the said cut-off date does not automatically follow from a mechanic application of the law: it involves a discretionary policy decision. However, when following basically the same approach as the Commission, a national court called upon to assess the legality of the voice telephony monopoly of the national telecommunications operator in the light of Article 86 EC (in conjunction with the competition rules), could in principle come to the conclusion that in view of the circumstances prevailing on the national market concerned, the voice telephony monopoly should have been abolished already many years before 1998. It is clear that the mere risk of such an approach would seriously affect legal certainty.

In the preamble of Directive 96/19, the Commission states that at the time of adoption of the first liberalisation directive in 1990, it had granted a *temporary exception* under Article 86(2) EC in respect of the said exclusive rights. However, the text of Article 86(3) EC does not provide for the granting of "exceptions" by the Commission. Article 86(2) EC contains a *de jure* exception, that applies irrespective of what the Commission may find. Indeed, neither the granting nor the non-granting of an exception by the Commission may impair the freedom of national courts to assess the application of Article 86(2) EC in individual cases. Incidentally, it should be noted that the (preamble of the) 1990 Directive does not mention the alleged granting of a temporary exception at all.

It is submitted that obligations for Member States of the (political) nature just described should be laid down in harmonisation directives based on Article 95 EC, and not on directives based on Article 86(3) EC. The use of Article 95 EC emphasises that when it comes to the liberalisation of entire sectors of the economy, secondary Community law, adopted by the legislative power appointed in the Treaty, should set the pace, and not primary Community law.

One further example may help to show why this should be held to be the right order. Within the framework of Directive 98/30/EC, the Member States should open up the gas sector up to at least a certain minimum level. They may go further, but

---

[53] Indeed, in the *dictum* of the judgment in case C-18/88, the Court uses such wide wording as well.

that is up to the national *legislators* concerned, and not up to the national courts applying primary Community law. It is clear that under Article 98/30/EC, Member States are not (yet) obliged to liberalise the supply of gas to domestic users. Where the Community legislator has made this choice, there should be no room for national courts to second-guess whether the Member State concerned should not have gone further and liberalise the entire sector at once in full. Where the Community legislator has decided on a gradual creation of an internal market for natural gas, the legislative framework may not be jeopardised by the application of primary Community law. This is, it is submitted, also one of main messages that may be drawn from the series of judgments in the so-called Article 37 cases. These cases had a clear political background: the Commission had opened infringement proceedings as a reprisal against the Member States' lack of cooperation in the legislative field. The Court, in turn, was not prepared to endorse an attack against elements of the existing national market organisation outside the context of an integral concept for an internal market for energy.[54]

Finally a word about drinking water. So far, the Community legislator has not undertaken any steps towards the creation of an internal market for drinking water. This should mean that in principle there should be no room whatsoever to challenge the legality of the existing national systems via the route of invoking primary Community law.[55] And that brings us back to the subject-matter of Section 2.

4. Liberalisation and Beyond

Only very briefly, this paper will address a number of issues that come up once the decision to liberalise a given (utilities) market has been taken.

As the – very different, because the sectors involved are so different – histories of the development of the internal markets for telecommunications services, electricity and natural gas show, difficulties only start once the basic decision to liberalise have been taken.

A crucial issue is that legal monopolies may in practice coincide with *de facto*, natural, monopolies. Some of those monopolies may be transient in nature – for instance fixed telecommunications networks, even including the local loop – others may be, or must be, assumed to be permanent – such as the distribution networks for electricity and natural gas – because they are *true* natural monopolies. In some

---

[54] And this is precisely also the reason why the approach followed by the Court of Appeal of Arnhem (n. 36, *supra*), should be dismissed. The Court of Appeal considered itself competent to review *ex post* the appropriateness of the national organisation of the public supply of electricity in The Netherlands the 1980, well before even the first Commission initiatives to create an internal market for electricity had been taken in the 1980s.

[55] See for an unsuccessful attempt to challenge the legality of a regional drinking water monopoly in The Netherlands in the light of (inter alia) Article 86 EC, *Hoge Raad* 12 October 2001, RvdW 2001/163. The applicants argued that the national legislation was in violation of the Treaty because they did not allow Third Party Access to the drinking water network. That, however, is exactly what the applicable Dutch law seeks to prevent in the interest of a safe and economically balanced public supply of drinking water.

markets, vertically integrated so-called incumbents may – irrespective of natural monopoly issues – foreclose newly opened markets to a significant extent using their remaining market power. More generally, incumbents may continue to yield considerable market power once their protected position has been dismantled. In those situations, the market behaviour of such dominant market players may require serious attention. This will be all the more necessary in those cases where liberalisation goes hand in hand with privatisation (i.e. in most cases). The ordinary competition rules may provide substantive guidance when it comes to assessing market behaviour, but the procedural framework of the (EC and national competition) laws do not generally facilitate pro-active involvement of competition authorities. Moreover, substantive competition law does not offer clear-cut answers to a wide area of relevant issues such as, for instance, pricing by dominant undertakings.[56]

The history of the liberalisation of the telecommunications sector shows that the Community legislator(s) have found it necessary to adopt a wide variety of binding regulations (in the legal form of directives) that affect very seriously the commercial freedom of incumbents as well as new entrants, dominant players as well as operators that have no market power at all. Liberalisation does not imply de-regulation, but rather re-regulation. Whilst too little regulation may have as a result that effective competition will not come off the ground at all, too much regulation may very well stifle innovation and economic progress, and substitute competition in court rooms for competition in the market place.

The telecommunications sector was the first to experience the creation of sector-specific regulators on a Europe-wide scale. Irrespective of the preferences one may have for either the creation of sector-specific regulators or concentrating sector-specific regulatory powers by a single supervisory authority for competition matters generally, it should be noted that differences between regulatory practices of national regulators may give rise to equally if not more serious distortions of the proper functioning of the common market than may differences between national laws. This may be clarified by an example. The Dutch regulator for the energy sector had in the first year of its existence drawn up highly detailed rules on the calculation of tariffs for transport of natural gas (allegedly applying principles of "normal" competition law), which if implemented in full would have forced the main Dutch transmission company to reduce its tariffs to less than half of what is the prevailing level in Western Europe. At first sight this may seem attractive for consumers, in reality it jeopardises the competitive position of the Dutch operator *vis-à-vis* its foreign competitors.

This is all meant to emphasise that regulating industries – more particularly utilities – is a cumbersome exercise. Experience on a European level is still quite limited. The experience built up with the telecommunications sector may only be of limited relevance to other sectors, if only because the various sectors are so different. It would not make much sense to state that the electricity or the natural gas sectors may see similarly spectacular developments as the telecommunications

---

[56] See in that connection my contribution to the 2001 Fordham Conference: "Excessive Pricing under E.C. Competition Law; an Update in the light of 'Dutch Developments.' "

sectors. Whereas, as a result of technological developments, both networks and services in the telecommunications sectors have made a tremendous progress over the last two decades, and demand for such services – notably transmission of data – has increased enormously as well, electricity and natural gas are homogeneous products for which demand may not be expected to increase dramatically within most national markets, if only because official governmental policies aim at reducing the use of energy.

When looking at the problems of regulated markets from the perspective of Community law, it is clear that the role for primary Community law – in particular the fundamental freedoms – decreases. Nevertheless, one should keep in mind that the essence of the whole exercise remains the creation of a true single market. So far, not even in the telecommunications market that aim is close to being achieved in full.

5. Concluding Remarks

As I hope to have clarified in this chapter, the assessment of legal monopolies under Community law has become increasingly complex over the last 20 years. Legal monopolies have come under serious pressure. I have, however, tried to make clear that the de-monopolisation development is primarily a politically driven and only to a lesser extent a legally driven development. Primary Community law may help to curb fringe cases involving clearly exorbitant and disproportionate monopoly rights; the intervention of the Community's legislative power will remain necessary when it comes to liberalising entire sectors.

Chapter 8

Changing Values in the European Community – A Commentary on the Papers

*Sheldon Leader**

This conference has provided a valuable set of observations that help us to address a general question. How, if at all, has the balance shifted in the European Community between the promotion of values associated with market integration and those that are independent of market integration? By "independent" of market integration, two things are meant:

One sort of independence refers to the content of values. There are those values which are directly promoted by market integration, such as the increased scope for consumer choice arising from competition among providers of goods and services. On the other hand, there are other values that are pursued for reasons that are quite independent of the market. They are values that the Community does not promote as means to the end of more complete cross-border exchanges, but for quite separate reasons. We find here, as examples, elements of social policy aimed at the decent treatment of employees; or the promotion of a European cultural identity.

A second sort of independence refers to the ability to resist control from the centre. Here we find a Community that gives varying degrees of freedom to member states to pursue an agenda that pulls them away from reciprocal relations with their partner countries. Their agendas might, for example, be the product of quite distinct cultural priorities, and at issue is how much a member state can have control over its own priorities.

If we go back to our initial question, asking about the balance between the promotion of values associated with market integration and those that are independent of market integration, we can see in the conference contributions these two distinct concerns: one about the content of values deployed, and the other about which part of the community controls the deployment. Sometimes, the balance between market and non-market values occurs at the centre only. That would be true, for example, with the balance between the need to protect basic social rights and the need to create an environment in which transfers of undertakings can take place efficiently.[1] At other

* Professor of Law, University of Essex, and chairman of the Pallas Consortium.

[1] This can involve, e.g. difficult questions about the timing and content of the requirement that workers must be informed and consulted before a transfer takes place. See the Transfers of Undertakings Directive (2001/23) Chapter III.

M. van Empel (ed.), "From Paris to Nice": Fifty Years of Legal Integration in Europe, 151–157.

points, however, the non-market values pursued also engage issues of levels of control. When a member state claims an entitlement to refuse one of the Community's market integrating demands, it might be doing so both on the strength of the cross-cutting value it wants to protect, and on the strength of its conviction that the appropriate level at which the character and weight of that cross-cutting value is given is that of the member state itself.

Consider, in the light of this, the following lines of possible tension.

1. Market and Non-market Values Balanced at Central Level

In Dr. O'Leary's analysis, it is the tension between values that stands out rather than tension between levels of control. Dr. O'Leary discusses the tension between values within Community social policy that are aimed at facilitating market integration, and those that are adopted for reasons that are independent of the imperatives of such integration. Her analysis contains the valuable general lesson that the differences between these two orientations cannot always be seen by looking at the content of the value being pursued. For example, the Transfers of Undertakings Directive guarantees certain basic rights to workers in the event of such a transfer. However, in the text and in its interpretations, she sees two distinct foundations for these rights. One aims at the protection of vulnerable workers as a value in its own right, and the other seeks to protect these rights because of the "... fear that disparities in employment protection legislation between Member States might have a deleterious effect on the transfers and mergers which it was in the common market's interest to bring about as a result of greater economic integration."[2] This is not just a distinct set of foundation principles but is also, as she points out, a source of tension. It is a "... tension between the Directive's social and economic facets [that] can be found throughout the case-law of the Court of Justice ...[which needs to] balance the employment protection objectives of the Directive with the need to ensure that there are no untoward disincentives to transferring business in an increasingly integrated and globalised European market."[3]

We find a similar tension between two foundations for the protection and promotion of cultural values in the Community. Lorna Woods contrasts the approach to culture that is rooted "... in the creation of the common market, which can be broadly characterised as a negative approach to culture", which confines the term to being an adjunct to the free flow of factors of production, and "... the more positive approach when the Community seeks to develop law and policy in this area...", because of the perceived qualities of the cultural values pursued.[4] As with rights of workers, it is not always possible to see these distinct foundations simply in the fact that a means of promoting a cultural value is being protected or promoted by the Community *per se*. Much depends on whether that protection or promotion is seen as part of the drive to further the integrated market, or is undertaken on a free standing basis. It is here, e.g. that we can locate her discussion of the Television without Frontiers Directive.

---

[2] Síofra O'Leary, *The Principle of Non-Discrimination and EC Social Policy,* p. 26 *supra.*

[3] *Ibid.*

[4] Lorna Woods, *Culture and the European Union*, p. 109 *supra.*

Cross border broadcasting can be seen as a further step in the creation of a single market, but it can also be seen as an important means of "establishing an ever closer Union amongst the peoples of Europe."[5] As a result, there is a tension between seeing this as "... just an attempt to generate a secondary market for European television programming", or as "... an attempt to ensure Europeans understand each other by virtue of watching each other's television programmes ... "[6]

2. Central Market Values in Tension with Local Non-market Values

Pijnacker Hordijk discusses the tension arising from the policies coming from Member State's creation of monopolies for certain services of public value, such as utilities or social insurance, and the increasing demands from the Community that the potential markets for these goods be open to competition.[7] In his analysis, we see that there is a clash between market and non-market values, but also an issue about appropriate levels of control over those values. Consider his points about the objectives that Member States might have when they establish certain monopolies they consider to be in the public interest. The ECJ allows Member States to fix the quality and level at which they wish to promote one of these objectives, and the control – in the name of the proportionality principle – is exercised over the means used to attain those ends. That manifests a deference to local decisions that is different from those cases in which the Court has been willing to force Member States to compromise both on ends as well as means. In the *Danish Bottles* case, for example, Denmark was obliged to accept a set of controls over the use of drinks containers that would marginally lower the level of environmental cleanliness it sought, in favour of greater access to the Danish market from drinks companies.[8]

As a second example of an issue that simultaneously raises conflicts of values and conflicting visions of appropriate levels of control, there is another part of Lorna Wood's paper. She discusses derogations from market access demands in order to protect local culture.[9] As with the previous example, the issue is not whether the derogations are possible per se, but what degree of autonomy states have in setting the terms for them. As Woods puts it, "derogation is about the space left to Member States. The question is, how big is this space, and has the ECJ taken a consistent approach to cultural questions?"[10] The scope for autonomy that is granted is affected by the initial view of cultural goods taken at the center, taking us back to the earlier distinction between valuing such goods for their own sake, or as part of the imperatives of market integration. For example, the scope that a Member State might have for imposing an export tax on artistic treasures depends on whether the article is

---

[5] *Ibid.*, p. 123 *supra.*

[6] *Ibid.*

[7] E. Pijnacker Hordijk, *State Intervention in the Economy: From State Monopolies to Regulated Industries* pp. 131 ff *supra.*

[8] *Commission* v. *Denmark Case* 302/86, [1988] ECR 4607.

[9] Lorna Woods, *Culture and the European Union*, p. 111 ff *supra.*

[10] *Ibid.*, p. 112 *supra.*

deemed as good for the purposes of free movement demands, or falls outside that category. The Court, she shows, has tended to the former solution.[11]

A further aspect of this tension over levels of control, as well as over values, concerns the Community's education strategy. Maria Sticchi Damiani describes different local conceptions of appropriate student evaluation in university courses in tension with centrally formulated standards coming from the CTS which are aimed to further the free movement of students between European universities.[12] To the extent that the latter are oriented towards extending that free movement, they come into potential conflict with local standards that are directed towards the distinct objective of quality assurance. She points out that the Community is also concerned about quality assurance, but the difference might arise over the level at which the appropriate mix is established between quality control and the objective of student exchange. A concrete arena in which this opposition plays itself out is that of recognition of the quality of foreign courses. As she describes the situation, such recognition is given more reluctantly when the coherence of the local programme, and local standards of evaluation are uppermost in the minds of the relevant education establishments; whereas the spirit of the common Community standard, more focused on the furtherance of student exchanges across borders, gives less weight to the preferred local pattern of teaching quality and control. Concretely, this can manifest itself in a clash between a domestic assessment of the amount of international teaching that is appropriate in a curriculum, and the call from the Community that "... some flexibility is used in determining the percentage of the whole study programme that is open to an international contributions."[13]

3. Central v. Local Non-market Values

Here, as an example, there is the difference between local and central conceptions of the appropriate balance between working and non-working time in employment. At both levels, securing an adequate amount of time away from work can and has been approached as a value independent of the imperatives of market integration. However, differences over the place to accord such a value have appeared between the Community and Member States. The conflict then becomes one of who has ultimate control over the deployment of this non-market value. This question manifested itself most dramatically in the litigation over the Working Time Directive,[14] with the UK making the unsuccessful bid for the legislation to be an instrument requiring its consent before it could become law: a consent it would have happily refused.[15] Balances of control in favour of the centre can lower as well as strengthen the levels of pursuit

---

[11] *Italian Art Treasures* Case, *Commission* v. *Italy Case* 7/68 [1968] ECR 428.

[12] Maria Sticchi Damiani *Legal education and international exchange.*

[13] *Ibid.*, p. 104 *supra.*

[14] I am here treating the mandate to the Community in Article 137 EC to *improve* workers' health and safety, as what is here called a 'non-market' value. As the Court makes clear, the Directive is not concerned to find a common denominator among existing practices of member states. See the *Working Time Directive case* (*UK* v. *Council* Case C-84/94 [1996] ECR I-5755 paras 47, 56, 59).

[15] See Case C-84/94 *UK* v. *Council* [1996] ECR I-5755.

of a non-market value. Dr. O'Leary makes this point when she considers how harmonisation of protection of pregnant employees at EC level meant that "... the more stringent protection sought by some Member States had to be sacrificed on the altar of compromise in order for [the Directive's] adoption to be secured."[16]

There are other lines of tension between values, and over levels of control, that could call for attention. But we have enough in hand to prompt some general considerations, in the light of these and some of the other conference papers.

3.1. Nature and rationale of harmonisation

Walter van Gerven explores the elements of diversity within the goal of harmonisation. As he indicates, the qualities of that goal have to be interpreted against the background of two distinct sets of needs: to provide room for diversity, but in doing so to avoid too much incoherence in the system. One of the key features of this diversity that he points to is that it can allow in greater participative democracy. It is not just a democratic involvement of Member States, but opens up the prospect of a greater role for "... private organisations and individuals participating in policy and law making."[17]

However, the earlier points considered could show that, on entering into such an endorsement of a partially democratic route to harmonisation, we need to have a prior understanding of the level and scope of legitimate democratic involvement being sought. This need not be a uniform understanding across all cases: it can vary with the issue. But without it, we risk raising more hopes than can be satisfied. For example, the project of harmonising laws in a given area requires an initial view of whether the values at work are those aimed at furthering market integration or stand apart from market values. The scope of legitimate working time regulation, to go back to that example, depends on that prior choice. If the Community had felt entitled only to seek the common denominator in health and safety policies, providing a level playing field for enterprises, then this would have provided a far narrower mandate than it had when it embraced the independent goal of improving health and safety. In turn, the scope for democratic dialogue in formulating harmonising laws will have a narrower focus in the former situation than in the latter. Those professional organisations that become engaged in the work of common deliberation in the setting of such norms would be clearly frustrated if they enter into the process thinking that their mandate is collective improvement of standards when in fact it is the collective coordination of standards. The same could be true for the process of harmonisation of rules on cultural activity. Whether this is a project for the collective promotion of cultural values as free standing objectives, or a species of market coordination, needs prior decision. This may well mean that the objective of harmonisation requires a judicial decision, establishing the character of the values that inform the project – from among several possible contenders. At other points, it is a political decision fixing the content of legislation that will provide the foundation.

---

[16] O'Leary, p. 24 *supra*.

[17] W. van Gerven, *Harmonization and Beyond*, p. 3 *supra*.

3.2. Member State autonomy

How can the objective of harmonisation and the demands of a margin of Member State autonomy be properly related to one another? In part, the difficulty in answering this question is captured in Prof. Van Gerven's treatment of the problem of coherence in the system. As he puts it, it is essential to try to avoid "... the incoherence which accompanies differentiation."[18] But coherence is a virtue that cuts both ways in Community affairs. What is coherent in domestic policy may disrupt the logic of Community policy, and what fits well with Community policy may introduce an incoherent element into a national system. The impasse can only be resolved if we address the issue both of clashing values and distinct levels of control over the content of those values, as portrayed in the earlier examples. Take the example of a situation in which the Community has decided to promote a non-market value, such as the aim of improving employee protection, which does not appeal to a member state because it does not fit coherently with its own set of fundamental policy choices. Why should the Community's demand for coherence win out at the expense of disrupting a Member State's different demand for coherence? Why should we not allow free competition between domestic policies, each with their distinct priorities, rather than impose uniformity?

This is a question raised by the contribution from Prof. Jan Wouters. He raises the prospect of competition among Member States as they fashion their rules for regulating corporate behaviour. As he points out, there is increasing enthusiasm for such competition in Europe.[19] However, there is persistent opposition from those for whom such rivalry between regulatory regimes provokes races to the bottom – a race at the expense of values that are independent of those which aim to further market integration. These values can include norms of adequate protection for employees, the environment etc.

Notice, however, that complaints about races to the bottom are broken backed unless it is first clear who is entitled to dominate a choice of values. In classic terms, made famous by economists such as Mancur Olson, a damaging race to the bottom can occur when a collective good, carrying risks and costs to produce, is being furnished and where the defection of any single participant enables him to get the benefits while avoiding the burdens of the collective scheme.[20] The evil wrought by a race to the bottom is that the defector agrees that what the others are producing by their cooperation is a benefit to him, but refuses to do his share. This can cause others also to defect, afraid of losing out on, e.g. a chance for a share of inward investment, and hence they are forced to abandon their initial goals. However, if we are in a situation in which Member States diverge over the content and weight to assign to the values of worker or environmental protection, then it is not so easy to make this complaint. For what seems to one country to be a value needing protection from

---

[18] *Ibid.*, p. 11 *supra.*

[19] Wouters, *Corporate Law*, sec. 3.2.3.

[20] Mancur Olson, *The Logic of Collective Action* (Harvard University Press, 1965), *passim.*

defection is in fact a value without much weight to the other. At that point, it is hard to convict the latter of taking the benefits but not the burdens. What the others see as a benefit, it does not. This has often been the UK's position on matters of employee protection. What the others think is a valuable improvement it thinks has no value – on grounds that have been quite coherent with the other parts of its social polity. It would indeed be happy if all others took the same view as it does. That is not the view of a free rider. It is only if values such as improvements in employee participation rights are placed firmly in the hands of a majority rule mechanism at the centre that it will be possible to then turn around and legitimately stop competition between regulatory regimes. Short of this, such competition seems quite legitimate.

With enlargement of the Union, and the redrawing of its constitutional framework, these related issues of competing values and competing visions of appropriate levels of control are becoming more acute. These papers help us to see some of the challenges quite vividly. It will be interesting to see what the authors have to say on the same topics in 10 years time.